MORAL REASONING FOR JOURNALISTS

MORAL REASONING FOR JOURNALISTS

Second Edition

Steven Knowlton and Bill Reader

Foreword by Jerry Ceppos

Westport, Connecticut
London

Library of Congress Cataloging-in-Publication Data

Knowlton, Steven R.
  Moral reasoning for journalists / Steven Knowlton and Bill Reader; foreword by Jerry Ceppos.—2nd ed.
      p. cm.
  Includes bibliographical references and index.
  ISBN 978–0–313–34548–7 (alk. paper)—ISBN 978–0–313–34550–0 ((pbk) : alk. paper)
  1. Journalistic ethics.   I. Reader, Bill, 1970–   II. Title.
  PN4756.K687   2009
  174'.907—dc22   2008033697

British Library Cataloguing in Publication Data is available.

Library of Congress Catalog Card Number: 2008033697
ISBN: 978–0–313–34548–7 (hc)
      978–0–313–34550–0 (pb)

First published in 2009

Praeger Publishers, 88 Post Road West, Westport, CT 06881
An imprint of Greenwood Publishing Group, Inc.
www.praeger.com

Printed in the United States of America

The paper used in this book complies with the Permanent Paper Standard issued by the National Information Standards Organization (Z39.48–1984).

10 9 8 7 6 5 4 3 2 1

What is a journalist? Not any business manager or publisher, or even proprietor. A journalist is the lookout on the bridge of the ship of state. He notes the passing sail, the little things of interest that dot the horizon in fine weather. He reports the drifting castaway whom the ship can save. He peers through fog and storm to give warning of dangers ahead. He is not thinking of his wages or of the profits of his owners. He is there to watch over the safety and the welfare of the people who trust him.

—Joseph Pulitzer

Contents

Foreword

I honestly thought it was one of my better ideas: For four years, I had heard that students frequently stole merchandise from stores in downtown College Park, Md., moments from the University of Maryland campus, where I was the editor of the student newspaper. I decided to demonstrate just how big the problem was—by assigning a reporter to shoplift.

Although almost every aspect of my decision can be criticized, the biggest problem 40 years later seems to me the complete lack of moral reasoning—or reasoning of any sort—behind my decision. Was undercover reporting called for? Was the story so serious that it was right to break the law? The answer is clear, at least to me: The depth of the shoplifting problem could have been explained more completely—and explained ethically—with a well-reported news story that included police information, quotes from merchants, and profiles of convicted shoplifters (if there were any; the "undercover" investigation didn't get into such minor details, as I recall).

On the other hand, some could argue that breaking the law perhaps was justified because the subject was so important to the safety of the community—but it would have been nice to have thought about that and talked it over with the rest of the staff, at the very least. As Steven Knowlton and Bill Reader write in this book, deception, let alone breaking the

Jerry Ceppos, in 2008, became the dean of the Donald W. Reynolds School of Journalism at the University of Nevada-Reno. His career in journalism was long and distinguished: He was the vice president for news for Knight Ridder newspapers and is a former executive editor of the San Jose Mercury News. He also served as an editor for the Miami Herald and the Rochester (N.Y.) Democrat & Chronicle.

law, should be used "rarely and, we should hope begrudgingly...as a tool of last resort for investigative journalists."

That's a crucial point, on a specific ethical issue. But, I pull an even more important lesson out of this book: the need to think in advance, before the challenging situation arises, about how we should make decisions. As the authors say, ethical decisions won't be made in the heat of the moment. "That's why it is so crucial that journalists think about ethics long before they go out on assignment," they write. "There rarely is much time in the field to bone up on the basic philosophy, let alone the particular principles to which journalists aspire."

In fact, thinking ahead is the authors' only inviolable rule. They don't even cast a blanket veto on breaking the law to get a story, although they aren't happy about it. Neither do they forbid the use of unnamed sources or of government-classified information.

They do exhort us to think before we act, to engage in what they call "ethical deliberation." When I was in charge of professional newspapers, none of my investigative reporters uncovered my thoughtless deception as a student, so I was free to argue what the authors argue, a point that would have served me well in the newsroom of the student newspaper: Lay out your ethical principles early and often to yourself or to your staff—and know how you'll respond when those principles are breached.

The case studies in this book, sometimes written by those who made the tough decisions, will help you understand those principles. Importantly, all of the studies are real cases, unlike so many taught in our profession. Again and again, you will appreciate the thought that many journalists gave to potential dilemmas before the dilemmas occurred—and occasionally you will agree with the authors that "many individual journalists, left to their own devices, will do all sorts of irresponsible things—invade others' privacy for no good reason, pander to their readers' and viewers' baser desires with gratuitous violence and titillating sex, sound the public alarm when there is no fire, and a host of other sins." But those who think about the issues in advance may well avoid those pitfalls.

Keep that thought and be sure to read the case about a journalist who used trickery to shine light on the ways that even the worst governments in the world can hire lobbyists to spiff up their images. You won't find crystal-clear answers to the dilemma of deceptive undercover reporting there, and, in other cases, you won't find perfect answers to the other tough moral questions surrounding our craft. But you will be forced to think about those questions in advance, which will put you far ahead of where I was 40 years ago.

—Jerry Ceppos

A Note to Our Fellow Journalists

Although this book is primarily intended for journalism students and instructors, it is actually written for anybody who wants to think seriously about journalism ethics, from veteran professionals at the world's leading news outlets to novice volunteers trying to keep their neighbors informed with monthly newsletters. Because the authors have been there and done that—we have been newbies and old pros, students and teachers, the critics and the criticized—we have put a lot of thought into how to make this book useful for many kinds of journalists at many different stages in their careers.

That said, there are many things about this book that make it unlike other casebooks and media-ethics textbooks now available.

First, the cases are real—not hypotheticals, not composites, and not made up from whole cloth. Hypotheticals and composites may be convenient and tidy because they can be constructed to illustrate exactly the points desired without the inevitable clutter that accompanies real life. However, their use is problematic for a number of reasons. For starters, journalism teachers insist that students be scrupulously accurate, and working professionals have little patience for colleagues who fabricate sources or play free and loose with the facts. Hypotheticals and composites fly in the face of such lessons and expectations. In addition, hypotheticals and composites generally aren't as messy as the real world, and they lead too easily to discussions that focus on absolute rights and absolute wrongs. Ethics aren't that easy. Most ethical decisions involve degrees of both right and wrong, with the goal being to tip the scales toward the former. Frankly, sometimes good people make bad choices for reasons that seemed good at the time. When it comes to ethics, we are all better off analyzing actual events that involved real people in real situations.

Second, this book is intentionally light on theory. For a more in-depth consideration of the theoretical underpinnings of journalism ethics, we recommend you refer to the companion book of this text, *The Journalist's Moral Compass* (Praeger, 1994), an anthology of foundational writings that have an important bearing on the moral dimensions of modern journalism. We don't expect that a working journalist, facing an ethical dilemma and a looming deadline, will always reach for *Moral Compass* to consult Plato or John Stuart Mill before deciding whether to use quotes from an anonymous source. However, we do maintain that the principles outlined in *Moral Compass* are part of the intellectual fabric of the journalistic profession, and as such are worth perusal and consideration by those who find themselves doing this work.

Third, this book tries to represent the breadth of journalism practice in the early twenty-first century by focusing on two important considerations: that journalism is a global enterprise and that there is more to journalism than the marquee news outlets of the world. Too many ethics books are focused exclusively on the United States, where freedom of the press may have been forged but which has no claim to sole ownership of such ideals. Online communication also has made it more difficult to focus on journalism as a national-level phenomenon—when cartoons published in a newspaper in Denmark can spark riots across southern Asia, or the front page of a tabloid in London can be downloaded in Mexico City, the idea of journalistic borders fades very quickly. Most books about journalism ethics also focus mostly on the moral conundrums faced by the so-called big media—the Associated Press, the BBC, the International Herald Tribune, Al Jazeera, and so on. Although it is important to discuss ethics in the context of the big leagues of world journalism, we must not lose sight that the vast majority of journalists in the world work for small newspapers, regional Web sites, small-market radio and television, niche magazines, and all manner of other journalistic media. Therefore, this book also includes examples from the small media world, where many committed journalists work hard to balance their professional standards with the moral values of their communities.

Fourth, this book is not an ivory-tower condemnation of the current state of journalism nor is it a naive enterprise in hero worship. It is, in true journalistic fashion, a good-faith effort to report on the foundations and applications of morality in a profession that is increasingly diverse and global in nature. After a combined sixty years of interaction with literally hundreds of working journalists, we are convinced that journalism is a deeply moral profession in which ethical lapses are uncommon but still openly admitted. As in most professions, there are charlatans and knaves at work in the journalism business, and there are hustlers, cons, and folks on the take. There are errors of venality and, far more common, errors of sloth and too much hurry. For all that, however, the great majority of journalists working for newspapers and magazines, TV and radio news, wire services, and online news sites are highly principled, deeply committed individuals who take the moral imperatives of their work extremely seriously. Both *Moral Compass* and this book are meant to honor the honorable who dominate our discipline, and to encourage them to continue their principled work despite increasing hostility from media critics.

When the first edition was published in 1994, an observation was made that "press bashing may be at an all-time high." In the years since, press bashing has increased, and now is a lucrative business for many bloggers, ideologues, and paid media critics—many of whom have never once set foot in a real newsroom or talked shop with real journalists. Another observation in that first edition was that despite such widespread criticism and hostility toward journalism, "the profession operates on a nobler plane than it ever has." That also appears to have been amplified over the past years. Despite shrinking newsrooms, fickle shareholders with no sense of public service, and widespread claims that the old media are circling the drain, we also see journalists being more willing than ever to go to jail to protect their sources, to put themselves in harm's way to get information that the public needs to hear and read, to contest secretive government officials (from township supervisors to heads of state), and, perhaps most telling, to police their own ranks. There have been many high-profile journalism scandals in recent years (some of them discussed in this book), but what many of the critics fail to consider or acknowledge is that the wrongdoing was, in most cases, revealed by other journalists, often coworkers or direct supervisors of the offenders. Rather than deal with such problems in secret, many editors and publishers have insisted on revealing those problems to their readers and viewers. We hope this book can serve not just as a guide, but also as a reminder that journalists are becoming increasingly moral and accountable.

Finally, this is a book about journalism ethics, not about the ethics of the mass media or mass communication, broadly defined. Journalism does use mass media to engage in mass communication, but it is not the same thing as public relations, advertising, television serials, or feature films. It shares some technical elements with those and other forms of mass communication, but journalism has its own history, its own philosophies, and its own problems to solve.

Part I

...

LOCATING ETHICAL JOURNALISM IN THE WESTERN TRADITION

1 ▪ ▪ ▪

Introduction to Ethical Thinking

Journalism as an American institution has taken quite a beating in public discourse in recent decades. In the generation since the go-go years of Watergate, journalists' credibility has fallen precipitously in the minds of the public, showing up in recent polls in the neighborhood of that of used-car dealers in the public's estimation. The broad assumption seems to be that *journalism ethics* is a contradiction in terms. Yet, research suggests that journalists today are more concerned about professional ethics than in any time in the past. Perhaps the missing morality isn't among journalists, but among those who perpetuate the myth that journalism and ethics are mutually exclusive.

Media bashing has become both a lucrative industry and an insidious political tactic, with new books, new talk-show discussions, and new blogs popping up all the time that are devoted to decrying the sorry state of the "mainstream media." "It's biased." "It's shallow." "It's boring." "It panders." Politicians always have beaten up on the press—and no wonder, given their adversarial relationship—but blaming the media for all of society's ills has become a stock part of any political campaign, right up there with kissing babies and honoring war veterans. In recent decades, politicians have been joined in the anti-journalism assault by full- and part-time media critics. Some of those critics are in the legion of academics who have little or no professional experience, yet make their careers in the university theorizing about why the press is so dreadful. Others are working professionals who sometimes agree with the academics that the press (in its generic sense) is a mess. There are few who will openly commend the press for its hourly endeavors to distribute news of importance, to hold authorities accountable, to provide forums for thoughtful opinions, and to document the many goods and ills of the human experience.

Leaving aside the complaints from the targets of vigorous press inquiry, who would naturally prefer to shoot the messenger rather than discuss the message, the most thoughtful (and honest) press critics usually cite these reasons for the sorry state of the news business:

• *Money.* Especially in television, truly staggering sums of money are involved. Competition is keener and the pressures to cut ethical corners are much stronger; some cable news networks have gone so far as to embrace blatantly biased socio-political positions, sacrificing good journalism for good ratings. Meanwhile, many newspaper companies are ignoring research findings that equate quality with profits, and instead are slashing their staffs and shrinking their news holes in the name of short-term profits. And, with the Internet maturing as a preferred source for news and information, some news companies are cutting budgets from the news side to reinvest in online marketing and development of new (not *news*) online products.

• *Spinmeisters.* The image builders for politicians, celebrities, and corporate leaders have come of age and are extremely good at what they do: making their employers look good, regardless of the facts. They also have become extremely good at making those who report the truth about their employers look bad—by seeding mistrust in the mainstream media, the spinmeisters make it easy to dismiss news reports of bad behavior and questionable conduct. The preferred rhetorical tool is (with apologies to our more sensitive readers) "bullshit," which renowned philosopher Harry G. Frankfurt describes as making statements of certitude with no regard as to the underlying facts of the matter. The result is image over substance, and the public is accosted daily by clever marketers posing as public-relations experts, or by actual PR people who ignore or dismiss the importance of serving the public good.

• *Tabloid journalism.* Scurrilous methods and sleaze have been a part of journalism for centuries, but in the past few decades, the sensational and the tawdry have gained far more visibility and clout than the more numerous news outlets that emphasize serious and important journalism. More broadly, many critics have seen a blurring of the real and important distinction between news and entertainment, leading to hybrids such as *docudramas* and *infotainment,* and, worse, the appropriation of news techniques for bald-faced marketing and propaganda in the form of *advertorials* (ads designed to look like news content) and *astroturf* (fake grassroots activity organized by large organizations).

• *Political bias.* Not since the early nineteenth century have there been so many claims of political bias in the press (and back then, the political bias was intentional). Critics within the academy most often assail the press as being hopelessly conservative—as being the tool, witting or not, of the capitalist ruling class. The critics on the TV and radio talk shows, meanwhile, often are political conservatives who insist that the news media are hopelessly liberal, forever covering up the sins of their political fellow travelers, whereas maliciously attacking all ideas from the right end of the political spectrum. There was a time not too long ago when an editor or news producer might look at complaints of bias coming from both sides and take satisfaction in being, essentially, in the middle; today, with the so-called culture wars raging in many corners of the world, those same journalists find themselves in very dangerous crossfire.

Perhaps there is a common thread running through these and other complaints about the state of today's journalism. Critics are saying that journalism has lost its way, that it no longer provides honest information in a form that readers and viewers can use. In the race for numbers—circulation, ratings, and page views; advertising dollars and profit margins—perhaps journalism has too often skipped the nutritious main courses of serious news and gone straight to the dessert of entertainment, which is tasty in the short run, but, in the end, neither satisfying nor sustaining.

Those are important concerns, and there are others, most with some measure of truth to them—although none as universally true as their proponents seem to believe. Although the criticisms vary widely, underlying them all is a presumption, spoken or unspoken, of *should*. The criticisms are that, because of corruption, bias, or sloth, journalists are not living up to their moral obligations to report and write certain things and in certain ways. Professional critics and lay readers respond with great vehemence to perceived shortcomings in the press because they see the lapses not just as mistakes but as moral failings; they also tend to overestimate the influence of media messages on individuals and on society such that they blame most, if not all, social problems on the media. Nevertheless, in the cacophony of press abuse (and, too often, self-righteous self-defense from journalists themselves) little constructive action is taken. Notions and accusations become certainties and convictions, informed debate on legitimate subjects of concern degenerates into mere shouting matches. Thought becomes noise.

Journalists of all kinds, be they students or seasoned veterans, need to be able to respond to the criticism and to join in thoughtful discussion concerning what newspeople do, how they do it, and why. That discussion must also include considerations of what journalists should do, how they should do it, and why. Journalists in many countries enjoy astonishing constitutional protections and wield awesome amounts of power.

The abuse of that power can have disastrous consequences for their governments, their societies, and their major institutions, including the press itself.

Before looking at the *should* of journalism, we need to look at the broader question: Is there a *should* at all? Do the very notions of *right* and *wrong* have any real meaning outside the walls of religious institutions or courts of law? Are there absolute rights and wrongs, or is there a range of *rightness* and *wrongness* by which to assess alternatives and make choices (i.e., is there not some right and some wrong in all choices)? Without a basic understanding of how moral decisions are made, a professional journalist might make the egregious mistake of simply doing what feels right, the common go-with-your-gut attitude that is far from reliable and almost never based on reason. In journalism, the stakes are simply too high for such gambling. What follows, then, is an introduction to the branch of philosophy called ethics, or moral reasoning, which is intended to help journalists understand the philosophy of making sound moral decisions.

A BRIEF HISTORY OF ETHICAL THINKING

According to the Greeks, who provided the foundation for most philosophical thought in the West, ethics was one of the fundamental branches of philosophy. Aesthetics was the study of beauty, epistemology was the study of knowledge, and ethics was the study of the good. The intention in all three areas was to get past the purely emotional, the subjective, and the intuitive and to arrive at a reasoned understanding or a thoughtful analysis. The aim was to avoid statements that began "I just think..." or "It seems to me..." and instead move toward statements such as "I conclude that..." or "The weight of the evidence indicates...." As such, we urge you to stop thinking of the terms *ethical* and *unethical* as synonyms for *good* and *bad*; rather, use *ethical* to describe choices that reflect reasoning, and *unethical* to describe choices based on assumption, emotion, or reflex (i.e., gut reactions). We also urge you (for reasons to be explained later in this chapter) not to confuse law and ethics as shades of the same color: the study of law is focused on what is allowed in a society, whereas the study of ethics focuses on what is possible. The two often intersect and synchronize, but that does not make them the same thing. Although somebody may be ethically compelled to be lawful, in a philosophical sense one cannot be compelled by law to be ethical. In the end, people must choose whether to obey, bend, or break laws, and ethics is devoted to the making of those choices—as well as choices that do not involve legal considerations whatsoever.

You should note that although the Greeks and their dedication to reason have had, and continue to have, a great influence on Western thought, their rationalism has by no means been universally accepted or gone unchallenged. The Romantics of the early nineteenth century, for example, were generally anti-rationalist and explicitly rejected the power of reason in favor of presumptions about natural folk wisdom, intuition, and so on. In many Eastern philosophies meanwhile, the strict separation of aesthetics, knowledge, and morality is generally seen as unnatural and untenable (as in the Buddhist principle of alleviating suffering through simultaneous control of the three aspects of self: the physical body, the conscious mind, and the unconscious mind). There also are any number of religion-based philosophies that eschew the Greek model of scientific reason in favor of dogma, scripture, and obedience to the teachings of elders. It would be folly to suggest that a traditional Western approach to ethics is the only viable approach. Yet, it is a proven approach, an effective approach, and, finally, the approach that led to the notions that all people have inalienable rights to freedom of speech and freedom of the press. For journalists, it is, at minimum, the best place to start thinking about professional ethics.

In a broad sense, ethics ask such questions as: What is good? Is it the same for each of us? Is good synonymous with pleasure (as the hedonists believed) or, perhaps, with excellence (as Aristotle argued)? Is it immutable, or does it change from time to time, from place to place, and from person to person? In a relativistic world that is leery of declaring that value *a* is better than value *b*, ethicists try to find a firm footing from which to judge right from wrong—not necessarily eternal verities in a religious sense, but principles grounded in something beyond expediency and impulse.

At this point, it is important to make the distinction between ethics and prudence. To be prudent means to be careful or circumspect, not rash or foolhardy. Both ethics and prudence suggest rational, thoughtful behavior, and a great many choices we make are both ethical and prudent. However, the terms are not synonymous because prudence does not require a moral ranking of the available alternatives as ethics clearly does. There is nothing wrong with being prudent—nothing necessarily immoral or unethical. Most of us make a great many decisions every day based on prudence—brushing our teeth, calling our friends, spending time with our loved ones. However, those prudent choices are not ethical choices.

Consider the question of whether to obey a speed limit. Many motorists drive within a few miles per hour of the posted limit. If you ask why, the most common answer would be to avoid getting a speeding ticket. That is a good reason; that is, it is a considered and careful one. Yet, it is not an ethical reason. The ethical argument for obeying a speed limit would be quite different and could go something like this: Statistics show that driving faster than the posted speed limit increases the chance of an accident and increases the chance that an accident would result in serious injury or even death for me or someone else. I have adopted as an ethical principle that I should cause no harm to myself or to other human beings without due cause. Speeding, or even the advantage of getting to my destination a few minutes sooner, is not sufficient reason to risk causing harm or death, so I will obey the speed limit.

However, what if you note that it is a clear day, your car is in excellent mechanical condition, and you are alert and attentive? Should you still be bound by a speed limit that was designed for average or even poor drivers, for all vehicles under all highway and weather conditions? Or you may even recall that some speed limits used to be higher, but they were lowered to save fuel during the 1970s' oil shortage and that they were not raised again in some areas because of political reasons. Alternatively, you may see that the majority of other drivers on the highway are speeding so why shouldn't you? In short, you might decide that the law setting speed limits is a bad law. Are you not free, on ethical grounds at least, to violate a bad law? Perhaps. Many noble figures, including Mohandas Gandhi and the Reverend Dr. Martin Luther King, Jr., have deliberately broken bad laws when the grounds were good enough. Also, the political revolutions that established the free states of the modern world were all examples of people breaking old bad laws to create new and better ones, not the least of which are constitutional protections of civil liberties such as freedom of speech and of the press.

However, there is a case to be made for choosing to obey bad laws, even unjust laws. For example, a democratic society, with its remarkable amount of personal freedom, exists primarily because the great preponderance of its citizens choose to obey the great bulk of its laws voluntarily. Indeed, in a democracy, the laws are essentially established by the people, and the people have the power to change the laws. If people stopped respecting and following established laws, the result would be either dangerous chaos or police state oppression, neither of which free citizens would find tolerable. Thus, for free citizens of the democratic world to preserve the kind of society most of them prefer to live in, they are obliged to follow the laws of that society, even if they encounter from time to time a law they find inconvenient or unjust (or, when they visit other countries, laws that are inconsistent with the laws of their home countries). If a law is particularly egregious or outdated, then citizens are obliged to work within society to change those laws rather than ignore or violate them.

That argument may seem far-fetched, but it is a variation on one of the most long-standing arguments for obeying even bad laws: Socrates' argument for not escaping from prison when he had the chance. According to Plato's account in *The Crito*, Socrates, who had been unjustly imprisoned and was facing execution, argued that the state was more important than any of its individual citizens and that obeying its laws was essential, even if, as in his case, the law was being unjustly applied. Thus, to escape would contribute to general lawlessness and a destruction of the social order.

Almost nobody today, it would seem, has the reverence either for the state or for the law that Socrates had, but the point is still valid: Widespread breaking of laws would almost certainly lead to social chaos and a society in which we would not care to live. There may well be grounds for breaking a law, but to do so requires a clearly stated appeal to principles that, in a given instance, seem to outweigh the dangers of promoting lawlessness.

To the Greeks, as in the example of Socrates, the key was in the *telos,* the ends or goals. In the study of ethics, *teleology* is that branch of philosophy that is focused on outcomes: For any ethical question, the reasonable way to determine the best choice from those available is to consider what would happen, or was most likely to happen, in each case, and then make the choice that would produce the most good. In *The Responsible Self,* a modern examination of this ancient problem, the philosopher H. Richard Niebuhr describes one model of the moral being as "man-the-maker." That figure is goal-directed and strives toward an end, much as a cobbler makes boots and a carpenter builds houses. Cutting leather and pounding nails are neither good nor bad, nor even important, in and of themselves; the value those activities have is in their outcomes. Niebuhr notes that "Aristotle begins his *Ethics*—the most influential book in the West in this field—with the statement: 'Every art and every inquiry and similarly every action and pursuit, is thought to aim at some good.'" Throughout the classical Hellenic period, this outcome-based moral philosophy, called *teleology,* was dominant.

However, with the emergence of strong, organized religions as major political forces in the early Middle Ages (most notably the Roman Catholic Church in Europe and *sharia,* or Islamic law, in the Middle East and Africa), a new way of determining right and wrong came to hold sway in those parts of the world. Religious institutions became most involved in moral questions, determined morality through a series of rules, the "thou shalts" and the "thou shalt nots" of religious orthodoxy. That rule-based ethical theory is called *deontology* (from the Greek *deon,* or obligation). Although deontology does not necessarily have to be based on religious rules, the influence of religion on many cultures does help explain the rules-focused approach many people take when determining right from wrong.

The deontologists argue that behavior has moral weight in and of itself, regardless of the outcomes. Certain things are right and other things, usually the opposites of the right things, are wrong. For example, killing is wrong and stealing is wrong, but compassion and generosity are good. For a millennium and more in the West, religious deontologists were virtually unchallenged in the ethics business. Religious leaders provided both the rules and the keys to their interpretation and understanding. That model is what Niebuhr calls "man-the-citizen," as opposed to his teleological notion of "man-the-maker." The citizen metaphor suggests that the world in which we live has laws that we are bound to obey. We might like to think of ourselves as wholly free agents to build whatever world we might like—to obey whatever principles we like—but, in truth, we are not.

With the Reformation and the Renaissance, Western minds began to turn from the hereafter to the here and now. One of the bedrock principles of the Reformation was a belief in the power and worth of the human mind, which was a monumental change in the way Western people saw their world and saw themselves in it. The human mind, Renaissance thinkers argued, was capable of rational thought. From the sixteenth century on, more analytical ways of thinking, with their origins in classical antiquity, increasingly challenged the spiritualism and mysticism of the church in Western society. (It should be noted that people in the East, primarily those of Taoist and Dharmic persuasions, had recognized the power of the mind at least a millennium before the Renaissance in Europe.)

It is not at all coincidental that one of the most profoundly important advancements of the Renaissance was the development of the printing press and, with it, the mass distribution of printed news. All across Europe, the explosion in the availability of printed materials following Gutenberg's developments in the mid-1400s fundamentally challenged the *ancien régime* and its previously unrivaled power. By making the printed word available on a scale unimaginable in the era of hand copying, the printing press showed people firsthand that their own minds were indeed capable of reason and rational thought. Teach people how to read and put books and pamphlets in their hands and, voilà! You have a completely new level of rational discourse. What people believed came to be vastly more important than mere physical prowess, and the ability to share radical ideas behind the backs of religious or government authorities became easy and commonplace.

The West's return to rationalism reached its zenith during the Enlightenment of the mid- and late eighteenth century, an era in which the rational mind was thought to be capable of solving all problems, working out all mysteries. To some, the human mind came to replace the omnipotence and mystery of an older god. To others, the realization of the astounding power of reason was proof anew of God's presence. Yet, however people saw God's role in this new scheme of things, the historical record is clear that many of the most advanced minds of the West were increasingly convinced that humankind could eventually approach perfection through the exercise of the human intellect. There was less and less room in this world for intellectual confidence in rules-as-rules, for people blindly and willingly accepting the dictates of their ancestors, nobles, or clerics, and devoting their best energies to trying to live by others' rules. Not that those rationalists discarded ethics. On the contrary, the can-do attitude led to the assumption that the intellect could fix moral problems and solve injustice just as effectively as it could turn steam power into textile factories and, a little later, iron ore into railroads.

In the field of ethics, such confidence, fueled in part by an emerging trust (if not faith) in science, prompted a return to the Greek notion of teleology, which many took as a challenge to the church's rules. What is morally right and wrong, this thinking went, is not blind obedience to a set of rules; instead, it is based on rational predictions of the consequences of certain acts. Two notable champions of that new way of thinking were Jeremy Bentham and his godson John Stuart Mill. The name they used for their outcome-based ethical system was *utilitarianism*.

The name *utilitarianism* is somewhat unfortunate because the term seems to contain, at least to modern ears, a sense of mere practicality or usefulness, like consumer ratings on a brand of toaster or the recommendation to inflate one's car tires to 32 psi. True, Bentham and Mill were very much intellectuals of this world and were concerned with the real-world application of their ideas, but utilitarianism is a good deal more than an overly simplified philosophy of whatever works best. Instead, the term *utilitarianism* means the philosophy of determining, as well as one is able, the most likely outcomes of the various choices under consideration and then acting on the choice that will produce the greatest possible amount of good for the greatest number of people, which Mill called the "greatest happiness principle." As a philosophy, utilitarianism is very consistent with populism and democracy, for it insists that each person is as important as any other and that all are entitled to their fair share of the good. For journalists, whose work derives from populism and democracy, utilitarianism is an efficient and relatively easy way to approach ethical dilemmas.

Some dispute the value of utilitarianism as an approach to moral reasoning. Many postmodernists, for example, might argue that the concept of a greatest happiness principle is merely an illusion of harmony that veils the fact that life is, finally, a power struggle with winners and losers—as philosopher Michel Foucault suggested, anybody who studies the history of a war must necessarily choose sides. However, the most common and long-standing complaint about Mill's greatest happiness principle is that it specifically denies any sense of right or wrong that is independent of outcome. Many of Mill's critics see this as a serious flaw, arguing that pure utilitarianism would allow a government to condemn an innocent person if the execution would calm an outraged populace and prevent a murderous riot. Mill does not deal specifically with that question in his book on the topic, *Utilitarianism*, but a close reading of the book makes the complaint seem specious. For Mill did stress the importance of impartiality and of providing people with their just desserts, rewards as well as punishments. Mill was, in fact, quite troubled by a sense of justice that he believed was both real and universal, but for which he could find no completely rational explanation. It certainly seems to be a violation of this sense of justice that the state, acting in our name, would condemn an innocent person in the name of social order. And, if we factor in the respect for law embodied in *The Crito*, it seems reasonable to conclude that Mill would have seen a blatant injustice like a show trial and unjust execution as a serious tear in the social fabric, one that would produce, in the long run, far more harm than good.

Regardless of the path taken, many philosophers have maintained that all people have a moral sense of some sort (e.g., someone who enjoyed maiming children would be found repugnant) that is wholly independent of whether good or ill resulted. Criminologist James Q. Wilson took a stab at defining and then finding that moral core in his book *The Moral Sense*. Wilson combed the social science literature, especially work in sociology and anthropology, looking for a Darwinian explanation of human morality. The studies he cites are consistent with such an evolutionary sense of morality, but, in all candor, they do not prove its existence. It is probably unprovable.

If the existence of morality cannot be proved, why bother with it at all? Is the question of morality, perhaps, outdated nonsense or a pleasant diversion for the idle rich? Aren't ethics just too, well, nice, for the rough-and-tumble world in which we live? Was George Bernard Shaw right in *Pygmalion* when he had Colonel Pickering react with dismay when Eliza Doolittle's father asked to be paid for his daughter in Higgins's famous test of his ability to teach proper diction to anyone, even a Cockney like 'Liza?

> "Have you no morals, man," Pickering thundered.
> "Can't afford them, guv'nor," the senior Doolittle answered.
> "Neither could you, if you was as poor as me."

There are two answers to those questions. Neither may be fully compelling, but between them they cover most of the necessary ground. There is an explanation grounded in theology, which may be satisfying for those who are themselves religious and those who acknowledge theological influences on their lives. Whereas the world's great religions differ in rites and details, all contain a core principle of concern and kindness for one's fellow human beings. Across the centuries, many philosophers have echoed the sentiments of Sir Francis Bacon, the great English philosopher, when he wrote at the beginning of the seventeenth century, "All good moral philosophy is but an handmaid to religion."

For those who deny not only all religion but also the moral worth of all religious teaching, there is a societal reason to behave ethically. For people to live in societies—and all of us do—those societies have to function. A society functions, even minimally, only if most members of that society obey its rules voluntarily. Take, for example, the very common societal dictum that people should tell the truth. It is not just that telling the truth is nice, pleasant, or even enlightening. More profoundly, it allows society to function. Here's why: One of the key features that distinguishes a genuine society from a mere aggregate of isolated individuals is the level of sophistication in our communication with each other. However, that level of communication presupposes that the information being transmitted, from the trivial to the crucial, is true. At the trivial end, if someone on the street asks you for the time or directions, you are expected to respond honestly. At the other end of the importance scale, what is at the root of the global malaise concerning elected officials? The conviction that many of them do not tell the truth. What is at the heart of all contract law? The insistence that all sides do what they say they will do.

The same is true in the animal world. Animal behaviorists bring us fresh data all the time to suggest that many species have far more sophisticated forms of communication than scientists had earlier thought. The same principles governing individuals in human society are true there as well. If a honeybee "dances" in the midst of the hive to give directions through a complex set of vibrations to the other bees to help them find a good field of clover, that information is valuable only to the extent that it is true. If the dancing bee were to transmit false information and thus send the other bees off in the wrong direction, the whole hive would suffer.

This argument gets into social contract theory, which is worth a brief explanation. At its most fundamental, social contract theory, espoused initially in 1651 by Thomas Hobbes in *The Leviathan*, argues that there was a time before society when people were born with the unlimited natural right to do just as they pleased, including the right to kill one another over food and possessions. However, that world of one-against-all proved unsatisfactory to everyone, for, as Hobbes noted, people are similar enough in both brains and brawn that no one is safe from attack—if not from an individual, then from a small gang assembled for the purpose. In Hobbes's most famous phrase, life under such conditions is "solitary, poor, nasty, brutish, and short." The solution to that intolerable situation, he argued, was for people to surrender voluntarily many of their natural rights, including their right to predation, in return for the collective security of not being preyed upon. That theory of how human societies evolved was refined and elaborated upon for the next century and beyond by John Locke, Jean-Jacques Rousseau, and many others, but the essential principle remained intact: People are not wholly autonomous agents. Rather, they are, by necessity, part of a larger unit called society, the survival of which is crucial to the survival of its individual members.

We are primarily interested, however, in how an individual comes up with an ethical philosophy, even as we recognize the inevitable overlap between any individual's sense of morality and the moral code into which that person was born and socialized. There has been a good deal of discussion among philosophers and students of ethics over the centuries about the role of the self in ethical thinking. If I am a teleologist and therefore decide that I will act on that choice designed to produce the greatest ratio of good over evil, I have to decide whose good I am interested in, or most interested in. Some philosophers have argued that all of us are, eventually, concerned only with our own well-being, and properly so. That way of thinking is called *ethical egoism*. If you are an ethical egoist, you are declaring: I will act upon that choice that will produce the greatest good for me. One ethical egoist was Friedrich Nietzsche, the German philosopher of the late nineteenth century most well known for two observations: first, that "God is dead," by which it is thought he meant that the era of Christian morality and theology was over; and second, that the world was properly destined to be ruled by a tiny group of *Übermensch*, or "overmen," who were not bound by the "slave morality" of the "herd" of the rest of humanity. Nietzsche saw himself as the prime example of that new breed of *Übermensch*. If Nietzsche was correct, then it is, morally speaking, perfectly acceptable for people to declare themselves bound by one set of rules and everyone else bound by another.

The problem with such thinking is that, by definition, ethical reasoning must be concerned with the notion of self-in-society, not merely with self. That is what Niebuhr called "man-the-answerer," as he stressed that moral behavior must be seen in the context of how our behavior affects others, the complex web of actions and interactions that make up human society. Even thinkers like Thomas Hobbes, who was convinced that people truly cared only for themselves, realized that it was in each individual's interest that the larger society continues to function. It must be noted, however, that Hobbes's views of people as wholly self-centered received a good deal of support in the twentieth century from psychologists and sociobiologists who believe that we are, in a sense, hardwired for selfishness. Nevertheless, even if there are innate tendencies in this direction—something that is open for debate—one can still contend that people can learn to overcome those selfish tendencies through intellect and force of will, just as all social conventions, manners, and mores are learned. In hot weather, there is no physiological need to wear clothes at all, but most people beyond the toddler stage wear clothes anyway.

Such social conventions are called *norms*, and cultural norms can be found in all aspects of society, from favorite foods to holiday traditions to what behaviors are expected (or forbidden) in various circumstances. For example, there are rules about when it is acceptable to engage in conversation—at the dinner table, it's expected; in the movie theater, it's rude. Whether norms are actually cultural rules can be debated, but in most cases norms are not laws—one can break with a norm without committing any crime. Yet, when one does break with a norm, there can be strong consequences, either positive or negative in nature. An audience member who interrupts a concert by taking a call on her cell phone breaks with a norm in a negative way; the moral objections to human slavery broke with (and in many nations ended) a brutish norm that was thousands of years old. When it comes to ethics, norms are important to consider because many times assessments of right and wrong are based on the norms of the day. Many of the journalistic norms professionals take for granted today—such as telling both sides of the story, not making up information or sources, and not misrepresenting what a source actually says—actually came to be because older norms (one-sided reporting, fabrication of information and sources, putting words in sources' mouths) were found to be lacking. And many of the more controversial practices of modern journalism—such as undercover reporting, the use of unnamed sources, reporting information that has been classified by governments— represent practices that the industry (and society) isn't ready to fully reject or accept as norms.

We mention norms because many journalistic organizations have taken to creating codes of ethics, which are lists of ethical norms that members of those organizations are expected to adhere to. The Society of Professional Journalists (SPJ), a United States-based professional organization, has one of the more widely consulted codes of ethics, and many newsrooms and journalism schools post the SPJ code in public spaces as if the tenets therein are to be followed as law. What is most interesting is that every few years, the SPJ's ethics committee meets to revise the code, sometimes rewriting it entirely, to remove tenets that may be outdated and to add tenets that address previously unforeseen concerns. The fact that ethics codes often change is indicative of the inherent problem with ethics codes—they are not (or at least should not) be considered anything more than contemporary guides for beginning the process of moral reasoning. There often are many situations in which the best moral choice—the one that will result in the most good—is the one that breaks with the norm. And it is because of such situations that a journalist should be concerned with ethics, not just rules.

If ethical deliberation is important, what are the most important guiding principles that good journalists should follow and why? What conflicts can they expect, and what are some of the variables that may influence their decisions? For answers, it seems reasonable to examine the same intellectual history that is the core of our collective sense of moral propriety and look for the special ethical obligations incumbent upon journalists. That is because the same intellectual forces that have led to the modern free democracies of the world have granted the press enormous freedom under their constitutions. The First Amendment to the U.S. Constitution states, "Congress shall make no law . . . abridging the freedom of speech, or of the press. . . . " In the European Union, freedom of expression and information is considered a "common value" under the Charter of Fundamental Rights—many argue that the nations of Northern Europe provide even more press freedoms than the United States. Even some small and poor nations, such as El Salvador and Cape Verde, provide broad press freedoms in their constitutions, suggesting that freedom of the press need not be exclusive to large, wealthy nations such as the United States. At the root of those freedoms is a belief that to function properly, a democratic society needs a communication system that can inform the public, investigate government, challenge orthodoxy, and facilitate debate. Journalism, in all its varied forms, is the foundation upon which a public can govern itself.

The idea that the press is more than just an industry invariably leads to a discussion of whether journalism is a profession or a craft. A case can be made for using each term. Those who argue that journalism is a profession note its similarities to other professions. Journalism, medicine, and law all have important public service roles, their own professional organizations, and their own codes of standards of behavior, including ethics codes. Those who argue that journalism is a craft and not a profession note that, unlike medicine and law, journalism does not require any special training or license and that, although journalists do have their own codes of ethical behavior, there is no governing body for journalists that has the power to prevent transgressors from practicing or to drum out miscreants. Therefore, they say, journalism is more like a traditional craft, albeit one with somewhat more individual autonomy than some other crafts. Academics often like to discuss such differences (as do lawyers—the difference between craft and profession has important legal ramifications, such as individual autonomy and its resulting implications for responsibility and liability). However, many working journalists consider what they do to be more like a calling; they think of journalism as both the bulwark of democracy and as the last and best defense of individual rights. That sense of ethical responsibility and duty, as we shall see, can be best understood in the context of the political, philosophical, and economic underpinnings of modern journalism.

The Political Case for Moral Reasoning in Journalism

To make the political case that journalists should (i.e., are morally bound to) get at the truth as well as they are able requires a review of the core political principle of democratic self-government, or *popular sovereignty*. The principle was largely developed in Europe and was exported to other parts of the globe through colonialism, postwar occupation, and the Cold War of the mid to late twentieth century.

As already noted, in the seventeenth century, and increasingly in the eighteenth, the leading intellects of Europe, particularly in England and France, came to believe in the power and value of the human mind. They came to appreciate that human intellect was a powerful force and that human reason could be brought to bear successfully on solving life's greatest challenges. The reasons for that development are complex and tightly woven into the fabric of history. It was closely connected to the great explosion of Newtonian science and, in other ways, was a direct outgrowth of the Renaissance, the Protestant Reformation, and the Age of Discovery.

The upshot for political theory was the growing belief that people were capable, under the right circumstances, of governing themselves. The belief in the possibility of self-governance was a frontal assault on what had been the dominant theory of government for thousands of years, the so-called divine right of kings. In brief, the theory held that kings were selected by the supernatural (in Europe and the Middle East, by the God of Abraham) to run their countries for the greater glory of their gods. In Europe, the belief in self-governance did not by any means deny the existence of God or diminish God's power and authority—although those ideas would come later for some—but it did hold that human life was well worth living and that human society was worth improving for its own sake as well as for the greater glory of God. Such political thinking mirrors the shift in ethical thought from deontology to teleology, a shift noted earlier.

The new line of thinking came to be called the Enlightenment. It held that kings and princes did not have divine appointments to their thrones. What gave a king the right and the ability to govern other people was knowledge, not godly intervention. Furthermore, Enlightenment thinkers believed that if ordinary citizens were educated and informed, they could govern themselves. At first, the task of governance would be assumed by each individual; as societies grew, that task would be taken up by representatives serving at the people's pleasure.

The most significant assault on the old theory of the divine right of kings came from Thomas Hobbes, who developed the natural-rights theory about the origins of government, which was mentioned in Chapter 1. In Hobbes's view, as laid out in *The Leviathan*, each person in the community or state started out with absolute rights, including the right to harm other people to benefit oneself. However, in Hobbesian theory, people voluntarily surrendered those rights to a government that was established to protect people from themselves. Hobbes had a bleak view of human nature and thought that without a very strong central government—indeed, an absolutist one—individuals or groups would overthrow the government and society would revert to its natural state of war, in which each individual was pitted against all the others.

A generation later, another English political philosopher John Locke revisited the world of Hobbes's Leviathan and came away with a view of government that is similar to Hobbes's in many ways, but that also has profoundly important differences. In 1691, Locke published his own theory of the foundation of government and the proper role of the state in managing the affairs of its citizens. That document, *On Civil Government: The Second Treatise*, begins with natural rights, as Hobbes did, which leads to the idea of a government created to provide services (including protection) to the citizens. However, there was a crucial difference. Whereas Hobbes saw people as depraved, always and inevitably looking out for only their own interests, Locke saw people as capable of great good and possessing a broad concern for the well-being of their fellow citizens.

It is impossible to know for certain why the two men differed in their views of humanity, but there is little doubt that a major factor was their religious views. Hobbes was not a religious man by the standards of his day. (He was not, however, an atheist in the modern sense of the word.

His detractors accused him of atheism, which has led to some misunder-standing, but in the seventeenth century, the term did not carry with it the modern meaning of a direct denial of the existence of a deity. Hobbes did believe in God.) Locke, on the other hand, was a deeply religious man and had studied for the Anglican priesthood (he left before ordination, he said, because he feared that he would be only a middling priest). People with proper religious training in morals, Locke argued, could be trusted to have a stable society with more personal freedom, and far less govern-mental coercion, than in the absolute state that Hobbes had envisioned.

The notion of where ultimate political power should lie is the single most important difference in the worldviews of Hobbes and Locke. In Hobbes's world, people initially held power through natural rights, but they surrendered it permanently and irrevocably to the government; they could not be trusted any other way. However, for Locke, ultimate polit-ical power—that is, political sovereignty—remained with the people. In Locke's view, the government worked for the people, not the other way around.

The people hired legislators and tax collectors and diplomats to do the people's will, and if those hired functionaries did not do their jobs to the satisfaction of the sovereign people, then the people were entitled to get rid of them, Locke said. If the governors would not leave office when told to do so by their masters, the people could throw them out by force, even with violence, as a last resort. Thus, within the concept of the people re-taining ultimate power—that is, popular sovereignty—Locke provided a philosophical justification for armed revolution (Locke's father had fought for the Parliamentarians in the English Civil War, and Locke himself was an ardent supporter of the Revolution of 1688 and the overthrow of King James II). That justification would be cited again and again by revolution-aries for centuries to come, including the revolutionary generation that led the armed breakaway of the American colonies in 1776, the French Rev-olution of 1789, and many other republican revolutions that overthrew monarchs and emperors the world over.

At the time when Hobbes was exploring the nature of political power, another Englishman was exploring the notion of free speech, although from quite a different starting point. That was John Milton, the most im-portant poet of his era and one of England's most famous intellectuals. In Milton's day—the middle of the seventeenth century—everything printed in England had to be published by the small monopoly of government-sanctioned printers or had to get approval from them before publication. The government monopoly on printing, called the Stationers' Company, was a holdover from the days of Henry VIII. He saw the first printing press come into England in the generation after Gutenberg and immedi-ately saw the potential power it contained. Trying to harness that awe-some power, Henry clamped tight controls on printing. The controls were continued under the reign of Henry's daughter, Elizabeth I, and were still in place at the time of the Stuart succession in the early 1600s.

Milton got involved in the free-speech question because he wrote a pamphlet advocating more liberal divorce laws, a political hot-button issue of his day. Milton was interested in liberalizing divorce laws because he wanted to divorce a young countrywoman whom he had married and then separated from. When strict divorce laws kept him from ending his marriage, Milton, in exasperation, wrote a scathing pamphlet essentially demanding that he, the mighty Milton, should be allowed a divorce if he wanted one. In the ensuing debate over the divorce pamphlet, some of his critics noted that Milton, either in his rage or his arrogance, had not secured the required stamp of prepublication approval from the government censors, causing the debate to shift from divorce to prepublication censorship. Milton responded to that new criticism with a thundering denunciation of the censorship statute and a request—or demand—that the British House of Commons repeal it. He made his appeal in the form of a speech to the Commons, and it was subsequently published as a pamphlet entitled *Aeropagitica*. In towering prose, full of classical allusions and ringing phrases, Milton made the case for abolishing prepublication censorship.

Although many of Milton's phrases were memorable enough to be adopted centuries later as newspaper mottoes, what is frequently forgotten is that Milton made his argument primarily on religious grounds, not political ones. In Milton's day, the leading indicator of political beliefs and loyalty was religious affiliation, whether one was Church of England, or Anglican (the church in the United States is called Episcopalian), or one was Roman Catholic. For more than one hundred years, since Henry VIII's famous break with Rome in 1534, religion had dominated English politics and had largely determined political loyalty. To the Protestants, a group that included Milton and every member of the House of Commons he addressed, the Roman Catholic Church was seen as narrow-minded, dogmatic, intolerant, and anti-intellectual. The church was also held responsible for the bloody Crusades in the Middle East, the infamous Inquisition, and the Index of Forbidden Books. Protestants, by contrast, saw themselves as broad-minded, tolerant, and intellectually curious. They believed their religion could withstand rigorous inquiry, whereas the Catholic religion could not. So Milton's ringing argument for free speech is an argument made by an Anglican to a room full of Anglicans, asking for a distinctly Anglican decision. The same speech that demanded, "Let her [Truth] and falsehood grapple; who ever knew Truth to be put to the worst, in a free and open encounter?" also went on to say, "I mean not tolerated Popery," that is, Roman Catholicism. To Milton, Roman Catholics were so intolerant, so opposed to free inquiry that they should be banned and their books prohibited. So although it is true that Milton demanded "the liberty to know, to utter, and to argue freely according to consciences, above all other liberties," it is a misreading of history to make him a champion of free speech in anything like the secular political sense of the Enlightenment.

That argument did not begin until after Locke's work on civil government and the origins of political power. Among the earliest and best of those who worked through the free-speech implications of Lockean popular sovereignty were a pair of eighteenth-century political journalists who wrote under the pseudonym of Cato.

Cato, the name of a Roman statesman noted for his honesty and integrity, was the pen name of John Trenchard and Thomas Gordon, who began a weekly column in 1720 for a number of liberal London newspapers. The column ran for four years and covered a wide range of political topics, including government corruption and foreign policy. The columns were extremely popular with the liberal political faction called the Radical Whigs. The pieces were frequently republished in popular anthologies and widely sold among progressive political thinkers, both in Britain and in the American colonies. It was Cato who first explored the implications for journalism within the concept of popular sovereignty. That argument, made in *Essay No. 15*, was the clearest statement yet of the *political* need for free communication. At its most basic, it says that if the people are sovereign—that is, they retain ultimate political authority over their hired governors and functionaries—then the people have to know how well or how poorly their employees are doing their jobs. Cato went further, arguing that even though other principles might be violated, popular sovereignty in effect trumps all. It was more important to keep the sovereign people informed than it was to keep people thinking highly of their governors. Nothing less than human liberty was at stake.

In a subsequent column, *Essay No. 32*, Cato took the notion of free inquiry even further, challenging the centuries-old notion of libel in English common law. Since the founding of the modern state, toward the end of the Middle Ages, one of the most serious concerns of any government had been law and order, mostly order. No monarch anywhere felt truly secure on the throne, probably with good reason. There was always danger about, usually in the form of a potential usurper trying to stir up discontent that could lead to revolution. Broadly speaking, *libel* entailed saying (in modern usage, it means publishing) something derogatory about someone else, either a private citizen or the government. In either case, according to the British common law, the government was entitled to prosecute. A person who was libeled had a right to sue, but the government also had a right to prosecute because the person who had been libeled might react violently against the assailant. The point of libel law was to keep the king's peace far more than it was to prohibit derogatory words, therefore, truth was not a defense for libel—in fact, it exacerbated it. If the defamation were untrue, the reasoning went, the defamed person could probably mount a successful verbal defense against the libel. Yet, if the accusation were true, the person being libeled was considered less likely to rely on mere words for a defense and more likely to resort to physical violence, thus violating the king's peace. Hence the popular aphorism: The greater the truth, the greater the libel.

That concept was firmly entrenched in law long before John Locke came up with the notion of a sovereign citizenry. Here was a direct clash of legal principles. Speaking ill of government officials was clearly libelous, but the press had to be free to do just that if Lockean democracy had a chance of surviving. Cato was clear: The libel laws had to go. "Truth," Cato wrote, "can never be a libel." It was another seventy-five years before that principle became law in either England or in what had by then become the United States, but it has been a bedrock principle of journalism ever since.

The Enlightenment was in full swing by the second half of the eighteenth century and was responsible, in large measure, for massive political upheaval in the two European nations where Enlightenment thinking had taken root most successfully. In France, the storming of the Bastille prison by a Paris mob in 1789 led to the overthrow of the monarchy. During the very height of the French Revolution, the radical Jacobin Maximilien Robespierre made an impassioned defense of liberty of the press, borrowing Cato's phrase about a free press being the "bulwark of liberty" and arguing that a free flow of information was essential, especially in times of tumult. "The liberty of the press is the only effectual check of arbitrary power," Robespierre told the National Assembly. The revolution in France sent tremors of fear throughout Britain and Europe because the French monarchy was the very embodiment of the old order, the *ancien régime.* However, France's revolution was the second of the great Enlightenment revolutions. In Britain, thirteen years earlier, the revolution happened not in England proper, but in England's richest and most important colonies in the New World, America. The intellectual leadership of the Colonial rebellion was determined to put into practice the Enlightenment theories that so stressed the power of the intellect. The founding generation went to great lengths to curb the power of the government they were building, borrowing heavily from English and French intellectuals the notions of checks and balances, divisions of authority, and protections against what they saw as the inevitable desire of those in power to try to gather more power for themselves at the expense of the citizenry. The American revolutionaries were determined to create, for the first time in human history on a massive scale, a country built on the Lockean notions of popular sovereignty. The citizens, not the politicians, would hold ultimate political power.

Of all the things the American Revolution did to try to ensure that political power would continue to rest with the people, nothing was more important than the guarantee of unfettered communication, of a free flow of information that the governors themselves could not control. Knowledge alone did not guarantee that the grand experiment in popular self-government would work—even the most devoted Enlightenment thinkers never made that claim—but a free flow of information made it possible. That is the thinking behind the famous words of the First Amendment to the U.S. Constitution: "Congress shall make no law ... abridging the freedom of speech, or of the press. ... "

The first fragile years of the United States of America saw a furious political debate over whether the high-sounding principles of the Enlightenment could truly be implemented successfully, and in that crucible was forged the most enduring principles of journalistic freedoms. American politics broke along a European fault line; the more conservative forces allying themselves with the Britain they had just quit and the more daring seeing great virtue in the revolution then going on in France. Those split allegiances led to the formation of two political parties: the Federalists, led by John Adams, and the Democratic-Republicans, led by Thomas Jefferson and James Madison. As the arguments raged back and forth, supporters on both sides tried to find the balance point between individual liberty and the civil state. Among the best of the Jeffersonian writers was a New York lawyer named Tunis Wortman. Wortman contributed very little that was truly original, but his 1801 book *A Treatise Concerning Political Enquiry and the Liberty of the Press* provided an outstanding summation of the Democratic-Republican position on the principles of free expression.

About the same time, another Jeffersonian, John Thomson, wrote *The Uncontroulable Nature of the Human Mind*, a remarkable book that evokes Milton's "truth will out" argument and neatly sums up the popular sovereignty arguments for a free press. Thomson also foreshadowed much of John Stuart Mill's argument in *On Liberty*, written half a century later. However, Thomson's main point, suggested by the title of his book, is that human beings start out as blank slates—shades of Mill's *tabula rasa*—and that they respond to external stimuli and learn, layer by layer, from experience. He argues that people thus have no control over their thought processes and that expression, written or oral, is merely a manifestation of thought. To Thomson, it is both wicked and foolhardy for a government— which is, as he points out, made up only of people—to try to control the minds and expressions of others when they cannot, in truth, control their own.

Mill, who contributed the concept of utilitarianism to ethical thinking, also argued for freedom of expression. By the middle of the nineteenth century, when he wrote *On Liberty*, he thought it safe to assume that there was a widespread understanding of and belief in freedom of the press—the popular sovereignty arguments of Cato and Wortman. He endorsed those principles in a paragraph, then went on to argue, as Thomson did, that free inquiry led inevitably to greater truth. If an argument is right, Mill argued, it should be expressed for all to hear it. If an argument is wrong, Mill said, it can be and must be successfully refuted by better thinking—thinking that would be sharper and more acute for the exercise. Moreover, if an argument is partly right and partly wrong, as Mill believed most were, both of the preceding principles would come into play.

There is another dimension to Mill's argument about the importance of refuting a bad argument. That is the notion of the *dialectic*, often called the Hegelian dialectic for one of its chief developers, the early nineteenth-century German philosopher Georg Wilhelm Friedrich Hegel. In the Hegelian dialectic, progress is always achieved by an idea, the *thesis*, coming into collision with its opposite, the *antithesis*. The result is a new entity that Hegel called the *synthesis*. The synthesis becomes the new thesis; it is in turn opposed by a new antithesis, leading to a new synthesis, and the process of refining ideas continues.

Mill also made a valuable point that is sometimes lost upon Americans because of their superficial belief in majority rule. Mill argued vehemently for minority rights within majority rule. In a famous passage, Mill argued, "If all mankind minus one were of one opinion, mankind would be no more justified in silencing that one person than he, if he had the power, would be justified in silencing mankind." Mill was so committed to the notion that the individual be fully free that he argued that human behavior should be limited only if it would cause direct harm to others. People engaging in intemperate, foolish, or even self-destructive actions could be argued with or cajoled, Mill said, but they should never be coerced unless their behavior would be harmful to others.

The Western democracies have long struggled with the idea of protecting minority rights. In the early nineteenth century, John C. Calhoun argued that legislation should be passed according to the principle of "concurrent majority," which would mean that the people affected by the legislation would have to concur with its passage, even if they were in the minority. In the late twentieth century, efforts to address the question of minority rights in the United States led to the gerrymandering of some voting districts to ensure political representation for minorities and to the idea of cumulative voting, espoused by the legal scholar Lani Guinier, to give minority candidates a better chance of winning elections. Many democracies in Europe, Asia, and South America restrict certain forms of speech to protect minorities—for example, in many European countries it is illegal to publish works that deny the Holocaust because such work is deemed anti-Semitic, and the post-apartheid South African constitution does not extend free-speech protections to "advocacy of hatred that is based on race, ethnicity, gender or religion, and that constitutes incitement to cause harm." A free flow of information is especially important for minority rights; even without political clout, the right of minorities to express and disseminate ideas is a crucial tool, perhaps their most powerful one.

However, journalism can bring people harm as well as benefits. One of the harms that bothers readers and viewers the most concerns the invasion of privacy. During periods of intense media attention to spectacular events, such as the accidental death of Princess Diana in 1997 or the untimely death of U.S. model Anna Nicole Smith in 2007, two seemingly contradictory things usually happen. First, the news media—from the staid newspapers to gaudy tabloid TV shows to the free-and-loose gossip sites on the Internet—focus massive attention on the events and on the backgrounds and personalities of the people involved. Second, hordes of media critics—a relative handful of professionals and many thousands of bloggers and writers of letters to the editor—complain that the press is invading the privacy of some or all of the people involved. The complaint is usually some variation of "How dare they?"

The notion of privacy seems almost intuitively to be part and parcel of what it means to be a free citizen in our society. Many countries today provide explicit legal protections of privacy, and some restrict journalists' access to private information, but the notion is relatively new in the legal systems of the world. For more than a century after the American Revolution, there was little attention paid to privacy as a legal concept in American courts. It was not until two technological developments of the late 1800s—high-speed newspaper presses and the halftone process, which allowed photographs to be run in newspapers—that privacy became a serious issue. It was a heyday of what we now call the paparazzi, the photographers who make a living shooting and selling photographs of the rich and famous without their consent, and the questionable ethics of such journalism has been used to justify the erosion of press liberties the world over.

In the 1890s, in the midst of a great outcry against this practice, two young Boston lawyers, Samuel Warren and Louis Brandeis (who would later become famous as a U.S. Supreme Court justice), developed the modern notion of the right to privacy. In a famous 1890 article in the *Harvard Law Review*, Warren and Brandeis went back to first principles and said they had discovered a fundamental right to be left alone. The argument builds its case on the familiar and cherished Lockean guarantees of life, liberty, and the pursuit of property. Over time, the young lawyers argued, the definition of property has expanded from the concrete to the abstract.

In the same way that the notion of property was expanded to include intellectual property, they argued, the idea of the right to one's person and estate should be expanded in law to include the right to enjoy those things away from public scrutiny. Just as Cato made a nod to privacy with the observation that some trivial things, even about public figures, were not worth knowing even if true, so Brandeis and Warren acknowledged that their notion of the right to privacy was far from absolute. In good Lockean tradition, they contended that matters and people of "public and general interest" were the legitimate targets of press scrutiny.

This concept of privacy is often at the very core of political restrictions against press freedoms. In India, which has the least restrictive press laws in southern Asia, reporters can face criminal defamation charges if they invade the privacy of individuals, including government officials. In Canada, which is generally considered a free-press nation, journalists can face prosecution for publishing information about criminal trials before a verdict is issued. Japan, also a free-press nation, has a system of press clubs, or *kishas*, which are cozy with government and corporate leaders and, as such, rarely challenge attempts to protect privacy at the cost of press freedoms. In some countries, where neither the law nor the culture restricts the press, media-hostile officials may resort to brute force, as in Kenya in March 2006, when the government, upset by reports in the news media about alleged private negotiations between political rivals, ordered police to raid the offices of the Kenyan Television Network and *The Standard* newspaper—in the raid, journalists were detained at gunpoint, expensive equipment was damaged or destroyed, and copies of *The Standard* were burned by police.

The concept of privacy parallels the concept of security, which is another and perhaps more troubling concern for those who believe freedom of the press is necessary in democratic societies. Whereas privacy laws are generally meant to allow individuals (even public officials) to keep personal secrets, security laws are meant to provide for similar secrecy by the government itself. A common argument in defense of such press limitations extends from the realities of warfare—commanders charged with planning and executing battles naturally would be at a disadvantage if journalists could reveal tactical plans or specific troop locations. During the Cold War of the mid to late twentieth century, governments became even more secretive on other matters of national security, particularly in terms of espionage, diplomacy, research and development of military technologies, and even international trade agreements. With popular support based on both real and perceived fears among the public, democratic governments were able to draft and implement laws that allowed for increased government secrecy, from closed-door meetings of local school boards and city councils to broad powers of presidents and prime ministers to classify documents in the name of national security.

The initiation of the global war on terror in late 2001—precipitated by a massive terrorist attack on the United States and aggravated by other large-scale attacks in Madrid, London, India, and Russia—has provided even more popular support for so-called security laws that either directly or indirectly limit freedom of the press. Some governments, most notably the United States and Russia, have dramatically increased the criminal prosecution of journalists who are accused of leaking government information, even information that has little or nothing to do with defense issues. For example, U.S. prosecutors took legal action against reporters who had investigated claims of illegal steroid use by professional baseball players—hardly a matter of national security.

Whether because of paparazzi like those who chased Princess Diana's car into that fateful tunnel in Paris, or because of aggressive investigative journalists who revealed secret details of anti-terror tactics of the White House under President George W. Bush, or because of the scores of incidents each year in which journalists cross lines that the public thinks should not be crossed, one thing is certain: The controversial decisions of a few journalists have been catalysts for political erosion of the freedoms of all journalists. Whereas the political case for journalism ethics is based on the very foundations of popular sovereignty, today, the most pressing reason for moral practice in journalism is not to honor traditions but to preserve press freedoms for the next generation.

3 ▪ ▪ ▪

The Philosophical Case for Moral Reasoning in Journalism

The most straightforward reason that journalists are morally obliged to tell the truth is that the search for truth is one of humanity's most powerful intellectual drives. In this regard, journalists are among the most important of a broad array of communicators. Journalists are voices of the citizenry who, to put it most simply, help us understand us, and who connect us with one another. Journalists inform scientists about sports scores, inform athletes about politics, and inform politicians about the arts—and so it goes. Journalists inform communities about the workings of local government and about fun activities in the public parks, and inform nations and continents about faraway wars and remarkable discoveries in remote corners of the world. Underlying the efficacy of those connections is the understanding that the information is, to the best of the journalists' ability, truthful.

The record of human thought is filled with efforts to know and to discern truth from illusion or falsehood. A brilliant early example is Plato's "Allegory of the Cave" from *The Republic*, written in the fourth century B.C.E. In the parable, Plato describes a row of people who spend their lives chained within a cave, their heads bound so that they can look only straight ahead. He further imagines that a fire is burning behind the prisoners and that puppeteers are positioned behind them as well, but in front of the light source, so that their puppets will cast shadows on the wall in front of the prisoners. Plato then suggests that one of the prisoners gets loose. He leaves the cave and discovers the real world beyond the shadows on the wall of the cave. Plato then discusses the difficulty the freed prisoner would have in returning to the darkness of the cave and trying to persuade the prisoners to believe his tale of what he had seen and heard in the world above.

The parable is a complex piece of philosophic thought, and readers over the centuries have found much in it to debate. In Plato's cave, those who have been chained together inside the cave are clearly not at fault, in the sense of being morally liable for some failing or shortcoming. However, Plato is quite clear that they are mistaken in believing that the two-dimensional shadows on the wall are reality. For journalists, it provides a good lesson in how long-standing is the human search for truth and a caution against relying too heavily on surface appearances. It also points to the complex and powerful influence of culture on perceptions—whether chained to a wall in a cave or fixated on a single news channel, people who can't (or won't) gain new perspectives are doomed to stubborn ignorance.

It is worth noting the context of the statement from Plato about the existence and the comprehensibility of reality. Plato is clearly arguing that a reality exists, but many of us are so blinded by our own circumstances that we neither see reality nor are aware that we do not. In this, Plato was arguing against the position held by a group of Greek thinkers called *sophists*, who were by no means convinced that there was such a thing as reality. The sophists were willing to argue any side of any question, contending that, in the absence of reality, it did not matter much which side one argued. The debate in early Greece over the existence of reality is strikingly familiar to the debate among intellectuals in recent years over a twist in cultural relativism: the question of whether there are enduring values—ideas and principles that are valid and valuable across time and space—or whether everything is relative, in which case no values would be better than any others, and none would be more true than any others, just different.

If Plato's fight with the sophists seems to have a familiar ring, so should the arguments for clearheaded thinking and objective analysis advanced in the early seventeenth century by the English philosopher Francis Bacon. Bacon, one of the earliest champions of the scientific method, agreed with Plato that truth was attainable, but hard to find. In his great work, the *Novum Organum*, he sought nothing less than a wholesale rethinking and codification of human thought. In a famous passage of the book, he listed four barriers—"idols," he called them—to true understanding. The barriers were the various traps of faulty reasoning and comprehension, beginning with humankind's general tendency to rely on perception alone and, as a result, get things mixed up, which Bacon called the Idol of the Tribe. On top of the general failings of human perception is the individual's propensity toward misunderstanding based on personal thoughts and opinions, which he called the Idol of the Cave (in obvious reference to Plato's cave). Next, he noted that when people talk to one another, the information transfer is far from perfect, a situation he called the Idol of the Marketplace—not in the sense of a marketplace where things are bought and sold, but in the sense of a place where people gather to talk and exchange information. Finally, Bacon described what he called the Idol of the Theater, the barriers to truth thrown up by the various schools of thought (religious dogma, secular philosophy, scientific axioms, etc.). He called it the Idol of the Theater because, he said, those systems of thought were "so many stage-plays, representing worlds of their own creation," rather than accurate and honest representations of reality. All four idols add up to a recipe for misunderstanding, Bacon argued, such that "what a man had rather were true he more readily believes. Therefore he rejects difficult things from impatience of research; sober things because they narrow hope; the deeper things of nature, from superstition; the light of experience, from arrogance and pride . . . [and] things not commonly believed, out of deference to the opinion of the vulgar." To overcome those barriers to understanding, Bacon argued, people must turn to empirical observations, even though there are daunting possibilities for error in that realm, and to pay strict attention to what later came to be called the scientific method.

Much has happened in the world of intellectual thought in the nearly four centuries since Bacon published his *Novum Organum* in 1620. Modern political theory was developed in those years, and democracy as we know it was not merely dreamed of, but implemented, however imperfectly, in many nation-states of the world. By the early twentieth century, mercantilism had largely been replaced by capitalism, but the Industrial Revolution and the horrors of the factory system, pointed out by Charles Dickens, among many others, cast serious doubt on its long-term survival. Yet, Marx and other major critics of capitalism seemed able to fashion nothing better. The Enlightenment, with its cool reason, and a successor movement, the richly emotional Romantic period, had come and gone. Freud had shattered, probably forever, the widespread optimism that progress was inevitable, or even likely. A war of unfathomable atrocity had bled the West into exhaustion, with an entire generation of the best and the brightest perishing at Verdun, the Sommes, Gallipoli, and Ypres.

In the years just after the horrors of World War I, perhaps the most prescient mind in American journalism was that of Walter Lippmann. He noted the massive complexity of then-modern life, at one point likening the contemporary citizen to a deaf spectator at a stage play—able to see and to understand a little, but painfully aware that much was going by without comprehension. Lippmann's solution was, essentially, Bacon's—recognize the pitfalls of the idols, challenge received information, and bench-test ideas. Apply as much mental rigor to news copy as to any other intellectual endeavor.

What Lippmann was advocating was essentially the often confused and maligned notion of journalistic objectivity. Although it seems true today that entire industries have sprung up to denounce the dreaded *O* word, the concept is quite simple. The job of journalism is to provide citizens in a democracy with the information they can use to make rational decisions about how best to govern their own lives. It is not to govern for them, nor to decide for them, but to provide the tools that people can use in making their own decisions. At the same time, Lippmann recognized that a mere collection of unsorted information was virtually useless; factoids, as CNN calls them, are amusing, even interesting, but hardly the serious stuff with which to build an informed citizenry. Information is all but useless without context, shape, color, and background.

It is important to note that the goals of objectivity and context often work against each other; the more one tries to achieve one of those goals, the more the other is jeopardized. In a given situation, it is fairly easy to arrive at a set of facts on which most reasonable people can agree. As an example, consider any news article about the incident at the end of the 2006 FIFA World Cup in which French player Zinedine Zidane flattened Italian player Marco Materazzi with a head-butt to the chest. In the incident, neither Zidane nor Materazzi had possession of the ball, and Zidane was walking away from Materazzi when he turned and rammed his head into the Italian player's chest. Most people would agree that those two facts are germane to the story, and nearly all journalists would include them in the account of the accident. What about the details that Zidane and Materazzi had sparred over the ball furiously in that game? That too would be considered germane. What about the facts that Zidane was the youngest of five children and was raised in a government housing project? Almost certainly not. Or that he was born to Algerian immigrants? Probably not. How about the fact that Zidane had a reputation for losing his temper on the pitch, and that in the 1998 World Cup he was issued a red card for stomping on the captain of the Saudi Arabian team, Fuad Amin? Yes. How about the fact that Materazzi had a reputation for being a bit of a bully on the pitch and was nicknamed "The Matrix" by his teammates for having a "complicated" mind? That is less clear. How about the fact that video footage showed Materazzi saying something to Zidane that could have provoked the attack (as was later discovered to be the case)? How about the fact that Materazzi had been expelled from an earlier game in the tournament? Clearly, if one were to include *everything* one could find out about the incident, the story would be hopelessly complex and loaded with irrelevant details. On the other hand, it is very difficult to say with great certainty just which details are illuminating and which are gratuitous. Nevertheless, agreeing on the pertinent details of thuggish behavior in a football match looks easy when compared with doing the same in a sexual assault case. How much of the suspect's background is pertinent then and how much of the victim's? Keep in mind that stories about crimes are relatively straightforward. Political stories can be vastly more complicated—the full story about a proposed piece of legislation would be nearly impossible to tell in a single article or newscast.

With that in mind, Lippmann provided an important reminder that journalism is not designed to supply, and is probably not capable of supplying, all the information citizens need. In his most famous book, *Public Opinion*, he suggested that journalism is much like a searchlight, moving here and there in the night sky, illuminating one small incident and then another, but never providing the broad, even light needed to conduct the public's business. The last generation has witnessed many demands on journalism—that it provide more trends and lifestyles articles, that it does a better job with traditionally underrepresented groups, and that it explains art and economics and a host of other subjects better than it did in the past. In addition, in truth, during the last generation or so, journalism has made enormous strides toward providing those things. Doubters should read newspapers, listen to radio archives, and watch television broadcasts from the 1950s and even the 1960s and compare them to news reports of today. Overall, news material from a generation ago is almost farcical in its triviality and superficiality when compared with the best of today's print, broadcast, and online journalism.

Still, it is valuable to recall Lippmann's disclaimer that newspapers (and now broadcast and online news as well) cannot convey all of the necessary or important information to a passively receptive public. Full participation in the democratic process takes considerably more than twenty-two minutes of the evening news, a glance through the local weekly newspaper, or a daily perusal of the Web site of the *Times*. A truly informed citizen needs to read books and magazines, attend public lectures, engage in discussions with friends and colleagues, and, perhaps above all in Lippmann's mind, have access to public policy institutions that aim to serve the public. The journalist can help, and the journalist may in fact be a critical element in all this, but, Lippmann said, news and truth are not the same thing as being there. News, at bottom, is an honest and comprehensible report of current events; truth is vastly more complex than any single article or series of articles can possibly convey, however artfully and honestly crafted.

One of the most serious problems that Lippmann noted in the journalist's quest for understanding was the rise of contrived events—the so-called news events and photo ops that are the products of public relations, which was a fledgling profession in Lippmann's day. The impact of such information manipulation was explored in great detail by Daniel Boorstin in his classic book, *The Image*. Boorstin, a former Librarian of Congress and the author of a number of important popular histories, devoted a considerable portion of his book to the rise of what he called the pseudo-event and the relationship of such events to newsgathering.

The pseudo-event, as Boorstin defined it, is anything that does not happen spontaneously but rather is deliberately staged for the purpose of generating news coverage. At its most extreme, a pseudo-event may be a political photo op (shorthand for photographic opportunity). Typically, a political figure appears to be doing something while photographers and camera operators capture the event on camera. It could be a president or secretary of state sitting in a formal office talking with a foreign dignitary, suggesting the importance of that foreign country in domestic policy, or a candidate walking through a veterans' hospital, suggesting that the candidate is both deeply patriotic and is concerned about military families. Ribbon-cuttings and check-passings are perhaps the most common photo ops at the local level. Typically, such photo ops are staged for photographers and TV cameras, but they aren't the same as press conferences. In photo ops, reporters are allowed to watch the "event," but they are usually not allowed to ask any questions on the grounds that questions might divert attention from the visual image that has been painstakingly organized by the politician's image handlers.

However, pseudo-events include far more than just picture-taking sessions. Other staged events are press conferences, most political rallies, civil rights and other popular demonstrations, and a host of other events that are put on primarily or exclusively for the benefit of the journalists who may cover them. They include, certainly, tidy political maneuvers, such as U.S. President Ronald Reagan having his picture taken in a working-class tavern in Boston to show his "sympathy for the working stiff"—as Reagan's media handler extraordinaire Michael Deaver put it—to the speech by Venezuelan President Hugo Chavez to the United Nations General Assembly in which he condemned the U.S. government for its perceived imperialism and called U.S. President George W. Bush "the devil." Today, they also include sports tournaments, awards ceremonies, and publicity tours. However, they also include less civilized actions, such as public assassinations and suicide bombings.

Boorstin does not blame the image makers entirely for the phenomenal growth of the staged event. He also blames journalists for swallowing such events whole, then demanding more. Publishers have known for more than 150 years that they stand to make a great deal of money out of selling information, provided it is lively enough and interesting enough for the consuming public. As a result, Boorstin argues, news outlets are set up to handle massive amounts of news, the "great yawning maw" of the news hole, as some reporters call it. If there are not enough real events to fill up the paper or the broadcast in a given news cycle, editors and news directors are extremely vulnerable to the lure of covering the staged event. For reporters who need to produce content on deadline, staged events are much easier to cover than real ones because little or nothing is left to chance. A contrived happening will be staged at a time and place convenient for reporters to get to, often with a coffee urn nearby. Anyone who has ever wandered through Disney World has certainly noticed the little yellow signs recommending where to take the most scenic pictures. Pseudo-events have their own versions of the little yellow signs, less obtrusive but just as manipulative. The production will be painstakingly set up, and the places for still and television cameras will be selected with care so the photographers will get what they want—compelling pictures—and the event's arranger will get the desired image across to the viewers.

The pseudo-event presents at least two serious problems for journalists, especially journalists who depend upon pictures to tell their stories. One problem is that the pseudo-event may not be news; paradoxically, the other problem is that the staged event may have considerable news value. A candidate's trip through a public school can be dismissed as a blatant attempt at news management, although TV stations will find it very difficult to turn down pictures of such a colorful event, particularly in markets with keen competition. However, the pseudo-event that produces real news is more troubling for the thoughtful journalist. In journalists' understandable effort to provide readers and viewers with as much information about their elected officials as possible, they have, in the last generation, considered newsworthy virtually anything that a head of state does. Knowing this, the image handlers are happy to provide opportunities for television cameras to photograph the president or the prime minister doing things that the image makers wanted him or her to be perceived as doing, knowing that journalists would be largely unable to resist. Yet, the payoff for journalists is that the leaders may go off script and let slip bits of important new information that reveal unforeseen truths about the inner workings of government or the true nature of our leaders—even the most accomplished spinmeister can't prevent a buffoonish leader from revealing his true colors with the cameras rolling. In today's heavily mediated world, the pseudo-event may well be a necessary evil in the pursuit of truth.

4 ▪ ▪ ▪

The Economic Case
for Moral Reasoning
in Journalism

One of the strongest values of a free press is that it must remain free of government control, and by extension that means it must also remain free from government financing. There are exceptions, most notably the world's largest broadcasting organization—the British Broadcasting Corporation, or the BBC—which is owned by the people of the United Kingdom, but remains relatively free of government control as to programming and news coverage. Less encouraging are examples of government media ownership in Asia, particularly post-Soviet Russia and modern China, where government exercises considerable influence (through law and/or intimidation) on journalists. However one argues whether journalism is a craft, profession, or even a calling, it is undeniable that in truly democratic societies, it is also a business, and it exists in the world of contemporary global capitalism for better or for ill. Even state-owned media, such as the BBC in Britain, and nonprofit media such as PBS and NPR in the United States, are heavily influenced by market forces in terms of both finances and programming. Therefore, a brief review of the world's dominant economic model is in order.

The basic text of capitalism's most fundamental features is *An Inquiry into the Nature and Causes of the Wealth of Nations*, written by Adam Smith and published in 1776 as an answer to the then-dominant economic model called *mercantilism*. At its most basic, mercantilism argued that nations should set economic policy designed to increase the amount of gold and silver in one nation at the expense of the amount of gold and silver in another. Mercantilism, which was popular in the sixteenth, seventeenth, and eighteenth centuries, was an early version of what in contemporary parlance is often called a zero-sum game. It argued that there was a fixed amount of wealth in the world and that governments should erect tariff boundaries to keep out imports, offer bounties to increase exports, and otherwise try to maximize the flow of money into the country.

However, Smith argued that economics is a win-win situation, if we can again borrow terminology from modern game theory. All nations could increase their wealth, Smith contended, if only governments would get out of the way and let natural forces take over. The term most often associated with Smith's economic policy is the French term *laissez-faire*, meaning let it be or leave it alone. Smith said governmental tinkering with economic matters only gets in the way of what he called the "invisible hand." That metaphorical hand, Smith argued, sets the natural price of goods and services. Two cobblers, for example, would compete with each other for customers by trying to make better boots and by selling them at a cheaper price. The result would be the highest possible quality of boots and the lowest possible price, consistent with the boot maker making a comfortable profit for the labor expended. If, because of better climate or cheaper raw materials, a French boot maker were to make and sell high-quality boots in England cheaper than an English boot maker could, everyone would benefit by having the English artisans seek a different trade in which to prosper. Smith argued that unrestricted competition would inevitably produce the best possible combination of price and quality for all goods and services. Any governmental interference, he argued, simply adds inefficiency to a natural system and interferes with the natural principles of supply and demand. All people should be allowed to follow their own best interests, and the "invisible hand" will guarantee that the result will be the best possible system, Smith said.

Wealth of Nations was published in the same year as the American Declaration of Independence. That is in some ways an unfortunate coincidence because it leads to the false assumption that the principles of laissez-faire capitalism are linked with the founding of the United States, giving free-market economics an even stronger position in American lore than it deserves. In fact, U.S. economic policy was interventionist from the very beginning because America's founders freely used fiscal tools and strategies to shape the type of society they wanted. As one example among many, consider the U.S. government's economic policy toward the news business. As noted earlier, the founders of the United States believed that a free flow of information was absolutely critical to the survival of the popular democracy they were trying to build. On the legal front, they protected the free flow of information with the First Amendment. On the economic front, the government granted important favors to journalists. Foremost among them was cheap postage—essentially a major government subsidy—that newspapers still enjoy and many rely upon more than two centuries later. The U.S. government bestowed other financial concessions on journalists as well: for example, building many roads and post offices that were very beneficial to newspapers but were otherwise not necessary. However, the proximity in time of the publication of the U.S. Declaration of Independence and that of *Wealth of Nations* has contributed to the notion, popular among many in business, that American-style liberty means nearly absolute economic as well as political freedom.

For the news business to succeed economically, all that was needed was a buying public large enough to create a huge market for news and a technology able to feed that market. Those two elements came into being in the 1830s with the birth of what is known, in historians' shorthand, as the *penny press*. The growth of major U.S. cities and the arrival of new printing technology enabled journalism to enter a powerful new phase. No one better represents that new world than James Gordon Bennett, who began the *New York Herald* in 1835. Bennett soon realized that journalism could not only enlighten its readers, but could also enrich its publishers.

More than anyone who had gone before, Bennett realized that people would pay for information if it was fresh and entertaining. Bennett confirmed on a new scale what had been learned much earlier, going all the way back to Benjamin Franklin a century before: Advertisers will happily pay for access to a newspaper's readers. What Bennett contributed was not the realization that advertising pays, but the idea that news itself pays, that information can itself become a mass commodity. Thus, with Bennett, the most enduring dichotomy of Western journalism truly began. Someone approaching journalism purely from its political, popular-sovereignty dimension is clearly interested in putting important information in the hands of as many people as possible because democracy depends upon broad participation. At the same time, providing interesting information, whether useful or not, can make its provider, that is, the publisher, wealthy. From Bennett's day onward, it has been difficult to separate the political and philosophical motives of journalism from the economic ones, especially because the freedom to make money—Smith's free-market capitalism—is as deeply ingrained in the Western psyche as is the political freedom to say what one chooses and the philosophical freedom to follow truth wherever it leads.

In Europe, where the Industrial Revolution came earlier than it did to the United States, Karl Marx, Charles Dickens, and other critics of the factory system pointed out that Smith's argument for free-market capitalism belonged to an era of individual artisans, when cobblers made their own boots. With the onset of the factory system, owners did less and less of the actual work of manufacturing; instead, they hired wage laborers by the hundreds and then by the thousands to run the machinery of the Indus-trial Age. The cost of that labor quickly became the most significant part of a capitalist's cost of doing business, so when Smith's invisible hand set to work controlling the price of goods, the first step in cutting costs was to reduce wages. As early as 1800, critics such as David Ricardo and Thomas Malthus were arguing that in the new industrial world, free-enterprise capitalism guaranteed massive human misery because the "iron law of wages," as Ricardo put it, would keep workers at no more than subsis-tence pay. By the early twentieth century, Marxism had been interpreted broadly throughout the West (and in the East decades later, most notably in China), leading to decades of Soviet-style communism in Russia and Eastern Europe and to the socialist democracies that dominate the West today.

For journalists, one of the most important influences of Marxism was a widespread sympathy for the working class and serious concerns about the social harms of the unrestrained accumulation of capital. Among the more interesting of such voices was that of Joseph Pulitzer, who in the late 1870s anticipated that which, a generation later, would come to be known as the *muckraking tradition*—the role of the press to investigate and report on the seedy underbelly of big business and corrupt government. Money brings with it power, Pulitzer observed, and money can and does corrupt the political and economic systems. Pulitzer's warning concerned a spe-cific U.S. Senate campaign in which wealthy industrialists were trying to buy their way into office (sadly, a problem to this day in most democratic nations), but his point is well taken on a broader level as well. The guar-antee of a free press was established, at considerable social cost, to enable democracy to work. If money corrupted that democracy, despite the free flow of information, then the political influence of that money needed to be curtailed. What the muckrakers were saying—and what Pulitzer re-ally was foreshadowing—was the idea that however well the press guard against the corrupting influence of wealth and greed on democracy and free societies.

The muckraking era proper got under way about the turn of the twentieth century. Although Pulitzer's *New York World* undertook many serious stories about corruption of the political system, especially by wealthy interests, most muckraking was done for magazines, which had more space and time to devote to the long, complex stories that muckrak-ing often entails. In a sense, it is unfortunate that Pulitzer was a muckraker at all, for the fact that he championed good causes adds to the confusion over the differences between muckraking and its ill-mannered cousin called *yellow journalism*, which has come to mean irresponsible pandering and focusing on salacious details of sex, violence, and wrongdoing. Yellow journalism is also associated with Pulitzer, especially during his great circulation war of the 1890s with William Randolph Hearst's

New York Journal.[1] There are several reasons why people often confuse the two genres: They were both at their height around the turn of the twentieth century; they had some overlapping memberships; and, less obvious but just as important, they were often deliberately misidentified by the people who were the objects of the muckrakers' attention. Then, as now, muckraking exposés of malfeasance had elements that were personally embarrassing to their targets, and those targets often fought back by labeling the attacks yellow journalism in attempts to discredit the reports. The answer from a responsible journalist, then as now, would be that the public interest served by publication overrode any concern about the private discomfort of powerful individuals. However much journalists dislike causing personal pain or embarrassment—and the good ones dislike it acutely—providing the information that citizens need to have to govern their own lives is paramount. The problem, of course, is that some information is embarrassing and important, whereas other information is merely titillating, and people of good will and bad may differ over which is which. Since Bennett's day, when pandering became extremely profitable, unscrupulous publishers have been willing and eager to confuse the two. The test of what belongs in the public arena may not have changed since Cato's day, but the financial stakes have gone up considerably.

By the 1920s, some of the best muckrakers turned their attention to the news industry itself. Upton Sinclair, a dedicated socialist, concluded sadly that the watchdogs had caught the disease they were trying to keep at bay. In *The Brass Check*, Sinclair argued compellingly that news organizations had themselves become big businesses and were no more honest and no more concerned with the real welfare of the working classes than were the lords of the steel, oil, and agribusiness industries.

A generation later, the press critic A. J. Liebling made much the same argument from a less extreme political perspective. Liebling noted the decline of genuine competition among news outlets and saw in that decline a loss of interest in ferreting out important stories. In the late twentieth and early twenty-first centuries, Ben Bagdikian, a veteran journalist and journalism educator, chronicled the trend toward having a handful of huge corporations controlling more and more of the U.S. nation's and the world's information providers. His argument is eloquent evidence supporting an argument Marx made more than a century ago, that capital tends to accumulate in fewer and fewer hands. With each new edition of Bagdikian's important book *The Media Monopoly* (renamed *The New Media Monopoly* in 2004), the author notes the dwindling number of corporations controlling the world's mass media. What is worse, some argue, is that most mass media companies are increasingly controlled by shareholders who have little or no interest in the philosophical or political obligations of a free press. We have witnessed that a few times in the first decade of the twenty-first century, as well-respected news companies such as Knight Ridder were hijacked by nonjournalist investors and sold out from under the journalists who worked for them and the communities they served.

Turning a profit and providing a democratic citizenry with the information it needs are both measures of freedom, but of different kinds of freedom. They may well work in tandem. As the respected journalism educator Philip Meyer has noted, there is an economic dimension to providing a credible news product. At one end of the credibility spectrum lie supermarket tabloids, newspapers filled with space aliens, Elvis sightings, Brangelina gossip, and other nonsense. What these papers are *not* filled with is advertisements for reputable products and services; the ads they do carry tend to be for diet pills that claim to work while you sleep and similar foolishness. Meyer points out that the range of advertisements is limited to products that only the most gullible of readers would consider purchasing. At the other end of the credibility spectrum lie the prestige publications and their corresponding Web sites—the *Wall Street Journal, The Economist, Die Zeit*—full of long, richly detailed, and meticulously edited articles about local, national, and world affairs. They also are full of extremely expensive advertisements for luxury automobiles, designer clothing, fabulous jewelry, cutting-edge, high-tech gadgets, and other goods and services befitting their upscale markets. The prestige news outlets of the world are perfect examples of doing well by doing good.

However, that does not always happen. In 1947, a commission of academics and professionals—usually known as the Hutchins Commission for its chair, Robert M. Hutchins, then chancellor of the University of Chicago—studied American news media of that era. The upshot of the commission's work was a new sense of *should* for journalists that has come to be called the social responsibility model of a free press. The commission did not really break much new ground; most of what it recommended comes out of the moral arguments made earlier in this chapter. The Hutchins Commission argued that the public needed, and was entitled to, an honest and accurate account of the day's events in a context that gave those events meaning and that journalists had a moral obligation to provide that information. This idea became what we now call the people's right to know.

The social responsibility model runs counter to what has come to be called the libertarian model of press behavior. Whereas the social-responsibility model suggests that freedom of the press is a contract that can be violated by irresponsible journalists, the libertarian model contends that freedom of the press is an inalienable right that is afforded to all people, not just journalists (whether responsible or not). The libertarian model denies that the press is obliged by government, readers, or morality to do anything. That concept of a free press says there is no such thing as the "people's right to know" principle; its adherents say that if there is a right to have information, there must be a concomitant obligation to provide it, an obligation that they do not recognize. The libertarians argue that the First Amendment guarantee of "no law . . . abridging freedom of speech, or the press" means exactly what it says: Government cannot control what journalists write, and neither can the readers demand coverage of, say, a city council meeting instead of a feature story about a new ice cream parlor.

The tensions between social responsibility and press libertarianism cuts across all aspects of journalism ethics. Any effort to curtail press freedom is dangerous, yet surely Madison and the rest of the founding generation of America had more in mind when they invented this government than simply encouraging media barons to get filthy rich with unlimited pandering. This much is clear: The First Amendment was written, not as an end in itself, but with a purpose, and that purpose has been replicated the world over in constitutional guarantees of press freedoms. Nevertheless, that freedom is not without its limits, and many have argued that speech that fosters democratic self-government deserves greater protection than speech that does not, regardless of whether the latter is more profitable in the short run.

However, there are enormous dangers in trying to compel journalists to be socially responsible—that they be fair, that they be accurate, that they be unbiased, and that they be comprehensive. However laudable those goals, this question immediately arises: Who is going to do the insisting? Insisting connotes some power of coercion, and the only institutions with coercive power are national, state, or local governments. However, constitutional guarantees of freedom of the press exist expressly to prevent the government from controlling the press because any such control would inevitably become corrupt. One answer to the question of "Who should be insisting on high journalistic standards?" is simple: journalists themselves. Today, the most rigorous and meaningful critiques and criticisms of the press come from within the journalism profession, including professional organizations and journalism schools. Yet, should journalists police themselves individually or collectively? In *Existential Journalism*, John C. Merrill argued that even though the Hutchins Commission came up with a laudable and reasonable concept of social responsibility, journalism must, in law at least, remain much closer to the pure libertarian model. The burden of responsibility must rest with the individual journalist, Merrill insists, because there is no one else with whom to entrust the awesome power of regulating what the press says and does.

There is also a great deal of evidence that many individual journalists, left to their own devices, will do all sorts of irresponsible things—invade others' privacy for no good reason, pander to their readers' and viewers' baser desires with gratuitous violence and titillating sex, sound the public alarm when there is no fire, and a host of other sins. We have seen that come to fruition in recent years, in the forms of vitriolic and polarizing prime-time talk shows, vapid "happy talk" morning shows, mean-spirited gossip sites on the Internet, and all manner of so-called news shows that capitalize on personal embarrassment and human suffering. For example, at the time this chapter was being written, the immensely popular cable channel MTV was launching a nonfiction show called *Scarred* that featured videos of "bone crunching, spine splitting extreme sports tricks gone wrong." Surely America's founders did not have that level of irresponsibility in mind when they were protecting the press.

Or did they?

Although limited in how it could present hateful speech and graphic depictions of sex, violence, and disaster, the press in the late eighteenth century was far more scurrilous than almost anything on the market today. Gentility in public commentary is a relatively new development, and the abuse that Jefferson and Madison had to put up with was far more hateful and vituperative than anything today's world leaders have had to endure. Yet, even if the abuse of public figures and the public trust is no worse than it was two centuries ago, the question remains: Is the greater good served by such irresponsibility?

One response would be to turn the question on its head: Would the public be better served by reining in the press? Presumably, some panel or board would be established to distinguish responsible from irresponsible journalism. Such boards or panels are common around the globe, with press councils in Australia, India, New Zealand, Canada, most European nations, Chile, Peru, and many other democratic nations. Such councils have not had much luck in the United States except for councils in a few states (Minnesota and the northwestern state of Washington) and a short-lived National News Council in the 1970s. In the United States at least, few news organizations will cooperate with such councils out of concerns that any institution designed to critique the profession could one day lead to organized, perhaps even governmental, infringements of journalistic freedom. Some news organizations have attempted instead to create their own internal system of checks and balances. One common approach is to hire an *ombudsman*, or public's advocate (some organizations call them "public editors"). Those ombudsmen have often done a good job of investigating readers' complaints and taking staff members to task for failing to meet high standards. However, their credibility has always been weakened by the fact that they are employed by the news companies they critique.

Perhaps one of the most important checks on journalistic integrity is the work of professional media critics—journalists who make a living covering journalism. Most media critics are well educated, well read, and open-minded about the important role of journalism in modern society, and are just as apt to find positives as they are to find negatives in the daily work of the world's news organizations. Even though it might sting, a thoughtful negative review from a respected media critic often can help a newsroom identify its flaws and work toward improvement. Unfortunately, there are a number of people who are media critics in name only—they really exist to only find fault with those news organizations they don't like and to prop up those that they do. For example, in the United States, the Media Research Center is a well-funded front group for a number of fierce neo-conservative ideologues, and it often employs sketchy research methods and slick spinmeistering techniques to prove that the media has a liberal bias. Another such organization, Fairness and Accuracy in Reporting (FAIR), takes a similar tack to criticize the press from the left, also cherry-picking anecdotes and questionable data to make claims that the American news media is hopelessly conservative. Nevertheless, even such inherently biased sources of media criticism provide an important public service—they sometimes make good points, and even when their research is shoddy, they constantly reboot newsroom conversations about what should and should not be done.

Could an independent, unbiased panel be set up in such a way as to make journalists more accountable to each other and the public without jeopardizing their constitutional freedoms? One could envision a council run by journalists, for journalists, that would not only praise the good and criticize the bad but would also play a role in helping the public understand how journalism works and why it does what it does. Unless journalists could be assured, however, that the opinions of such a council could not be used against them in court by plaintiffs in libel or privacy lawsuits, the council could well exert a chilling effect on hard-hitting journalism, and that would be a price too high to pay. The best cautionary note may have been sounded by the late Alan Barth, a longtime editorial writer for *The Washington Post*. "If you want a watchdog to warn you of intruders, you must put up with a certain amount of mistaken barking," Barth once wrote. "If you muzzle him and teach him to be decorous, you will find that he doesn't do the job for which you got him in the first place. Some extraneous barking is the price you must pay for service as a watchdog."

5 ▪ ▪ ▪

The Principles of Ethical Journalism

Each profession has basic principles that are supposed to guide the day-to-day work of its practitioners. In medicine, physicians are generally guided by the principle of do no harm, and, in law enforcement, a common motto is to protect and serve. In journalism, it is generally seek truth and report it. More than mere mottos, such statements of principle provide constant reminders to the professionals about what it is they do, and at the same time, they establish certain public expectations for those professions.

So far in this book, we have discussed the *why* of journalism ethics. Now we turn to the *how*. Although "seek truth and report it" pretty much sums up what journalists do, the aphorism is far too imprecise and open to interpretation for those who want to think seriously about the ethics of the profession. More importantly, it's too simple: Journalism is much more complicated and challenging than simply sharing what you know. Journalists are researchers, artists, statisticians, editors, negotiators, proofreaders, technicians, counselors, students, and teachers—usually all at the same time. Add to all of those duties the constant struggles to keep their biases in check, to keep their cool with hostile sources, to be sensitive toward people who may be rude or suspicious or scared, and it becomes clear that just doing journalism is hard enough, and doing it ethically is a daily challenge. Journalism isn't like taking a stroll around the block on a Sunday afternoon—it's more like flying an airplane on a stormy night.

The ethical journalist, therefore, needs a more well-defined set of principles than a simple motto. The following list is what we believe are the most important principles to which journalists should aspire. The list is by no means comprehensive or universally accepted, and the distinctions made between each principle should not suggest that dilemmas can be easily classified under any one concept (more often, even the simplest of ethical speed bumps will exhibit characteristics of two, three, or more concepts). The principles also should not be read as proscriptions of "thou shalts" and "thou shalt nots," as one might find in the ethics codes of some professional organizations. Rather than rules to live by, these principles are ideals to which we who call ourselves journalists should aspire.

OBJECTIVITY (VS. BIAS)

One of the most important principles in journalism—and probably the least understood—is the notion of *objectivity*. The concept is popularly described in simple terms: An objective journalist is one who is detached, neutral, impartial, and unbiased. The problem, of course, is that it is difficult, if not impossible, for a human being to be those things. A journalist who aims for total objectivity will inevitably fail, and a public that demands all journalists be objective will be perpetually disappointed. As such, the concept of journalistic objectivity has honestly bewildered many and has been deliberately misunderstood and made into a straw man by many more. Many of journalism's critics have defined objectivity as something that approaches perfect truth and then dismissed the term so defined as an absurd idea. Because of the misunderstanding, many of objectivity's defenders have grown fainter in their support. The 1987 iteration of the Code of Ethics of the Society of Professional Journalists (SPJ) considered objectivity a fine goal, but the wording was tepid. A decade later, the SPJ code didn't mention the word objectivity at all.

That's too bad, because there is much of value in the concept and its application to the work of journalism. In fact, objectivity is what delineates journalism from other forms of mass communication, particularly journalism's close cousins and frequent collaborators, public relations and advertising. Particularly in the early twenty-first century, when advocacy seems to dominate the media landscape in the forms of punditry and partisanship, journalism needs to cling to the idea that it is, largely, information presented with an effort to suppress bias and to reach objectivity. The reason to strive for objectivity, even while recognizing that it may sometimes be impossible to attain, is that those who try to achieve objectivity will get closer than those who do not. Closer is better.

The notion of *objective* journalism came into common use only in the 1920s. The notion of *neutral* reporting goes back another three generations to the 1850s, but the impetus for neutral reporting was more a matter of money than morality. In the early days of the telegraph, newspaper publishers created press associations as a way to share the costs of distant correspondents. When publishers had to pay for each telegraphed word, flowery prose went out of vogue. When newspapers of very different political persuasions shared the cost of a single correspondent covering distant events—for example, the Mexican-American War—a down-the-middle report had enormous advantages. And when telegraph transmission problems (such as cut or fallen wires) could interrupt a story at any point, putting the essential facts at the beginning of each transmission was a prudent idea. Yet, nobody called that objective journalism, even though, in today's parlance, objectivity certainly connotes neutrality, impartiality, and a reliance on facts without embellishment.

The term objectivity came into being just after World War I as a possible cure for the problems then besetting journalism—decades of scurrilous yellow journalism, fierce competition with other forms of mass communication, growing faith in science and diminishing trust in the rationality of human beings, and increasing expressions of diverse and dissenting opinions to those held by the public. As Professor Richard Streckfuss put it, "Objectivity was founded not on a naive idea that humans could be objective, but on a realization that they could NOT. To compensate for this innate weakness, advocates in the 1920s proposed a journalistic system that subjected itself to the rigors of the scientific method."[1]

The answer, according to leading journalists such as Walter Lippmann and others, was to borrow from the hard sciences. Many disciplines in the social sciences—political science, economics, sociology—were adopting the scientific method, so why not adapt the same approach for journalism as well? The entire philosophy that is embodied in the term *scientific method* cannot be compressed adequately into just a few words, but some of the most fundamental ideas can be. It relies on evidence, not conjecture; on testing, rather than guessing; and on concluding, rather than imagining. Under that system, metaphysical explanations may lead to faith, but scientific ones lead to understanding. Journalists were encouraged to take the latter approach.

One of the greatest misunderstandings about objectivity is that it is bloodless, or mechanically balanced. Objectivity does not demand that reporters treat all sides of a story equally. On the contrary, it requires that they exercise their best and most honest judgment and then report stories from there, not from the dead center. Eric Severeid, a longtime reporter for CBS, first on radio and then on television, spoke during a retrospective on his late boss and mentor Edward R. Murrow by saying, "Murrow always tried to be objective, but he could not always be neutral. There is a difference. To some stories," Severeid said, "there were not two sides, only a side and a half or a side and a quarter." Murrow, he said, "reacted accordingly, especially if the story concerned human justice."

Scott Simon, the host of National Public Radio's *Weekend Edition* and one of America's most highly respected reporters, essentially agreed when reflecting on coverage of the Yugoslav wars of the 1990s. "I have been outspoken about the terrible crimes that have been occurring in Bosnia. I don't think that it would give us any satisfaction to look back on it years from now and think that we were evenhanded about that," Simon said. "I think the real truth of the story is not evenhanded." Being objective "doesn't mean that you don't ask tough questions and that you don't report the other side," Simon said. However, he added, "It is ridiculous to pretend that all sides of that question are morally similar. Is there another side to a massacre in Srebrenica?"

Perhaps the greatest failure of the "objectivity movement" was to conflate a set of observable practices with what is really a state of mind. When one is trying to be objective, one is engaged in an internal struggle to suppress biases; there are no outward indicators of that struggle, and, in the end, the only person who can tell whether a journalist is being objective is that journalist. Fortunately, the outwardly observable aspects of objectivity have remained stalwart principles of modern journalism, and have become even more of a focus of contemporary journalistic practice: fairness and balance.

FAIRNESS AND BALANCE

Many times, journalists and journalism scholars utter the statement "fair and balanced" as if the terms are both inseparable and interchangeable, but the two are quite different and serve very different functions. Both terms do relate to the behavior of journalists while they are on the job. Yet, there are many situations in which journalists are being fair when they are not being balanced, and balanced when they are not being fair. Like a pair of figure skaters, each has its own role to play, but they will be judged not independently, but on how well they work together.

In terms of journalism ethics, *fairness* is best defined as the manner in which journalists interact with people, and *balance* as the manner in which journalists gather and present information. In other words, journalists who treat sources, colleagues, and audiences with dignity and respect (fairness) and who continually seek out and report multiple points of view (balance) are those who live up to the most basic standards of the profession. In the decades since objectivity became, to many, an unattainable ideal, the combination of fairness and balance has become a very attainable substitute.

Like objectivity, however, both fairness and balance are tricky to both fully understand and to adequately implement. That's because they aren't binary concepts—one isn't either fair or unfair, balanced or unbalanced. Rather, each is a continuum, with "totally fair/balanced" on one end, "totally unfair/unbalanced" on the other, and each of us moving between the two as we deal with ethical dilemmas. In some situations, trying to be fair can be easy—for example, an interview with Bono about his latest campaign for global justice isn't likely to turn hostile. However, it may take all of a journalist's self-control to keep cool during an interview with a bigoted, megalomaniacal talk-show host. Likewise, presenting both sides of a debate over a plan to build a new airport is no real challenge, but achieving balance is something else entirely when an event to honor Holocaust survivors is interrupted by neo-fascist protestors.

Most often, the principle of fairness is applied to people who are unwittingly (and often unwillingly) thrust into the public spotlight. For example, in the autumn of 2006, a deranged gunman barged into a one-room Amish schoolhouse near Lancaster, Pennsylvania, and killed five young girls before killing himself. The Amish are a religious sect of farmers and craftspeople who eschew most modern conveniences and who mostly keep to themselves and maintain intensely private and insular communities. For the Amish, the heart-wrenching loss of their daughters was made all the worse by the swarm of media attention. Because their county has a large number of Amish communities, the two local newspapers— the *Intelligencer Journal* and the *New Era*—already had experience in dealing fairly with the Amish. Not so with some out-of-town journalists who moved into the quaint Amish community to cover the big story. *Intelligencer Journal* editor Ray Shaw, in an interview with *Newsweek*,[2] recalled a few incidents in which some out-of-town reporters disguised themselves as Amish to get into funerals, or cases in which photojournalists simply trampled onto private property to get photos of the camera-shy Amish for the news-hungry public. For some journalists, fairness is too easily surrendered for the sake of getting a story, and the unfair actions of a few too often tarnish the reputations of all the other journalists who tread more carefully when innocents are involved.

Many times, though, the first step toward being fair is to seek balance— to gather information that helps journalists and their audiences to understand what different people value and believe. Although often defined as getting both sides of the story, balance is usually much more complicated than tit for tat. First off, there rarely are only two sides to any story—what is more common is that a journalist only has enough time and space to research and present two sides. Given more time to report and more space or time to present the information, a journalist could get a third side of the story, and a fourth, and a dozen more. In fact, it is often those third, fourth, and fifth sides that are more measured and thoughtful in their responses to any given issue, and, as such, are more useful to the public.

Finding artificial balance—an opponent to every view, a naysayer for every advocate—is both easy and bad journalism, according to NPR's Scott Simon. In journalism, he said, "Too often we just get the tub-thumpers because they're the easiest to bump up against each other. The fact is, that's not really engaging the issue." Simon said it is "much more fair and rewarding to the audience to find moderates than extremists." As Simon prepares a story, he said, "I like to look for people who have the strength of their doubts as well as of their convictions." Such people, he said, have things to say that the audience "can connect with and begin to run around in their own minds," which is much more rewarding than simply finding people "on opposite sides of the tub, thumping."

Therein lies the challenge of fairness and balance in journalism—to achieve either, one must genuinely strive for both. Simply going through the motions of being nice or getting both sides of a story may get the job done, but in the end is it a job worth doing? As stated earlier, journalistic objectivity isn't cold and mechanical, and neither should be fairness and balance. Objectivity, for a journalist, should be the ideal state of mind. Fairness and balance, when done right, must come from the heart.

INDEPENDENCE (VS. CONFLICTS OF INTEREST)

Beyond the internal struggle to suppress bias and the need to demonstrate fairness and balance, the most common ethical challenge faced by working journalists is to maintain professional independence by minimizing conflicts of interest. *Conflict of interest* is another one of those terms that is often used to critique journalists' performance, but the term frequently is used without precision or consistency. Confusing conflict of interest with simple bias is the most common error and, in most cases, the result is utter nonsense. Does a British reporter's personal preference for the Labor Party preclude her from fairly covering a campaign event of the Conservative Party? One might just as well argue that a mother's affection for her child precludes her from disciplining the child for not doing his homework. Conflicts of interest are much more substantial than the inevitable tensions between personal feelings and professional obligations. Rather, they are situations in which journalists misuse their professional influence to serve their personal interests, or as the late journalism scholar H. Eugene Goodwin defined it, "a situation in which you find one of your jobs, interests, activities, or duties can be advanced only at the expense of another of your jobs, interests, activities, or duties."[3]

Most often, conflicts of interest arise because of two powerful temptations: money and power. We see examples of those conflicts often, in the form of journalists who take bribes and give preferential coverage to businesses they invest in, or journalists who use their news reports to benefit their friends in public office. However, conflicts of interest also can be precipitated by more substantive human needs: security, comfort, friendship, love. It is one thing to lambaste a food critic who accepts free meals in exchange for favorable restaurant reviews; it's another thing entirely when a newspaper editor anguishes over whether to print photos of a fatal car accident when the victim is a personal friend. As in all things related to journalism ethics, there are few black-or-white solutions to resolving conflicts of interest.

Complicating the issue is that conflicts of interest come in two flavors: real and perceived. Real conflicts of interest are demonstrable and measurable—as in the case of Armstrong Williams, the American newspaper columnist and news analyst who secretly accepted thousands of dollars from the U.S. government to promote the No Child Left Behind education policies of President George W. Bush. Although embarrassing and troubling, at least real conflicts of interest, once discovered, can be dealt with—in the case of Williams, his syndicate dropped his column, his on-air appearances dwindled (other than a few appearances in which he tried to defend his actions), and he suffered professional disgrace. Beyond that, the media outlets that once gave ink and airtime to Williams implemented policies against such abuses.

Perceived conflicts of interest are much more difficult to manage, because no matter how hard a journalist works to mitigate perceived conflicts, critics will always seize upon those appearances to find fault. A prime example is News Corp., the massive, global media company that owns many influential news outlets in the English-speaking world—*The Times* of London, Sky News, *The Weekly Standard*, many influential Australian newspapers, Star News network throughout Asia, and Fox News in the United States. The company also owns many entertainment media outlets—most notably 20th Century Fox, which produces dozens of popular films and television shows each year. When a new 20th Century Fox blockbuster is released, the perennial question is whether News Corp. journalists have an inherent conflict of interest when discussing and reviewing the movie. The same questions could be applied to journalists working for CNN or *Time Magazine* when a new Warner Bros. movie is released—they're all owned by the same company, Time Warner. Or to reporters working for state-owned media such as *The China Daily* in China or *Trud* in Russia (the Russian government owns controlling shares of *Trud*'s parent company, Gazprom). Those issues always arise when media owners become political leaders, such as the Bloomberg news service (its owner, Michael Bloomberg, was elected mayor of New York City) and Italy's national television stations owned by Italian Prime Minister Silvio Berlusconi. In such situations, many media critics refuse to consider that individual journalists can remain professionally independent from their owners, no matter how hard those journalists try. Of course, many media owners exercise tight controls over their rank-and-file journalists, but there are many who respect the need for their journalists to remain independent. Regardless, perceptions too often are more powerful than realities, and many independent-minded journalists are burdened with the perceived biases of their owners.

Journalists have developed a number of practices to counteract the problems of both real and perceived conflicts of interest. Real conflicts are often addressed in terms of employment contracts and employee handbooks—no-compete agreements, restrictions on fraternization with sources or coworkers, strict prohibitions against accepting gifts, meals, or graft. Perceived conflicts are more often addressed with attempts at transparency. The most common solution is simple disclosure—when writing or speaking about their parent companies, journalists will often simply mention that their news organization is owned by the same company. Some news companies have strict policies regarding perceived conflicts, going so far as to restrict journalists' free-time activity, such as prohibiting them from participating in political rallies or being members of certain types of organizations.

Another common practice is for journalists to actively avoid conflicts of interest. If a city hall reporter gets romantically involved with a member of the mayor's staff, for example, the reporter will generally ask to be re-assigned to another beat (or, in the case of some cold-hearted editors, the reporter will be told to not pursue the relationship). Of course, the best policies allow for some flexibility, particularly when it comes to the family and friends of journalists. An example is the case of Kathleen Rutledge, editor of the *Lincoln Journal Star* of Nebraska, whose husband, Ted Kooser, was the U.S. Poet Laureate from 2004 to 2006. "I stay out of it entirely," Rutledge said of her newspaper's coverage of her famous husband. Instead, Rutledge relinquished editing duties to her colleagues when her husband was in the news. "And we remind people all the time that I'm married to him," she said at the time.

Avoiding conflicts of interest is not always possible, particularly in small communities. At a small-town newspaper with a staff of two or three reporters, finding a colleague to take over when a conflict arises isn't always possible. Nor is it reasonable to ask reporters and editors to not get involved in community activities that might end up in the news, like being a volunteer coach for a youth sports league or helping to organize a fundraiser for the local humane society—in small towns, such organizations are in the news all the time, and volunteers willing to serve are few. In such situations, maintaining journalistic independence is often an effort in compartmentalization, with individuals fulfilling many roles but trying to keep those roles separated as much as is humanly possible (not unlike any other workplace where people must differentiate between professional roles and personal friendships with coworkers). When a small-town newspaper editor sits on the board of a local nonprofit agency, she often has to take off her journalist's hat and put on the hat of an advocate for the agency, and then leave the advocacy hat at home when she goes back to work in the newsroom. Most often, just being aware of and sensitive to conflicts can lead journalists to be more responsible toward maintaining their independence.

PRIVACY VS. THE PUBLIC'S RIGHT TO KNOW

The fourth principle of moral journalism is a balancing act. It involves dealing with the tensions between the desire for privacy on the part of news subjects against the public's right to know about what is going on in government and, at a broader level, all of society.

There is no area in contemporary journalism that bothers students, and probably most other readers as well, as much as the journalist's apparent willingness to invade other people's privacy. Many believe that they see in journalists a cavalier attitude toward the sensibilities of those they write about, an indifference to—or even real pleasure in—the embarrassment and pain they cause with their probing questions, their intrusive microphones and harsh lights, their willingness to print and broadcast names and addresses and all manner of intimate details of people's lives. Nevertheless, it is important to recall that a free flow of some kinds of information is clearly and unambiguously in the public interest and essential to democracy.

Most certainly, that includes the on-the-job behavior of public officials, which means the debates, hearings, votes, committee meetings, and all the other activities involving officials who have been hired with the people's money to perform the people's business. It also has come to include the off-duty behaviors of public officials that come into conflict with their public duties (such as shady business deals, giving jobs to underqualified friends and relatives, accepting lavish gifts from campaign donors seeking favors, etc.), and, more controversially, peccadilloes of their private lives. Related to information about public officials is information about public procedures—hearings, investigations, trials, permit reviews, and the like, in which private information is made a matter of public record. This involves the involuntary surrender of privacy rights, as in the criminal justice system where both defendants and victims are thrust into the public spotlight. As will be discussed in later chapters, journalists face particularly delicate dilemmas when covering criminal investigations and trials.

On the flip side of purely public information is information about private citizens maintaining their own affairs, bothering nobody and endangering nothing, which is certainly not essential to an enlightened citizenry. Whether your neighbor collects stamps or coins is really no business of yours; likewise if he is an alcoholic or cheats on his wife. Individuals have a right to be left alone, to live their lives as they choose without the prying eyes of their neighbors poking into their affairs, as long as their affairs do not bother or interfere with others. The fact that some private choices require some public paperwork is generally irrelevant—the fact that two people apply for a marriage license doesn't mean everybody is invited to the wedding or that the public has a right to know where the couple will spend their honeymoon.

Where journalists have the most trouble is with a third category of information, those things that are not clearly public, but not clearly private either. What if the neighbor down the hall or across the street moves from collecting stamps and coins to collecting poisonous snakes or high-powered assault rifles, or starts having loud drinking parties every other night? Does the right to privacy still trump the public's right to know?

Many journalism ethicists make clear distinctions between the public's *right* to know and the public's *need* to know, and they are distinctions worth constant consideration. Determining the right to know is mostly (though not entirely) the purview of the law, whereas the need to know is much more an issue of ethics. However, in a free society, there is a moral imperative for citizens (including journalists) to resist supplanting the public's hard-won legal rights to access information with short-term concessions to the individual's desire for privacy. As Cato (i.e., John Trenchard and Thomas Gordon) wrote in his essays, it is far better to have a society in which vile lies can be published than to have a society in which important truths can be suppressed. Without the right to know, the needs of the public can be too easily ignored, and that is why scores of nations today have instituted open-records laws that guarantee the public's right to access information about government. Yet, such laws are not always enforced, and are too often ignored or modified by government officials. We witnessed that in the early twenty-first century, with the War on Terror being used to justify secrecy about U.S. government abuses and corruption the world over. Therefore, defending the *right* to know is a moral imperative not just of journalism, but of all citizens of democracy, to ensure that everybody can obtain the information they *need* to know.

One simple tactic for defending the public's right to know is to exercise that right on a regular basis. Journalists sometimes flex their right-to-know muscles by obtaining and publishing simple information about public entities: the salaries of public school teachers, the property-tax records of local business owners, lists of vendors hired by a city council in the past year. Sometimes, journalists team up with their colleagues and competitors to conduct open-records audits, in which they fan out across regions, states, even whole nations, playing the roles of average citizens and asking low-ranking public workers to provide the most mundane of public documents (lists of police calls, official minutes of county board meetings, the mayor's expense records, etc.). The results of those audits often are disappointing, with wary government workers most often denying requests in defiance (or, more often, ignorance) of the law—for example, an audit by the Canadian Newspaper Association in 2005 resulted in nearly one-third of public-records requests being denied or only partially fulfilled.[4] Given the trivial nature of the information sought, such resistance to disclosure might be a symptom of simple human suspicion—if the public employees see no public need for disclosure, and the reporters posing as average citizens don't articulate why they need the information, it is hard to establish even the most rudimentary basis of trust. And without trust, even simple requests can meet with resistance.

Trust is very much at the core of the private-versus-public balancing act. Citizens entrust their governments with all manners of personal information, from statements about charitable donations on tax records to the most intimate justifications for divorce in court affidavits. Although that information will be in a file that could be accessed by the public, most people understand that the crushing volume of public records makes their individual records little more than needles in haystacks—anybody *can* access the information, but nobody will *want* to. Except, of course, for the news media, which have the means to uncover, amplify, and broadcast that information without even notifying the people who submitted it. It only takes a few such instances for individuals to feel that their initial trust was betrayed, and then for them to demand more restrictions on what information the government can gather and what government-held information the public (really, the press) can obtain.

Anybody who has spent time with public records knows that they are fascinating—each aging folder in the recorder-of-deeds office contains a lineage of ownership for a piece of land, every docket entry in a clerk-of-courts database a detailed account of a premeditated murder or a harassment dispute between neighbors. As storytellers, journalists are drawn to those records, as they provide the raw materials for engaging tales of humanity. What journalists too often forget is that those folders and data files are not just attached to information, but they also are attached to people—people who lost their marriages to infidelity or to inattention, lost their life dreams to bankruptcy, or lost their dignity before a jury of their peers. Sometimes those stories need to be told, if not for the greater search for truth than, at least, as cautionary tales for all of us fallible humans. However, those stories shouldn't be told simply because the law says they can be. As journalists exercise their rights to access information, they should always remember the act of individual trust that put that information in the public's hands in the first place, and try to live up to that trust by turning the spotlight onto that information only when the public needs it.

SENSITIVITY VS. RESPONSIBILITY TO INFORM

Closely related to the private-versus-public principle is the journalistic principle to balance one's own sensitivities against the demands of the job to not only seek truth, but to report it. Whereas private-versus-public considerations often are decisions involving empathy for the privacy of others, sensitivity versus responsibility to inform is about considering the welfare of everybody else involved in intensely emotional situations—the sources, their family and friends, the audience, even the journalists themselves.

This principle is most commonly in play with disturbing information—photographs of fatal car accidents, video of public suicides, and similar coverage of violence, destruction, despair, and suffering. In such situations, the public's need to know is implicit; what's at issue is just how much information the journalist is comfortable gathering and sharing with the public. There are few reasonable people who would argue that the public doesn't have a need to know about the horrors of a deadly tenement fire, but showing those horrors live and in color on the evening news will always be a matter of extreme controversy. When the news itself is disturbing, journalists often find themselves in a no-win situation. Show too little, be branded a coward; show too much, be branded a fiend.

That difficulty might explain why so many aspiring journalists seem to gravitate toward the soft-news side of the profession—food and fashion, sports and leisure, arts and entertainment. When it's all fun and games, there is little worry about death and destruction. However, even the soft-news departments are not havens from the mean aspects of life, such that sports journalism is as much about injuries and accidents and bad behavior as it is about skill and strength, and too often the journalists who cover glamorous film stars must reveal details of dysfunctional marriages, drug addiction, and personal tragedy. A journalist may be able to reduce the chances of facing hard emotional choices, but can never avoid them entirely.

One of the easiest approaches to dealing with sensitive issues is to take the "if I were in their shoes" test—imagine you were the one facing the difficulty and project how you would feel when approached by reporters. Although useful to a point, the problem with the "in their shoes" measure is that it only deals with one-half of this principle—the sensitivity part—and usually dismisses the part about informing the public. Journalists who simply don't want to hurt people's feelings may become too timid to ask difficult but essential questions, or to reveal uncomfortable truths about the world in which we live. However, an even more serious and less conspicuous problem with that approach is the limitation of imagination itself. Journalists often have to cover disasters that affect communities with which they are not familiar, and, with no personal experience or in-depth knowledge about those communities, journalists often project their own values and beliefs on others (as Walter Lippmann argued in his concept of the pseudo-environment, we really can't know what somebody else is thinking). Without actually walking in somebody's shoes, we can't really imagine what it would be like to be in their shoes.

The reverse can also be problematic, particularly when journalists become intimately familiar with their communities. Up until the turn of the twentieth century, major newspapers were deeply and often passionately involved with the cities and towns in which they were published. William Randolph Hearst's *New York Journal* and Joseph Pulitzer's *New York World* were prime examples of news organizations dedicated to improving the lives of their home cities. However, after World War I, when the new notion of objectivity became dominant, such conscious involvement began to be suspect in the eyes and minds of most thoughtful journalists. It began to be seen as *boosterism*, as something that threatened to turn reporting into cheerleading. Journalists began to keep their distance, and then greater distance still, in an effort to find a neutral vantage point from which to report the matters of interest and importance to a paper's readers.

In recent years, there has been something of a backlash as some editors began saying that news outlets had gone too far in distancing themselves from the cities and towns they served. Journalism professor Jock Lauterer of the University of North Carolina-Chapel Hill, a noted expert on the community journalism movement of the past twenty years, argues, "In community journalism, that detached attitude amounts to a death wish . . . The better community papers have historically and naturally embraced their reciprocal relationship between their community (their public) and their mandate to provide coverage of civic and public affairs that is bold yet benevolent, success oriented and positive without pandering."[5]

The flip side of being positive without pandering is to be negative with compassion—being capable of breaking bad news in a manner that minimizes harm. Certainly, a good rule of thumb is simply to care about people, both those in the news and those receiving the news. Yet, often that means caring enough to tell the uncomfortable truth, even when that truth is harsh, grisly, and emotionally troubling.

VERIFICATION AND ATTRIBUTION

When the legendary American newspaper publisher Joseph Pulitzer famously wrote the words "Accuracy, Accuracy, Accuracy" on the walls of his newsroom, he was signifying one of the hallmarks of quality journalism: Verify information before you publish it. Going hand-in-hand with verifying information is attributing that information to its source. To working journalists, the procedures of verification and attribution are as automatic as breathing in and out. However, underlying the most autonomic of journalistic practices are the very essences of moral journalism: truth and trust. Certainly, there are legal reasons for verification and attribution—the truth is the best defense against a libel case, and attribution allows journalists to blame their sources for published lies and misleading information. Beyond the law though there is an inherent moral value to making sure the information you publish is true, or at least accurate, and that the person providing that information is duly credited to encourage accountability.

Journalists are taught to approach both verification and attribution with a certain degree of skepticism, to challenge claims of certitude regardless of the trustworthiness of the source. Too often, what starts as respectful and reasonable skepticism can transmute into crass cynicism. The late University of Kansas journalism professor John Bremner was noted for advising his students with this journalistic adage: "If your Mom says she loves you, check it out." Although good for a chuckle and for toughening impressionable young minds, such a philosophy taken too seriously can undermine the spirit of trust and goodwill that journalists should cultivate with their sources. Why not just give Mom the benefit of the doubt? Or, more to the point: People in their early twenties will know full well whether their mothers love them, and may have no reason to doubt Mom's veracity.

Journalistic cynicism is not without some justification. Over several centuries, many journalists have been burned by lying hucksters, vindictive pranksters, and sleazy politicians. Such incidents have led to a professional culture in journalism in which all politicians are seen as inherently corrupt, all business leaders as inherently ruthless, and all celebrities as inherently shallow and self-absorbed. Perhaps the greatest inspiration for mistrust has been the pseudo-event, the made-for-the-media speeches and spectacles in which public figures command the spotlight of public attention, and the journalists simply record what is said without validating claims or checking sources. Ron Fournier, longtime political writer for The Associated Press, advises his colleagues to be more discerning about what they report from public figures: "Just because a public official says it doesn't mean you need to put it in your story or give his claim equal billing to what you know to be true. We have an obligation to write factual and fair stories, but we are not obliged to print attacks, spin, or distortion under the cover of 'fair comment.'"[6]

Today, that cynicism is fueled by a robust cultural phenomenon that capitalizes on the egalitarian nature of the Internet. In the blogosphere, it seems no public figure can make a public speech or presentation without fans and critics alike recording and deconstructing what was said, often just moments after it is said or, in the case of live broadcasts, in real time. Often motivated by passion and zeal, bloggers can find fault in even the most mundane of verbal or visual gaffes. Add to that the seemingly infinite storage capacity of the Internet, and we now have a world in which nobody can ignore his or her past: What a politician says about immigration policy today will be compared to what he said about the issue just a few years ago, or will say about it years from now.

This at-large approach to verification has also turned the tables on journalism itself, as the mistakes made by journalists in their reporting and attribution get noticed, documented, and amplified. There are some organizations, usually with strong partisan or ideological bents, that exist solely to ferret out examples of shoddy reporting. One of the most famous of such incidents was the 2004 Memogate scandal, in which the CBS news magazine *60 Minutes* claimed to have obtained documents from a reliable source that suggested U.S. President George W. Bush had shirked his military duties in the 1970s. Several bloggers had noticed that the typography on the alleged memos was not consistent with typewriters used by the U.S. government in the 1970s. In the end, it was revealed that the memos CBS received had been forgeries; as a result, several high-level employees of CBS resigned in disgrace, most notably lead news anchor Dan Rather.[7] (The Memogate scandal is discussed in more depth in Chapter 22.)

Principles that for decades have been seen simply as standard procedures of journalism have once again become important enough to write on the walls of every newsroom. "Accuracy, Accuracy, Accuracy"—now more than ever, journalists must carefully and thoroughly verify information before publishing it, be open and frank about the sources of information, and hold sources accountable for the information they provide.

AVOID DECEPTION (AND OMISSION AND OBFUSCATION)

Whereas much of journalism ethics involves making choices about how much information to give to the public, and in what manner, an awful lot of time is spent deciding what not to publish. That leads to the journalistic principles regarding the withholding of information, whether that information is being withheld simply as a matter of pragmatism (not enough space, not enough time) or for somewhat more devious purposes—protecting corrupt sources, misleading the public, or telling out-and-out lies.

Because omission alone is such a routine activity of everyday journalism practice, it often isn't viewed as an ethical dilemma at all. Nevertheless, in a profession in which the whole point is to publish information, what could be more problematic than deciding what information *not* to publish? Omission is difficult to avoid entirely, simply because omission is essentially part of the routine: cutting a twenty-minute interview into a two-minute report, or summarizing a three-hundred-page research project into a three-paragraph news brief, or deciding which one of three dozen photographs to publish. Omission rises to the level of ethical dilemma when journalists leave out important information in lieu of more titillating or less controversial fare. Typically, these dilemmas involve embarrassing personal information about public figures—the proverbial skeletons in the closet. Such tidbits are almost always interesting, and sometimes important (particularly when dealing with candidates for high public office), but what somebody smoked or snorted three decades earlier, or what marital problems an official is dealing with, is generally not newsworthy.

Another common quandary involving omission is what is said *off the record* or *on background*, which is journalistic code for "you should know this, but don't publish it." If a journalist promises confidentiality, she is obligated to keep that promise; but if the source interrupts an on-the-record interview with "don't print this, but," the journalist has to make a very quick decision—offer confidentiality or warn the source that the request won't be honored. After all, an interview isn't a confessional or a doctor's office—journalists are in the business of sharing information, not keeping secrets. As such, the journalist is the one who makes the ultimate decision about what information not to publish.

Naturally, much of the information a journalist happens across is insignificant, and the decision to omit trivial details is easy and automatic— few people would care that the mayor started his press conference three minutes late or that the actress had spinach in her teeth during a lunch interview. Who really cares if there was a dangling modifier and two pronoun errors in a press release from the local university? In addition, journalists rarely include detailed information about how they go about gathering information and preparing their reports, except for the occasional mention that it was a telephone interview or that the source explained his position in an e-mail. The editing process of journalism is even more of a behind-the-curtain thing, with the public rarely getting a hint as to how news products are made. Yet, what about more significant details that so often get left out of news reports, such as detailed descriptions of the methods scientists use in their research (how many people were in the study? What were the research questions?), extensive historical background on cultural clashes (what is the difference between Sunni and Shi'a? What is the history behind The Troubles in Ireland?), or comparative data that provide big-picture perspectives (at this writing, one Thai baht was worth about three U.S. pennies (US$0.03). Is that a favorable exchange rate or not? What can one thousand baht buy in Bangkok's famed Chatuchak Weekend Market?). It would be absurd to argue that journalists are obligated to provide such detail all the time and in a manner that would satisfy all people, but it isn't a stretch to argue that journalists should provide as much useful information as they possibly can.

As recently as the 1990s, most journalists felt little obligation to provide that level of detail in their reports—they didn't have the time or space for such background, and had to trust that people with enough interest in the topics would dig up more information on their own. The Internet has changed that. Recognizing the demand for less omission, many news outlets have expanded their online offerings to include extended interviews or complete interview transcripts, links to original documents and more extensive background information, archives of related articles, even unedited raw data that the public can review and analyze on its own. This trend, often called *value-added journalism*, raises a whole host of new ethical dilemmas for journalists—if the technology allows us to omit very little, what happens when we have information that should be omitted? How do you omit an off-the-record comment from something billed as a complete transcript of an interview? Simply delete it and pretend it never happened? Black it out with a note explaining why the passage was deleted?

This gets beyond mere omission and enters a much more dicey area of journalism practice—obfuscation. *Obfuscation* is the act of obscuring or hiding information, and in journalism is most often related to the use of anonymous sources. When a high-ranking government official is quoted in a news article, the journalist is obfuscating the identity of the official in exchange for an on-the-record comment and, more often, a relationship in which the high-ranking official may become a regular, trustworthy source of exclusive information. Obfuscation also is used to protect the privacy of the powerless or vulnerable, such as the common practice of using first names only in articles about children, crime victims, or innocent bystanders. In Japan, for example, TV journalists who interview eyewitnesses of accidents or street crimes often only show those witnesses from the neck down, to protect the identity of the people they interview. Other tricks of the trade include blurring the images of people's faces in photographs and film, masking their voices on video and audio clips, or simply being very careful in print not to reveal unique information that could reveal a secret source's identity.

When used judiciously, obfuscation allows journalists to verify and attribute information while respecting the privacy of individuals and being sensitive to their personal well-being. However, when used too much or when abused outright, journalistic obfuscation can undermine trust and veracity—people cannot judge the trustworthiness of a source if they don't know who that source is and, by extension, may not trust the journalists who give ink, airtime, and bandwidth to such sources. Nor can they judge the motives of those sources; in fact, many people assume that a source who wants to remain anonymous has devious motives or, at minimum, something to hide. To put not too fine a point on it, obfuscation is often seen as walking hand-in-hand with outright deception.

It's bad enough when a source lies to a journalist, but when a journalist lies to a source, the damage can be far, far greater. Worse still is when the journalist deceives coworkers or the public at large. Because journalists are in the business of seeking and sharing truth, those who lie come into stark conflict with their calling—a journalist who deceives is like a police officer who flouts the law or a doctor who enjoys causing pain and death.

It's no wonder that the two most serious sins of professional journalism—fabrication and plagiarism—both involve deception. Those found guilty of either or both sins face the harshest punishments of the journalism world—a public firing followed by the pillory of bad press.

For all that, deception has not been wholly ostracized from the canon of ethical journalism. It is used—rarely and, we should hope, begrudgingly—as a tool of last resort for investigative journalists. Journalistic deception is generally only justified when it is the only way to obtain important information (as philosopher Sissela Bok argued in her book *Lying*, telling a lie is only acceptable when telling the truth is not a viable option and when the lie can later be corrected and justified publicly). It is the highest-risk enterprise of modern journalism, even riskier than sending reporters into hostile war zones—a reporter who dies in the line of duty is remembered as a hero upholding the highest ideals of the industry, but a reporter who botches an undercover job disgraces not just himself, but his entire profession.

One of the most notable success stories of deceptive journalism occurred in the late 1970s in Chicago's Near North neighborhood, when the city's *Sun-Times* newspaper, in collaboration with the Better Government Association, covertly purchased a rundown pub and reopened it as the Mirage Tavern, complete with "more code violations than barstools," all ready to test the integrity of city officials.[8] The brainchild of award-winning investigative reporter Pam Zekman, the Mirage was staffed by reporters posing as bartenders and photographers hiding in the ductwork, and within a few months had documented several incidents of corruption, from easily bribed code inspectors to accountants who showed the bar how to avoid taxes and advised the owners to avoid bribing the police—because the cops would allegedly keep returning for more payments. The Mirage Tavern investigation prompted significant anti-corruption reforms in Chicago, was nominated for a Pulitzer Prize, and remains one of the most storied journalistic stings of modern history.

Of equal notoriety is a deception that went awry—the May 1998 report by the *Cincinnati Enquirer* that made allegations of questionable and illegal business practices by Cincinnati-based Chiquita Brands International, the global distributor of bananas and other foods. The deception here involved reporter Mike Gallagher, who in his one-year, around-the-globe investigation, illicitly (and without telling his editors) accessed Chiquita's corporate voice-mail system to verify the allegations of wrongdoing. Although the reporting involved scores of interviews with plantation workers, government officials, and even several Chiquita executives, and even though the facts of the story have never been formally challenged or proven false, the deceptive nature of Gallagher's use of the company's voice-mail system triggered the *Enquirer* to fire Gallagher, retract the story, publish a front-page apology to Chiquita (and republish it for several days), and to pay Chiquita a \$10 million settlement.[9] (It should be noted that in early 2007, less than ten years after the *Enquirer*'s report, Chiquita was fined \$25 million by the U.S. Department of Justice for illegally hiring Colombian paramilitary groups to provide protection for its employees in Colombia's banana-growing region.[10])

The most obvious lesson of the *Enquirer*–Chiquita affair is that even when the facts aren't in dispute, deception can taint the journalism, even if the deception pales in comparison to the wrongdoing being revealed. What is less clear from that incident is whether the *Enquirer* was obligated to retract the report altogether, rather than to admit to the illicit manner in which some of the information had been obtained. Retractions are very rare in professional journalism, but are generally reserved, not for reports that involved deceptive journalism, but for reports that are factually incorrect.

CORRECTION AND CLARIFICATION

The final principle of ethical journalism is the one that applies after mistakes are made. Because journalism is a thoroughly human enterprise, even the most careful and experienced journalist will occasionally get the facts wrong, misquote a source, or misunderstand an opinion. Such errors could be as simple as misspelling the name of a city street or as serious as accusing the wrong person of a serious crime. Any reputable news outlet will quickly and dutifully publish corrections for factual errors or clarifications for news items that were originally confusing or misleading. More serious errors might include a formal, public apology from the editor or news director, as well as disciplinary action against the journalists responsible for the mistakes. Sometimes, the news outlet will republish a corrected version of the report, whether it is a large, serious exposé of public fraud or an everyday obituary or birth announcement.

The most common moral problem regarding correction and clarification is overcoming simple human pride. Factual errors are not only damaging to the truth, but they also are damaging to the reputation of journalists and the news outlets they work for. Too often, prideful journalists who don't want to deal with the embarrassment of admitting mistakes will try to avoid making corrections or will minimize the corrections' notoriety. It is very common for a newspaper to run a small correction on the bottom of page three for an erroneous headline published the day before on page one, or for a TV station to correct a prime-time mistake with just a brief mention during the next day's noon update or a small note on the station's Web site (even though viewers may never log onto that site). Some journalists try to talk irate sources out of demanding corrections, essentially resolving the issue under the table. Before the Internet, many news organizations could get away with simply ignoring their errors altogether.

However, a number of highly damaging and embarrassing journalistic errors in recent decades have made journalists much more aware of their obligations to correct errors and much more willing to not just issue corrections, but to explain how they happened and take steps to prevent them. One such incident was the infamous case of *New York Times* reporter Jayson Blair, a young reporter who joined the *Times* right out of college. For several years, and despite a track record of shoddy reporting and many complaints from sources and coworkers about his erroneous reporting, Blair was given many high-profile assignments, including coverage of the 2002 Beltway sniper shootings in Washington, D.C., and national stories related to the U.S.-led wars in Iraq and Afghanistan. The accusations against Blair become more serious in April 2003, when it was discovered that his story about the mother of a U.S. soldier who was missing in the war had been plagiarized from an article in the San Antonio *Express-News*. Unable to disprove the allegation of plagiarism, Blair resigned, and the newspaper launched an investigation into the hundreds of articles he had written for the *Times*. That investigation revealed not just a long list of factual errors, but also several articles in which Blair had either plagiarized other news reports or fabricated sources and lied about interviews he never conducted on reporting trips he never took. On May 11, 2003, the *Times* ran an exposé about the scandal on its front page, a massive 7,200-word article under the headline "Times Reporter Who Resigned Leaves Long Trail of Deception." Beyond that unprecedented correction on the front page, the *Times* also responded with the resignation of executive editor Howell Raines and managing editor Gerald Boyd and changes to its newsroom management system, including the addition of a new position, that of the public editor, to investigate public complaints about the newspaper. (The Jayson Blair case also involved some racial tensions. Blair is an African American, and some, including Raines, claimed Blair's lapses had been excused because of his race. Others have said Blair was singled out for public punishment because of his race. Blair himself has blamed his lapses on drug addiction and mental illness.)

Noted media critic Seth Mnookin has noted that the Jayson Blair scandal at the *New York Times* has dramatically changed the way journalists respond to corrections. In an interview for the media-monitoring *Regret the Error* Web site, Mnookin said, "In a pre-Jayson Blair world, journalists for the most part had the feeling that if you could talk someone out of asking for/demanding a correction, that was a good thing. Corrections were thought to say something bad about your skills as a reporter...But if the public can begin to feel that we're not trying to cover up our tracks, or trying to pretend we're infallible, or trying to hide our mistakes, they might be more willing to accept what we do in its entirety."[11]

A year after the Jayson Blair scandal broke, the *Times* again engaged in an unprecedented exercise in correction and clarification, when it ran an article titled "The *Times* and Iraq" in which the newspaper's editors apologized for what they saw as incomplete and questionable coverage of the U.S. government's justifications for invading Iraq in 2003. The article detailed specific articles and their shortcomings, but made this general statement:

> [W]e have found a number of instances of coverage that was not as rigorous as it should have been. In some cases, information that was controversial then, and seems questionable now, was insufficiently qualified or allowed to stand unchallenged. Looking back, we wish we had been more aggressive in re-examining the claims as new evidence emerged—or failed to emerge.
>
> The problematic articles varied in authorship and subject matter, but many shared a common feature. They depended at least in part on information from a circle of Iraqi informants, defectors, and exiles bent on 'regime change' in Iraq, people whose credibility has come under increasing public debate in recent weeks...Complicating matters for journalists, the accounts of these exiles were often eagerly confirmed by United States officials convinced of the need to intervene in Iraq. Administration officials now acknowledge that they sometimes fell for misinformation from these exile sources. So did many news organizations—in particular, this one.[12]

The *New York Times* is not the only news organization to have finally discovered the morality of the mea culpa; it seems as if a week can't go by without some news organization, large or small, announcing that it has disciplined or fired a journalist for plagiarism, fabrication, conflict of interest, or some other serious ethical breech. Many editors these days are quick to write lengthy columns apologizing for mistakes, explaining controversial news choices, or even clarifying facts that can be confusing, as with this June 2007 example from *The Star* of South Africa: "An article appearing on the front page of *The Star* yesterday, under the headline 'Bafana Bafana star accused of threatening to shoot gatecrashers,' referred to Kokstad resident Scelo Mthethwa. Johannesburg advocate Sicelo Mthethwa wishes to point out that the story in no way referred to him."[13]

In an era when public trust in their news media is generally pretty low and its ability to point out journalistic errors is at an all-time high, it makes sense for journalists to be more willing than ever to correct mistakes and clarify misunderstandings, perhaps even before the public catches those errors.

Although each of the previous principles could easily be the subject of a book of its own (and some are), these brief overviews should provide journalists with enough information to help them understand just how complicated and multifaceted the pursuit of journalism ethics is. In the second part of this book, we will look at each principle in much more depth by considering various cases in which professionals dealt with (or largely ignored) those principles. However, before getting to the case studies, there is one more important discussion to have about the overall topic of journalism ethics—not just why ethics matter and how ethics are applied, but what journalists can do when faced with a serious ethical dilemma. What follows is a short chapter offering a workable, commonsense procedure that working journalists can use to identify and deal with the ethical dilemmas they will most certainly encounter.

6 ▪ ▪ ▪

How to Solve Moral Dilemmas: Balancing Competing Elements

Almost without exception, the interesting ethical decisions for journalists, as for everyone else, involve dilemmas. A dilemma is not a mere problem or question—ethical problems come up all the time, and ethical questions can be asked about every aspect of journalism practice. A dilemma is something more substantial—a situation with no easy solution and few attractive alternatives. In a dilemma, there is a downside to whatever choice one has to make whereas a question or a problem may well have a clearly right answer and at least one wrong one. That is a point that even serious journalism scholars often miss. Consider an article from the late 1990s in a top journalism research journal, in which the author discussed the following hypothetical situation: A television crew is covering a foreign war that involves the United States and is traveling with a patrol of the Americans' enemy when the patrol comes upon an American squad and prepares an ambush. The question for the television crew is whether to warn the American troops or cover the ambush. In a panel discussion of the case broadcast on public television, the late ABC network news anchor Peter Jennings declared at first that he would warn the U.S. troops. Then Mike Wallace of CBS argued that the better journalistic choice would be to cover the ambush, and he persuaded Jennings to change his mind. Jennings agreed with Wallace that the television crew members had essentially already decided to be neutral observers when they first planned to travel with the enemy forces. Jennings said he had "chickened out" earlier in deciding to warn the American forces of the ambush. The author of the scholarly article argued, "Both of these outcomes cannot be right...At least one of them must be wrong."[1] Ethics don't work that way—they are not tidy or binary, there are no black-and-white solutions, just shades of gray somewhere between completely wrong and totally right. The point here is not to decide whether Jennings was right at first when he decided to warn the Americans or whether Jennings was right later when he changed his mind and agreed with Wallace that the better course would be to cover the ambush as a neutral observer. The real point here is that there is no clear right or wrong answer to the dilemma. There are serious problems with both choices—conflicting loyalties, conflicting obligations, and many lives on the line on both sides. The hypothetical is also a bit too tidy. Had the situation been real, there would have been even more variables to consider: the purpose of the war, public sentiment toward the conflict, the journalists' own experiences with covering combat. Had more journalists offered different alternatives, there would have been serious problems with those choices as well. What matters isn't who is right or wrong, but rather what the arguments are each way, based upon an understanding of the moral underpinnings of professional journalism and the principles outlined in the previous chapter. The reason no one can insist that warning the American troops is the only right answer and photographing the ambush is the only wrong answer, or vice versa, is that nobody can say with certainty how much each element should weigh in making the decision. Journalists are people, too, and they try to prevent harm when they can. However, neutrality enables journalists to inform people about both sides in a conflict, and that neutrality would be jeopardized if journalists used the information they gathered from one side to warn the other side. Dilemmas are not puzzles that can be solved; they are conundrums that can only be managed.

What matters even more is whether a journalist in such a situation would be able to make the most ethical choice possible in the heat of the moment. It's not as if the reporter could have called a time-out, sat down with this book, and pondered the dilemma for several hours before making a decision. Journalists have to make ethical decisions quickly, sometimes in mere moments. That's why it is so crucial that journalists think about ethics long before they go out on assignment; there rarely is much time in the field to bone up on the basic philosophy, let alone the particular principles to which journalists aspire.

Making ethical choices involves being aware of our own limitations, considering the principles of our profession, and balancing our alternatives. Some call this ability a *moral compass*, a mental tool that can help point each of us in the direction that is the most right and the least wrong. Given the complexities of journalistic work, a more apt metaphor might be a *moral instrument panel*, like the dashboard of an automobile, with various warning lights, indicators, and gauges. Most of the time, we keep our eyes on the road—that is, on the task of reporting, editing, planning, and so on. Nevertheless, we frequently glance at the instrument panel to make sure the car itself is in good shape—acceptable speed, plenty of gas in the tank, but the CHECK ENGINE light suggests it might be time to pull over for an oil change. Just like drivers who know how to read a dashboard are better drivers, the more familiar journalists are with the issues and standards of the profession, the more comfortable they are in assessing even complex choices. In the end, they may not satisfy everyone, but they will have made a decision that can be explained and defended.

Determining the relative importance of each factor in the dilemma is up to the journalist making the decision and is relative to the situation at hand. This is not to say that there are no standards at all and that any decision is as good as any other. The more familiar with the principles the journalist is, the more likely she or he is to weigh all of the important variables, think about them, and make wise decisions. Yet, it remains true that experienced journalists of great intellect and integrity can differ as to how much value to assign to one element or another. Reasonable people may disagree. That does not make one of them wrong.

What *is* wrong is when the journalist doesn't consult the instrument panel, and instead bases a decision on impulse alone, reacting to the situation without really thinking about it. That is sometimes called going with your gut feelings, but there is a serious problem with that approach to journalism—it leaves ethics out of the picture. If a gut reaction leads to a satisfactory outcome (as sometimes happens), that's lucky, but what if the gut reaction leads to a disaster? The effects of journalism on people can be far too serious to leave such choices to instinct and chance. A quick decision doesn't have to be thoughtless, and, therefore, it shouldn't be.

Today's journalists have the benefit of learning much about the dilemmas faced by those who came before. Although each case that comes up has some unique elements to it, none is wholly original. Therefore, although each case must be weighed on its own merits, the weighing process is not brand-new each time. Experienced thinkers, like experienced cyclists, find that much of what they do the tenth time, or the hundredth, is made easier by all the efforts that came before. Fortunately for those just starting out, journalists spend a great deal of time thinking about moral questions, weighing the pros and cons of each decision they make. And, because they are journalists, they tend to write down their thoughts, which means that there is a large body of thoughtful work by skilled writers available for study by those just starting out. Journalists are storytellers in essence, and they like to tell stories about themselves as much as they like to tell stories about others.

Of course, what journalists have done in the past does not provide absolute marching orders for the present. Standards of taste and public morals change, technological advances bring new problems and new ways of solving old ones, and so on. However, voyagers who refuse to look at any of the existing maps before starting out are bound to waste a great deal of time discovering many things they could have easily known in advance. They will probably also get thoroughly lost.

The following procedure for dealing with ethical dilemmas is derived largely from the works of others who have considered these important questions (including the procedure laid out in the first edition of this book ten years ago). It has been tested in the classroom and in the field, and is just as useful for seasoned professionals as it is for novice journalists. At minimum, it should help journalists kick-start and guide newsroom conversations about how best to deal with dilemmas quickly and effectively without cutting corners or leaving too much up to chance.

Step 1: Challenge Your Gut Reaction

Challenge does not mean ignore, nor does it mean dismiss. Your first impulse when facing a dilemma is not without merit, as it often will bring to the fore your emotions, biases, and values. However, basing a decision on your first feelings can be misleading and, as we stated earlier, far too reliant on luck. Acknowledge your gut reaction, respect it, but have the temerity to set it aside for a moment while you give the situation some careful thought.

Step 2: Consider the Facts

This step involves both honesty with oneself and honesty about what's going on. Start by considering your own barriers to the truth. Do I have my thumb on the scales? Am I deciding the merits of a political debate because I like the mayor or because I dislike him? Do I think the school superintendent is incompetent because she expelled my child, or the child of a friend, for misbehavior? Many philosophers have come up with different models for tackling this sort of problem, but they all come down to this: Am I being fair and honest in assessing this case, or am I allowing my personal politics, my loyalties, my social or religious affiliation, or some other personal factors to distort my thinking? And beyond that, what are my personal limitations of knowledge and experience?

Once we have a reading on our own personal limitations and biases, it's time to think about the others who will be affected: Who wins and who loses? It is a blunt and unavoidable fact that almost anything a journalist does will benefit somebody and quite possibly harm somebody else—not just those who will be directly affected, but also their families, neighbors, coworkers, and many others, the great majority of them completely innocent of any wrongdoing.

When considering who will be affected, we must be careful not to project our own personal values onto others. Just because one person is opposed to premarital sex doesn't mean everybody is, and just because you wouldn't mind having your age and income made public doesn't mean others wouldn't want to keep that information confidential. When in doubt, and whenever possible, it can be very helpful to simply ask people what they think, and incorporate that feedback into the decision-making process.

Step 3: Consider the Principles

The third step to consider is: What principles are involved in this case? Is it a situation where my personal biases compromise my ability to be objective? Am I having trouble being fair and balanced? Do I have a conflict of interest? Is privacy an issue, and how legitimate a claim for privacy do the parties have? Would I want such information published if it were about me? Things that are important count more than things that are merely amusing; things that are interesting fall somewhere in between. Is it newsworthy or is it pandering?

Remember that the principles of ethical journalism go well beyond the decision of whether and how much to publish. Also in play are obligations to verify information and to attribute information to sources, choices about which information to leave out, whether to obfuscate the identity of sources, and sometimes whether telling a lie might reveal a greater truth.

Another useful part of this step is to ask what do we usually do in cases like this? Precedent is not infallible, but it certainly counts for something. Consistency is a major element of fairness and, therefore, it takes more compelling reasons to do things differently than to do things the way they were done the last time this sort of problem came up. If the precedent doesn't seem good enough, consider if maybe it's time to establish a new precedent. If we usually provide addresses of crime victims to warn people where the dangers are, do we have to give the widow's exact address, along with the information that she lives alone and will soon receive a big insurance settlement? Maybe just a block number or a neighborhood will provide the necessary warning without telling would-be burglars the exact address of an easy target.

Step 4: Consider the Alternatives

It's now time to work on some choices. This can be done alone, but it usually goes smoother with help from fellow journalists, either coworkers or just some college friends who are working elsewhere. Ideally, you will come up with two or more alternatives. Just one idea is better than none, but you aren't really making a choice unless you have at least two alternatives. Each approach needs to be reasonable (meaning it will address the principles in question) and attainable (meaning it's something you can actually accomplish); if you come up with two or more, then each also must be distinct (meaning they really are two alternatives, not just aspects of a single one).

Sometimes, *do nothing* creeps onto the list of possible approaches. That is almost never a good idea because ethical dilemmas have to be dealt with, not ignored. Giving up when the going gets tough isn't very defensible from a moral standpoint. It also doesn't say much about a journalist's character.

It also can be misleading to treat dilemmas as binary choices—do the interview or don't do the interview, publish the photograph or don't publish the photograph, name the source or don't name the source. Such simplistic debating can be misleading because if *don't publish* is a reasonable option, then *publish* likely never was reasonable at all. Likewise, if there is a valid public need to publish the information, then *don't publish* also is unreasonable. Ethical problems that can be resolved with a simple yes or no are usually not dilemmas at all, but just common, run-of-the-mill questions. True ethical dilemmas require much more rigorous consideration.

Most ethical dilemmas also have layers, and those need to be considered as well. Like the Jayson Blair scandal at the *New York Times*, many situations involve problems within the news organization as well as problems with sources, competitors, and the public at large. Beyond deciding how to handle the problematic information, ethical journalists must decide how to handle problematic colleagues and explain the situation to the public at the same time. For supervisors, that often involves disciplining subordinates, apologizing to the public, and developing new procedures to prevent similar dilemmas in the future. For lower-level journalists, the problem can be compounded by insecurities, vulnerabilities, and feelings of isolation. The way an editor deals with a reckless intern is very different from how an intern challenges an editor who is making a poor choice.

Coming up with alternatives can be difficult and at times frustrating, but it is always time well spent. That's especially true when the discussion involves multiple people—reporters, editors, interns, even support staff (never assume that the janitor or the receptionist won't have keen insights and clever ideas). Many times, a good group of people that ponders an issue carefully will come up with a creative idea for turning a lose-lose dilemma into a win-win decision.

Step 5: Decide

This step may seem obvious, but there are many people who ponder journalism ethics who never get to this stage. You could read this book cover to cover, discuss it with classmates and colleagues, read another four or five books on media ethics, and still never have to make an ethical decision. In the classroom or the conference room, all of this stuff is pretty academic and hypothetical; in the newsroom, it's all too real. Even the best role-playing exercise or heated classroom debate can't compare to the cold sweats, knotted stomachs, and sleepless nights caused by a true newsroom dilemma.

A journalist never feels as alone as when he or she makes a tough ethical choice, acts on it, and waits for what happens next. Even if the choice was developed with a close-knit team of coworkers and comes with the blessings of the highest officials in the company, that limbo between enacting the choice and response from the public can be long and foreboding.

Because you won't be able to concentrate on much else during that time anyway, you may as well put it to good use. Use those sleepless hours to write a memo of the steps you took thus far, from the frank admissions of your initial gut reaction through your consideration of your own biases and the limits of what you know, from a discussion of which journalistic principles you are upholding (and why) through the process of developing alternatives for dealing with the situation. Chances are good that you will have to write such a memo anyway—editors and news directors will need detailed accounts of what transpired for when they explain the situations to their publishers and station managers. However, writing the memo also prepares you for the sixth and final step, which generally begins in the form of a nasty e-mail or an angry phone call early the next day.

Step 6: Articulate Your Decision

In journalism, every ethical dilemma is immediately followed by another. After dealing with the primary dilemma, the journalist must then decide the most ethical way to deal with the unavoidable criticism to follow. Some choose to ignore it, others to fight it, but the best approach is usually to embrace it as an important part of the ethical process.

There is nothing more unethical than for a person or group of people to make a decision that affects another person and then refuse to explain that decision. It is the very definition of tyranny, especially when the latter is powerless to challenge such tyranny. Because journalism is all about people, and can (and often does) have profound and enduring effects on people's lives, it is unconscionable for journalists to not, at minimum, explain their actions. Press freedoms have been written into law the world over so that journalists, and through them the public, can hold their governments accountable. Journalists who aren't accountable to the public in turn would appear to be hypocrites.

If finding truth and building trust are the goals of ethics, then accountability certainly must be its modus operandi. In her important book *Lying: Moral Choice in Public and Private Life*, philosopher Sissela Bok made this most poignant argument: "Moral justification . . . cannot be exclusive or hidden; it has to be capable of being made public." She precedes that statement with this one: "To justify is to defend as just, right, or proper, by providing adequate reasons. . . . Such justification requires an audience;

it may be directed to God, or a court of law, or one's peers, or one's own conscience; but in ethics it is most appropriately aimed, not at any one individual or audience, but rather at 'reasonable persons' in general."

That detailed memo you write immediately after taking action is an important part of justifying your moral choice, because it starts by justifying that choice to yourself. After giving a copy to your supervisors, you can hand it out to coworkers to help them understand the effort and thought that went into the decision. It also can be excerpted, expanded, and annotated to become the justification to any journalists' real bosses—not publishers or station managers or (certainly not) shareholders, but the public at large.

That first angry phone call or flaming e-mail responding to your decision is not just a response. It's a test. It's a challenge to your integrity, intellect, and all of the thought and anguish you put into making a difficult decision that you thought was right. It's a challenge from somebody who relies on journalism but has little idea about how it works or the people who do it. And it is coming from somebody who cares enough to get involved, to ask the question—to make a connection.

At the very beginning of the first chapter, we mentioned how journalism credibility has fallen among the public, showing up in polls in the neighborhood of used car dealers. We'd like to take a moment to defend used car dealers—we've known a few in our time, and although some live down to the stereotype, many have been decent, honest people who enjoy making a fair sale and providing excellent customer service. They are good people in an oft-maligned profession who sincerely want to build solid, trusting relationships with people in their communities.

That vitriolic e-mail at the top of your inbox is from somebody who is looking for a fair deal and good customer service. If the press truly is a mess in the early years of the twenty-first century, journalists are the only ones who can clean it up. They can start by explaining their ethical decisions, with respect and integrity, to the public at large, even if they have to do it one citizen at a time.

Part II

■ ■ ■

CASE STUDIES

TOUGH CALLS FROM THE FRONT LINES OF CONTEMPORARY JOURNALISM

7 ▪ ▪ ▪

Objectivity vs. Bias
How Close Is Too Close When the Subject Is a Little Girl?

For good reasons, journalists usually try to stay out of their own stories. In the name of neutrality and objectivity, journalists usually consider themselves obliged to keep from becoming part of the stories they cover. The thinking behind this premise is simple and straightforward: The journalist is morally obliged to be as honest as possible, both with the subjects in the article and with the readers or viewers. One of the great journalistic sins is getting too close to a source, or becoming so friendly with a news source that personal feelings impede the reporter's ability to report honestly and fairly. It is relatively rare that journalists actually fabricate stories out of whole cloth on behalf of news sources—to do that would be such a blatant violation of the principle of honesty that few reporters are seriously tempted. It is much more common—because it is much less clearly wrong—that a journalist will play down a negative aspect of a story because of personal friendship or loyalty.

This wariness about reporters getting too close to news sources is behind the common newsroom policy to regularly rotate reporters from beat to beat, moving the city hall reporter to the public schools beat, or reassigning the high school football reporter to cover women's sports at the local university. The idea is that after some period of time—a year, two years, or sometimes longer—the reporter is apt to have made personal friends among the regular news sources on the beat and be unable to cover them objectively, that is, without personal bias. The other end of the argument, of course, is the realization that such policies sacrifice experience and expertise that can only be gained from years of working a particular beat. Most beats are complicated matters and it takes time to understand the dynamics of any area of public affairs. Each beat inevitably has its own players, its own issues, and its own institutions, which have their own unifying forces and divisive fissures. Almost any beat worth covering will have its own set of publications and its own jargon. It takes time to come to understand all these things, and a neophyte is more likely to make serious mistakes or be manipulated deliberately.

Sometimes it can be very hard to stay out of a story, as was discovered one day by Michael Dillon, now a journalism professor at Duquesne University in Pittsburgh. He was a reporter at the Bloomsburg, Pennsylvania, *Press-Enterprise* in 1988 when he wound up at the very center of a story he was covering, a spot made all the more uncomfortable because it was a bitter custody battle. Here is his account of what happened.

THE DAY THE NEWS CAME TO THE REPORTER[1]

It's not often the news comes to you, and rarer still when you wish it hadn't.

On a quiet Friday morning in October 1988, frantic voices on the police scanner reported a little girl abducted from the county courthouse with police in pursuit of two suspects. The newsroom was still relatively empty, but before I could alert colleagues and join the chase, there was a commotion at the receptionist's desk. There was no need to go looking for the little girl, eight-year-old Amanda Petock, because she was standing in the lobby with her grandparents, sobbing and shaking while they cast nervous glances out to the highway.

Before Amanda left the newspaper several hours later, my newspaper and I would be drawn into the center of an ugly story involving allegations of child abuse and judicial neglect. Not only were we covering the story, we were also negotiating the conditions under which police and social workers could take the girl out—they showed little taste for running a gauntlet of photographers to take her by force.

The facts are these: Amanda Petock had spent the summer with her mother and her mother's new husband. During her visit, the couple asserted, the child had told them that her father, Eddie Petock, had abused her and that she did not want to return to his custody at summer's end. The couple violated the visitation agreement by keeping Amanda longer than they should have and answered a court order to appear before the judge to argue that she should not go back to her father. The judge refused to hear their arguments and ordered Amanda returned to her father. That's when her mother Anita Walewski and her new husband Stanley, along with Rita and Buddy Lutsky, her grandparents, grabbed Amanda and fled. Police followed Anita and Stanley. The Lutskys brought Amanda to the Bloomsburg, Pennsylvania, *Press-Enterprise*, where I was a reporter.

I spoke to the girl's grandparents and then, accompanied by a female office worker, with the little girl. Their stories matched. Eddie Petock, at the very least, had beaten the child. Dark hints of sexual abuse also arose from our conversations.

Eventually, the Walewskis called the newspaper, and I persuaded them to join their daughter. After receiving assurances that social workers would investigate the abuse allegations, the Walewskis surrendered to police. Amanda was taken to the Child Protective Services headquarters and later, because she would not repeat the abuse allegations she had made at the newspaper, was returned to her father.

The story seemed clear: Desperate mom and heroic grandparents defy an uncaring judge and rescue child from abusive dad.

It did not turn out to be quite that simple.

By the time Amanda had been carried, screaming, from the newspaper by a sheriff's deputy, and Rita Walewski had been helped from the sidewalk where she had collapsed in tears as the child went away, it was almost 7 P.M. I had done most of the negotiating with the police, the parents, and the social workers. Another reporter suggested that perhaps he should write the story because I had become so enmeshed in it. I snarled and told him to put his notebook away.

I refused to give the story up. In doing so, I suppose I violated textbook canons concerning conflict of interest or interference in the course of a story. But this wasn't a textbook. It was a little girl. Journalists should not rush about trying to shape or direct the news, and they should resist getting emotionally embroiled in the stories they cover. But this story was unique. The Lutskys brought Amanda to the paper because they saw us as a sanctuary, a court of last resort. I was part of the story whether I liked it or not.

To me, at least, there was a more important issue involved: right and wrong. Not just what's right for journalists, but what's right or wrong for people. My personal values would not allow me to walk away from the story, but my professional values would not allow me to cross the line to unquestioning advocate for either set of adults or officials fighting over the child's fate. The kid was a different story. I was on her side.

But the clock was ticking, and I was nervous. Ethically and legally, I had a problem with running a story containing vivid abuse allegations without giving Eddie Petock, the father, his say. But Eddie was nowhere to be found. He had left the courthouse. He had not gone home. His relatives and lawyer claimed not to know where he was. Darkness was falling when I drove to his parents' rural home to ask their help in finding him. No need. He was there. And so was Amanda.

The little girl clung devotedly to her father. She smiled as he tousled her hair. Her mother, Eddie told me, had "brainwashed" the girl to make allegations against him. "I'm going in the paper as an abuser no matter what happens now, aren't I?" he asked sardonically. He let me speak to Amanda alone. She told me she had not lied when she made the allegations at the newspaper and pleaded with me to "not tell Daddy what I said." She added that her father was not cruel and that she did not object to living with him. She protested going back to him "because I didn't want to hurt Mommy's feelings."

The story I wrote for the next day's newspaper was circumspect. Every paragraph that contained an allegation of abuse was followed by one that mitigated that claim. Stylistically, it was no masterpiece. In the end, attention was drawn to the practices of the judge who had handled the case, but Amanda remained with her father.

I learned three things that day. One I already knew: that when moral right or wrong comes into conflict with journalistic right or wrong, I will base my actions on the former.

I also was reminded of the power of newspapers to serve as a court of last appeal—without the glare of publicity, no investigation of the girl's claims would have been conducted. We should not shrink from this power. It is worth more to the integrity and future of journalism than all of the marketing surveys we endlessly ponder.

Finally, more than any other, Amanda's story made me feel the full weight of the responsibility reporters assume in depicting those they write about. Eddie Petock had never been in the newspaper before Amanda's abduction. What I wrote about him—for better or worse, fairly or unfairly—will forever define him in the rural community in which he lives.

How will his neighbors judge him? Those who read closely will judge him on the facts. Those who didn't will see him and instantly think of the words "Child Abuser." No matter how fairly I wrote the story, he will have to live with that. And, so will I.

Dillon's first concern, what he describes as the conflict of personal morality and journalistic morality, is not as serious as it may first appear. The conflict is not really between competing moral standards, but between a deeply held moral sense on the one hand and an item on the checklist of appropriate journalistic behavior on the other. The underlying principles are not really in conflict. He is quite right in noting that many ethics codes caution against reporters writing about things if they are too close to them. The reason for this sanction is to preserve the honesty and integrity of the story, even if the journalist is confused by strong personal biases. Many competent professionals would recommend just what Dillon's colleague at the paper suggested: that someone else write the story of the bizarre custody fight. However, Dillon chose to write the story himself and took great pains to be fair and balanced to all sides, even though his personal objectivity was clearly compromised. In a sense, he was choosing to remain on the beat on the grounds that he understood the story's complexities rather than hand it off to another reporter to maximize impartiality. That is not a question of right and wrong, either in the sense of correct and incorrect or in the sense of moral and immoral. Instead, it is a case of different people with the same fundamental principles assigning different weights to the different parts of the question.

His second lesson, the reminder that people turn to their news organizations in times of need, is an important counterargument to periodic poll data showing a decline in public confidence in the news media. True, this incident took place twenty years ago, but local newspapers to this day get calls and walk-ins of citizens who want reporters to investigate allegations of injustice. In such major disasters as the London Underground bombings and the space shuttle *Columbia* explosion, through such armed conflicts as the Iraq War to such private tragedies as the custody fight Dillon discusses here, people frequently turn to news organizations for help and information when there is nowhere else to turn. Dillon's story is unusual in that the fugitives actually came to the newspaper office, but the principle is commonplace: Citizens generally expect their news media to hear them out, to hold bureaucracies accountable, and to make right the wrongs done to them. Any telephone operator or receptionist at almost any news organization will say the same thing: Whatever people say in the polls, large numbers of them have a strong sense of the news media's public service obligations. It is a good thing that they do; it makes the journalist's job a great deal easier, but even more importantly, it makes the job more meaningful.

The third lesson Dillon writes of is also important to remember: Most citizens who do not have public-relations professionals on the payroll are largely at the mercy of journalists. What journalists do and do not write about people makes an enormous difference in their lives, a difference that in many cases will linger long after the reporter has moved on to other stories. Recognition of the lasting impact of our work does not necessarily mean that we should weigh things differently, but it is a caution against weighing them haphazardly or considering the outcome trivial.

Real human beings occasionally suffer real harm in the course of much public work. A judicial decision to jail a felon nearly always causes harm to the defendant's relatives. Failing to incarcerate him or her may cause more harm to future victims. An executive decision to cut off or reduce social services in tight times causes harm to the poor who most need the help. Refusing to curb spending may cause harm to all taxpayers. Rarely is the question of avoiding harm simple.

In this case, there might have been some harm done to the child's father by putting the story in the paper at all. Nevertheless, the greatest harm to the public would have occurred if the paper had lost credibility by not covering the story. Readers trust the news media to inform them about issues of public interest and importance. This story surely qualifies. Failing to report it would have been an abdication of duty. Some readers would have never known about the case. That is the lesser problem. The more serious problem is that some readers would have known of the incident and looked to the paper to provide a full and impartial report of the day's events. Not finding it, they would have been entitled to conclude that, through ignorance or design, the newspaper was not objective in telling them of important events around them. Dillon's solution—a course of action that most responsible reporters would choose as well—was to write the story and use extreme care to be as objective as possible.

QUESTIONS TO CONSIDER

1. Would you have published the story? If you had been in Dillon's position, would you have written the story or would you have handed it off to another reporter?

2. Dillon was certainly involved in the story. Does that mean that he was not objective?

3. What should Dillon have done if he had not been able to track down Eddie Petock? Should he have written the piece and said Petock was not available for comment?

4. You probably came away from Dillon's account unsure about whether the girl had been abused or not, and that he had an unusual amount of access to the girl—two face-to-face interviews. In many, maybe most, cases, reporters feel that they do not have all the information they would like to have about an issue—information that would enable them to make a definitive case instead of writing an article that reads like a debate. Those kinds of stories often irritate readers and listeners, who would like to know if something is right or wrong, safe or unsafe. Would it be better if reporters waited until definitive answers were available before reporting on such issues? What if sources deliberately delayed providing information to prevent journalists from publishing anything at all?

5. If the girl had told Dillon in the second interview that she was afraid of her father and wanted to go back to her mother, what should he have done?

6. Assume the case wound up in court and Dillon was subpoenaed to testify about what the girl and the adults in the case had told him—all of it, not just what had appeared in the newspaper article. What would be the ethical response to such a subpoena? Would his obligations as a journalist point him toward the same decision as his feelings as a person, or would they be in conflict?

8 ▪ ▪ ▪

Objectivity vs. Bias
Keeping Cool When You Get a Hot Quote

The previous chapter discussed a case in which a reporter at a small-town newspaper had his objectivity challenged when he unwittingly became embroiled in a local news event. This chapter considers a case in which a reporter's objectivity was challenged by a slip of the tongue on the stage of international politics.

In early March 2008, at a critical juncture in the U.S. Democratic presidential primary campaign between U.S. Senators Hillary Clinton and Barack Obama, Obama's chief foreign policy adviser, a Harvard professor named Samatha Power, caused controversy when she told a newspaper reporter that Clinton was "a monster." In the next breath, Power told the interviewer, Geraldine "Gerri" Peev of *The Scotsman* in Edinburgh, Scotland, that the phrase was not to be published—it was off the record in journalistic parlance—and went on with the interview.

Perhaps the situation would have been different had Peev's interview with Power been about the Obama campaign. However, the interview was actually about Power's tour of Britain to promote her latest book, *Chasing the Flame: Sergio Vieira de Mello and the Fight to Save the World*, a biography about the late Brazilian diplomat for the United Nations who was killed in 2003 when terrorists bombed his hotel in Iraq. Power's comments about the political campaign back in the United States was only tangential to the interview, and her "monster" comment came after Power had taken a phone call and learned details of Obama's recent loss in the important Ohio primary election.

Despite Power's request that the impolite comment be ignored, Peev included the name-calling in the story that ran the next day, and the incident became front-page news in the hotly contested race in the United States. The Power interview caused a good deal of embarrassment to the Obama campaign, although it is impossible to quantify any harm it may have done to his quest for the presidency. For her part, Power apologized profusely and resigned from Obama's campaign.

Comments whipped around the blogosphere, many of them settling on the partisan implications of the "monster" comment – Clinton backers in high dudgeon over the insult, Obama's backers agreeing with the sentiment expressed, if not the word choice. Many comments also were leveled against the reporter for using an off-the-record quote in the first place.

In terms of journalistic objectivity, this case illustrates a common challenge for reporters who cover politics. In the course of interviewing newsworthy politicians (and their advisers), reporters often hear comments that the interviewees do not intend to be published. That's just human nature—people often say things out loud that they immediately regret. In a private conversation with friends or family, such comments can often be mitigated with apologies and further discussion. However, in conversations with journalists, such comments can slip straight from the politician's tongue onto the Internet for the whole world to hear. Especially when the comment is inflammatory and regards a high-profile situation, a journalist's objectivity is challenged in many nuanced ways.

In this situation, the challenge to the journalists involved began with whether Power's off-the-cuff comments about a political campaign she was working on were more important than the primary reason for the interview, which was Power's book tour. It then became an issue of whether to honor Power's after-the-fact request that the comment not be reported, that it be considered truly off the record. That latter dilemma is the stickiest in this case.

Off the record is a powerful term and one that has made its way into all sorts of areas beyond where it rightfully lies: at the professional core of how a reporter deals with a source. As journalists use the term, and as knowledgeable sources use it, it has a very specific meaning, although a fairly nuanced one. It is extremely important for journalists to understand the meaning of the expression, "That is off the record," and knowing when the action can be invoked and when it can't.

Simply put, "off the record" means a newsworthy individual will tell a reporter something that the source does not intend to be made public, but only if the reporter agrees not to mention the statement or the source in a report about that issue. It is generally not a unilateral condition imposed by a newsmaker upon a reporter; it is an agreement between journalist and source.

Such agreements should be rare, however, and should be justified on moral grounds, because reporters are in the information business, not the secrets business. There are exceptions, but the default position is anything and everything a reporter hears can be used and used in full—quotes, names, other pieces of identification, everything. As this book has made clear in many places, the core function of journalism is to ensure that the citizenry is informed and can manage its own affairs, including its own government. Thus, whatever a reporter comes across that is deemed to be in the public's interest to know, the reporter has not only a right but an obligation to provide.

In addition, journalists must not only be fair and open, but they also must appear to be so. On any given story, a reporter may withhold some piece of information that tilts or seems to tilt the balance of a report in one way or another. For a reporter with a strong emotional attachment to one party or one side of a story, it is tempting to give in to such personal biases. Who will ever know what was said but not reported? The audience may never be the wiser. However, in the long run, that sort of information has a way of getting out. Remember: by the time a reporter knows almost anything, somebody else—and usually a lot of somebody elses—knows it, too. That is particularly true in the current age of citizen journalists, bloggers, and any bystander with a video-capable cell phone and Internet access. The modern reporter who tries to withhold important information is quite likely to be discovered. Once that happens, bad things happen to the story, to the journalist who wrote it and, by extension, to all of journalism.

So, by default, anything that a journalist picks up may well wind up in a news report—just as Power's "monster" comment made it into Peev's article for *The Scotsman*.

Why then do some things not make it into the story? There are three main reasons. The first two are relatively easy, at least in extreme examples. First, and easiest to dispense with, are those details that are clearly unimportant. At the time of almost any given story, it is almost certainly either raining in Seattle or it's not raining in Seattle, yet Seattle's weather is left out of most stories—it is true and accurate, it is objective and fair, but it is irrelevant. Second, there is information that is true enough, but that someone legitimately wants to be kept out of the public domain and there is no legitimate reason for including it. All American citizens have a Social Security number and so do the authors of this book, but except in the most extraordinary circumstances, those numbers will never appear in a news story.

The third and most challenging reason for not publishing important comments regards situations in which a news source is willing to tell you something newsworthy, but either doesn't want to be identified as the source of the information or doesn't want the information to be made public. Reporters usually don't like getting information that way, but it is often the only way to get certain kinds of information—for example, tips about corrupt government officials from a whistleblower from within that government. Many times, the source agrees to provide the information so long as he or she is not identified in the report—what is typically referred to as *anonymous sourcing* (anonymous meaning "without a name"). Other times, the source may agree to provide information *on background*, which means the information will be provided on condition that the source not only be kept anonymous, but the information not be published until it is attributable to some other source (such as a public document). In rare instances will a source insist that information be completely off the record— that it neither be mentioned in any news report, ever, nor in any fashion, even generally.

Professional journalists are extremely loathe to accept information off the record for a number of reasons, but mostly because the information is of no use to them; they can't use it in their stories nor can they pursue the issue through other sources. So the sorts of information that wind up being off the record are usually the sorts of things that a news source wishes to be at ease in saying without the fear of seeing part of a conversation wind up in the news. If a reporter and a source share a casual meal, for example, or attend the same social event (both happen a great deal, particularly in state and national capitals), the source may wish to make the whole conversation off the record. A reporter may agree to the terms, saying, essentially, "I'm off duty tonight. Relax." Many reporters defend that sort of practice and regularly engage in it, arguing that it is only by getting to know public figures in informal settings will they be able to cover them adequately in more formal settings.

Here is the critically important point, and one that cuts to the core of the case of Samantha Power's "monster" comment: The reporter and the source have to agree that the information is off the record *before* the information is passed to the reporter, not after. That is also true in cases in which a source insists on anonymity or agrees to provide information on background—the source and the reporter talk about the nature of the information to be passed from source to reporter. The source then says, in effect, "I'll tell you, but. . . . " Then there is negotiation between reporter and source, the reporter trying to get as much information on the record as possible, primarily for reasons of credibility. Only when the deal is struck is the information passed. However, if the deal ends in an off-the-record agreement, the reporter is promising to keep a secret. Whatever the information is, the reporter is not to use it in any form, at any time, unless the source later agrees to put the information back on the record.

Now, all this bargaining to get things on (or off) the record applies mostly to politicians, entertainers, athletes, and other public figures who regularly talk to reporters and know the differences between anonymous sourcing, on background, and off the record. Most reporters believe they have a duty not to try to drive such hard bargains when talking with unwary private citizens with little or no experience talking to reporters. In a sense, they should feel obliged to protect private citizens from their own naiveté. The elderly widow you interview for a story about a local crime spree may tell you that she keeps an extra back-door key under the doormat, but you probably wouldn't put that in your story, even if the nice woman didn't have the presence of mind to ask.

With public figures who know all about how to interact with journalists, however, striking deals before hand is very important. If it was possible for a source to go off the record after the information had been passed, people being investigated for any wrongdoing by any reporter could easily put themselves in the clear by admitting everything and then putting that information out of reach by going off the record. "Yes, I took the money," or "Yes, I stuffed the ballot boxes," but "that's off the record so you can't ever put that in a story." That is why reporters tend to be less accommodating to public figures than to private citizens, and why the responsibility for starting off-the-record negotiations begins with the public figure, not the journalist.

Samantha Power is just such a public figure. At the time, she was an unpaid and outspoken adviser to Obama at the zenith of the long, contentious primary campaign in the United States. Power herself is a former journalist (a veteran war correspondent) who became a professor at the prestigious Kennedy School of Government at Harvard University. She is the author of *A Problem from Hell: America and the Age of Genocide*, which won the Pulitzer Prize for nonfiction in 2003, and, as mentioned earlier, she was in the United Kingdom promoting her latest book, *Chasing the Flame: Sergio Vieira de Mello and the Fight to Save the World*. As part of the book tour, she agreed to an on-the-record taped interview with Peev, who normally covers the British Parliament for her paper. There was nothing at all in the case to suggest that anything Power would say in the interview would be off the record.

The interview was on March 6, 2008, less than forty-eight hours after the critically important presidential primaries in Ohio and Texas, which Hillary Clinton had won and in so doing breathed new life into her flagging campaign. In the middle of the interview, Power got a phone call and excused herself. When she returned, she was clearly agitated, explained that the phone call was from the campaign headquarters, and concerned the just-concluded primary in Ohio, in which Clinton had adopted a stronger line of attack against Obama.

To quote Peev's story the next day in *The Scotsman*, here's what happened next:

"We f***** up in Ohio," she admitted. "In Ohio, they are obsessed and Hillary is going to town on it, because she knows Ohio's the only place they can win.

"She is a monster, too – that is off the record – she is stooping to anything," Ms Power said, hastily trying to withdraw her remark.

Power said of the Clinton campaign: "Here, it looks like desperation. I hope it looks like desperation there, too.

"You just look at her and think, 'Ergh.' But if you are poor and she is telling you some story about how Obama is going to take your job away, maybe it will be more effective. The amount of deceit she has put forward is really unattractive."

The Clinton campaign complained loudly and, within twenty-four hours, Power had resigned from Obama's campaign (and continued her book tour). Peev wrote of the incident in her paper the following day. "I didn't set out to cost anyone their job," she said, but added that she "thought it was incredibly important to underscore the tensions" in the campaign. "No one had quoted an adviser who had been as candid as Ms. Power had been. So I thought it was my duty to actually report what was said," Peev wrote.

Under a strict interpretation of reporter–source relationships, Peev was certainly within her rights to quote Power, and Power, herself a veteran journalist, while apologizing for the statement, has never complained that she was treated unfairly.

And yes, in one sense, the quote came in the middle of an on-the-record interview and Power had no right to ask, after the fact, that something she said to a reporter with a recorder running be considered off the record. On the other hand, Power agreed to an interview regarding her new book, not about the primary campaign back in the United States. Returning to the interview about her book from the interruption of the phone call was, in a sense, beginning the interview anew, and the comments about Ohio and the Clinton campaign were both an explanation for the interruption and an unscripted outburst of frustration. Given that, and given that Power immediately declared the outburst to be off the record, it is highly likely most political reporters would have agreed not to use the "monster" quote.

Nevertheless, *The Scotsman* is a very aggressive newspaper and, in the same story, has at least two statements that do not stand up to serious ethical scrutiny. Here are the first two paragraphs of Peev's story in *The Scotsman*:

Hillary Clinton has been branded a 'monster' by one of Barack Obama's top advisers, as the gloves come off in the race to win the Democrat nomination.

In an unguarded moment during an interview with *The Scotsman* in London, Samantha Power, Mr Obama's key foreign policy aide, let slip the camp's true feelings about the former first lady.

In a political context, the boxing metaphor about taking off the gloves suggests that, from that point on, the campaign would be a bare-knuckle fight—that is, brutal by contemporary standards. It certainly implied volition. However, consider the circumstances in which the Obama campaign ostensibly decided to turn negative. It beggars belief to suggest that the Obama campaign decided to turn nasty by having an unpaid staff adviser speak ill of Clinton while on an unrelated book tour in Europe.

The second paragraph is even more of a reach. Neither Peev nor anybody else can say that Power's comment represents the Obama campaign's true feelings about Clinton. It is highly unlikely that the whole campaign staff feels alike on anything beyond hoping their candidate wins. And certainly a part-time adviser on an unrelated book tour in Europe isn't up to speed on what a campaign thinks or feels. Most importantly, Power certainly did not indicate that she was speaking on behalf of Obama and his campaign staff, or that the "monster" comment was anything other than an aside to a conversation about a whole other matter (i.e., Power's new book).

Reporters who regularly cover a subject area, *a beat* in newsroom parlance, are often gradually, over time, granted latitude to interpret events along with reporting them. In other words, reporters put statements and events into context. However, putting things into context is always risky business, for it is exactly there that the imprecision of the journalism business is most apparent, when cool reason is most subject to being swamped by emotional heat. A reporter's bias toward getting a juicy story can overcome the obligation to put controversial comments in the proper context.

The context into which Peev put Power's "monster" comment is that the Obama campaign was turning aggressively negative and that Power's word choice represented the campaign's "true feelings" about Clinton. That was unlikely at best.

A far more likely context is this: Power was on a European tour to promote her latest book and, as part of that, set up an interview with Peev. In the middle of that interview, she got a phone call regarding her work for Obama, which bore bad news about the Ohio primary and, apparently, an assessment that Clinton's negative ads had worked. Perhaps because she had just gotten off the plane after an overnight flight to London and was a bit jet-lagged, Power unwittingly and candidly gave the gist of the call that interrupted the interview, immediately regretted making the comment, and asked the reporter for a courtesy. The reporter seized upon the "unguarded moment" and turned a tangential discussion into a front-page story in a major English-language newspaper that was picked up by major news media the world over.

We may conclude that Peev's use of the "monster" quote was within the bounds of journalistic propriety because there was no agreement beforehand for an off-the-record comment. Nevertheless, by not putting that quote into the proper context, Peev was reaching well beyond the boundaries of objective journalism. In the course of an interview about one matter, Peev came to possess an inflammatory comment about an unrelated matter, one that *The Scotsman* inflated into the lead story from the interview and, at best, exaggerated well beyond the context of the interview. Power certainly should have been more careful in her dealings with a reporter, but one wonders if the reporter could have been more considerate of Power's immediate regret over a slip of the tongue.

QUESTIONS TO CONSIDER

1. The on-the-record interview between Samantha Power and Geraldine Peev concerned Power's new book, not the U.S. presidential campaign. The quote about Clinton being "a monster" came in another context entirely. Does this have any bearing on whether the quote should have been used?

2. Most journalists consider politicians to be fair game because they live in the public spotlight and understand the norms of behavior that they and reporters operate under. Similarly, most journalists figure that purely private citizens are entitled to a little more leeway in letting sources retract errant comments and so on. Should this apply to going off the record? What about the spouse of a politician? Should a spouse be treated as a private citizen or held to the stricter standards of a politician? What about a politician's child? Does it matter if the child is fifteen or nineteen? Living at home or on her own?

3. Why not let a politician—or anyone else, for that matter—take any statement off the record at any time? Does the *pas de deux* between journalists and sources actually make for better journalism? Why or why not?

4. People routinely say things that they immediately regret and wish to retract, but those who do so when talking to reporters have no power to stop those comments from being published and, as a result, entering the public record. How much accommodation should reporters give to sources who want to retract or modify statements they immediately regret saying?

9 ▪ ▪ ▪

Objectivity vs. Bias
First-Person Journalism:
The Challenge of Perspective

Not too long ago, the use of first-person in journalism was largely frowned upon by daily news journalists and was left mainly to the adherents of New Journalism writing think-pieces for literary magazines (the work of writers such as Truman Capote, Hunter S. Thompson, Joan Didion, and P.J. O'Rourke). But the words "I," "me," and "my" almost never appeared in anything but direct quotes in newspapers or the six o'clock news. The idea was that only by having a degree of personal detachment from the people and events in the news could a report provide a relatively objective account of what transpired. What's more, a reporter's use of first-person pronouns (I, me, my) was seen as a rhetorical indicator of personal bias, which has long had no place in the reporting of "straight news."

Today, first-person is becoming more common in news reports of daily newspapers, accounts on national broadcasts, and, of course, in the blogs of professional reporters. Although first-person is commonplace in the blogosphere and in "crowd-sourcing" accounts from eyewitnesses to breaking news, the use of first-person by professional reporters is still seen as something that should be used sparingly, and then only when the journalist's personal stake in something is an important part of the story. Consider the following statement from Nicole Bode, who in 2005 was a reporter for the New York *Daily News* sent back to her hometown of New Orleans to cover the flooding triggered by Hurricane Katrina. Bode's assignment was complicated by the fact that her father was trapped by the flooding in the New Orleans suburb where Bode was raised. She told Poynter Online:

> The most difficult part of writing this story was the period immediately following it, when I lost the layer of separation that normally helps me—and I imagine many reporters—trying to function in places of great trauma. For the following day or two, every person I talked to cut me to the bone.
>
> It really took me until today to get back to a place where this is just a job. It built up to the point that people's pain was just staying with me and I couldn't let go. . . .
>
> I hoped that by telling the experience of what we were going through we would help people understand the scope of what was happening. . . . I hoped that this was a story that was worth telling.[1]

Sometimes a journalist's personal experiences with important issues can be as informative and thought-provoking as the more common practice of "reporting it straight." One particularly powerful example of that was the "My Cancer" series by the late Leroy Sievers, which was broadcast on National Public Radio (and published as a blog on NPR's Web site) from February 2006 until Sievers's death at age 53 in August 2008.

Sievers was a veteran broadcast journalist, not an upstart video-blogger with no professional credentials. Sievers had worked for CBS News for almost a decade and for ABC's *Nightline* program for fourteen years, including four years as executive producer. He had covered wars around the world, from the first Gulf War in 1990–1991 to Somalia to Nicaragua to the most recent war in Iraq (for which he was embedded with U.S. troops along with *Nightline* host Ted Koppel). He had won a dozen national Emmys and two Peabodys. He was responsible for the controversial *Nightline* report called "The Fallen," in which the entire show on Memorial Day weekend of 2004 was devoted to reading the names of U.S. soldiers killed in Iraq and Afghanistan. When he left ABC in 2005, NPR quickly hired him to be a commentator on world affairs. He was a journalist's journalist, and rarely worked in the spotlight; as a reporter and producer, his work was largely behind the scenes.

But in February 2006, Sievers stepped out into the open and quickly became something of a celebrity journalist. From the opening lines of his first NPR commentary—"My doctors are trying to kill me"—Sievers began a series of first-person accounts of his fight against the disease and his immersion into what he called "the world of cancer." With tumors in his brain and lungs stemming from colon cancer, he was given six months to live, but he held on much longer, and his "My Cancer" reports continued for nearly two and a half years, right up to his death on August 15, 2008.

Sievers was not the only reporter to cover a serious illness from the personal point of view of a victim. The first edition of this book discussed the case of Jeffrey Schmalz, a reporter for *The New York Times* who wrote in that newspaper in the early 1990s about his suffering with AIDS. At the same time Sievers was working on "My Cancer" for NPR, Lauren Terrazzano of *Newsday* chronicled her three-year battle with lung cancer in a weekly column, "Life, With Cancer," until her death in 2007 at age 39. Even if Sievers's first-person approach to writing about his own illness was not new, it was by far one of the most recognized of such efforts in the mainstream media, attracting, according to NPR, tens of thousands of people as readers, listeners, and contributors to the accompanying online forums.

All of Sievers's reporting in "My Cancer," from the on-air commentaries for NPR's *Morning Edition* show to the sometimes short daily postings on his blog, was intensely personal. He concluded his first on-air commentary, broadcast February 16, 2006, with this:

> Now I live in a different world than most of you. The world of cancer. In my world now, when you meet another patient, you don't ask, 'What do you do?' Or, 'where are you from?' You ask, 'What do you have?' And, 'What are you taking?'
>
> Unfortunately, it's a much bigger world than you might think, because one way or another, cancer touches all of us.
>
> I'm not spending my time thinking, 'why me?' though. I don't have the time. I think about the old saying, 'We aren't given the burdens we deserve, we're given the burdens we can bear.'
>
> "I have work to do, because I'm going to fight like hell.

What followed was a regular, candid, and often humorous accounting about trips to the hospital, discussions with doctors about the progression of his disease, struggles at home dealing with nausea and pain between treatments, and a lot of general philosophizing about life, illness, and death. His on-air commentaries and accompanying blogs discussed chemotherapy, radiation treatments, even an experimental radio-frequency treatment. His blogs included such topics as "Pain Takes the Spontaneity Out of Life" and "What's A Spinalectomy?" He also used the blog to talk about others who suffered from cancer, from Elizabeth Edwards (wife of former U.S. Senator and presidential hopeful John Edwards) to his own mother, June Sievers (who died of cancer at age 84 just months before Sievers died). Of his mother, he wrote on March 24, 2008: "I thought long and hard about whether I should write anything in the blog about her. In the end, I didn't see how I could go without saying something about her life, and her death. I think I probably learned how to fight this disease by watching her. What better gift could she have given me?"

Although most were about personal thoughts and experiences, many of Sievers's reports also contained general information about cancer itself—what scientists know about the disease and its many variants, the effectiveness and side-effects of different treatments, advice from physicians who treat the disease and counselors who help patients and their families cope with the emotional trauma. He often wrote about his own ways of simply living with cancer—the different ways he talked about his illness with co-workers, people he met, close friends, etc., but also how he dealt with the mundane aspects of daily life that were made difficult by his disease. He also commented on public policy toward cancer and health care in general, such as the particularly moving report from May 30, 2007, titled "Adding Insult to Injury," in which he wrote:

> Being treated for cancer is expensive, very expensive. Without insurance, I couldn't pay for it. Some numbers: $80 per pill, a procedure that may cost $15,000, or more. Whether those prices are valid is a whole different issue. For the time being, those are the prices that are charged.
>
> Even with insurance, the costs that the patient pays can be a hardship. Insurance doesn't cover everything. The co-payments, the deductibles, the uncovered items, can bleed you like slow torture.
>
> If you don't have insurance? Cancer takes your health, but it can also take your job. That can mean no insurance. Or what if the care you need is in another city, or another state? Can you afford to move? If you don't have insurance, are you sentenced to death, knowing that the treatments to help you exist, and you just don't have access to them?
>
> There's truly something wrong when how much money you have determines whether you're given the most advanced treatments, or whether you're treated at all.... The fact that the system adds insult to injury is just plain wrong. We, as a country, should be ashamed.

Taken as a complete body of work, the "My Cancer" project on NPR is perhaps one of the most comprehensive collections of reports, commentaries, and audience feedback focused on the issue of cancer that has ever been undertaken by a mainstream news organization. The amount of content Sievers produced is impressive enough, but the ancillary content adds considerably to the complete package.

If anybody was troubled by Sievers's lack of objectivity in covering his own battle with cancer, it wasn't evident among the thousands of responses to the "My Cancer" series. In fact, many of the responses to the "My Cancer" commentaries demonstrated an unusual level of thoughtfulness and resonance—and plain old interest—from a news audience.

Some of Sievers's blogs drew literally hundreds of responses, nearly all of them offering encouragement to Sievers and gratitude for his work, and many of them were statements of solidarity from other cancer sufferers. A virtual community formed around "My Cancer," and sometimes Sievers would mention people he had met, either virtually or in person, through the blog. In an August 2007 posting, Sievers used the term "us" to refer not to himself and his fellow journalists at NPR, but rather he and his fellow cancer patients:

> We have all learned so much, lived so much, and yet there's really no way to pass on a lot of that knowledge. And no real way to pass on the stories we tell each other. I have the great fortune of having this blog, but I just wonder if there isn't something else we should be doing. Granted, you can be told about cancer, just as you can be told about war. But unless you live it, it won't mean much. There is knowledge, hard-earned knowledge, that each of us now possess. . . . Maybe we should think about some sort of oral history project.

To which a reader named "Kathleen" responded (within 45 minutes of Sievers's post, according to the time stamp on the blog): "This blog is already 'an oral history project' par excellance! . . . Our collective wisdom is here for those with the will to seek out and take in. Bless us one and all—we are all living legacies."

Sievers made regular posts to the blog, almost daily. On the days when he was too ill to post, one of his NPR confidantes or his wife Laurie Singer (a television news producer for NBC) would post a notice to that effect. He also became the subject of a Discovery Channel documentary (by his former *Nightline* colleague and friend, Ted Koppel), and was sometimes a featured guest on other NPR shows, such as the call-in show *Talk of the Nation*. His death was widely reported in major news outlets, as were remembrances from his colleagues. NPR's *Talk of the Nation* devoted an entire segment to remembering Sievers (with Koppel as a guest). In the final analysis, "My Cancer" and the journalist behind it, Leroy Sievers, was held up as a triumph of national journalism.

And yet, the project raises a number of important ethical issues.

The first is, of course, that "My Cancer" was saturated in bias. Sievers made no claim to the contrary; his work was openly and intentionally told from his point of view, and the inherent value of "My Cancer" was that it wasn't "Somebody Else's Cancer." But telling a personal story in a personal way is not bias. The bias came in when Sievers became a news source to old friends and colleagues who interviewed him. Because those interviewing him were not just his colleagues, but in some cases his friends, the ability of those journalists to remain objective was dubious at best.

And yet, that familiarity between those reporters and their source allowed for some frank and difficult questions to be asked, the kinds of questions few reporters would feel comfortable asking a stranger they knew to have cancer.

Another issue is that, having worked for some of the largest and wealthiest journalism organizations in the United States, Sievers enjoyed a level of income and, more importantly, health-insurance coverage that relatively few Americans have. Without the universal health care common in much of the industrialized world, the level of care Americans have varies. Sievers himself commented that he was lucky to have the kind of health insurance and income that allowed him to get some of the best treatment possible.

He also had the kind of access to leading cancer experts that generally only comes with being famous. In an August 18, 2008, retrospective on *Talk of the Nation*, Ted Koppel remarked on that point, saying "The fact of the matter is that, A, he did have good insurance, and, B, because he had been a prominent journalist for years and had friends with connections, too, he was able to get access to absolutely the finest medical care available in the United States." Sievers received his treatments at Johns Hopkins Hospital, consistently ranked at or near the top of the best hospitals in the U.S. The popularity of "My Cancer" and the prestige of NPR also clearly gave Sievers much greater access to cancer experts at other major hospitals— and their expertise—than the average American has. The prominence of his project also surely made his blog not just a well-read feature, but also a point of contact to literally thousands of others whose experiences and insights guided him in his own struggle.

Finally, in "My Cancer," Sievers dealt with a danger that all reporters either experience or fear they will—getting so close to their subject that they lose the professional distance that makes them credible reporters. In most of his work for "My Cancer," Sievers did not lose that distance— although he often talked about how the cancer was a major part of his life, Sievers clearly put his role as a journalist above that of being a cancer patient. His commentaries were more like reports on his personal journey, and his presentation generally seemed much more like "this is what is happening" rather than "this is what bothers me today." "My Cancer" was, first and foremost, a story about cancer, not a story of "my."

The same sort of question arises on a much less powerful scale in newsrooms all over the country, and regarding a variety of personal issues. Especially among young or inexperienced journalists, the temptation to use their positions as journalists to explore their personal lives can be great. The basic questions of bias often are framed as such: Should, for example, a gay man cover gay issues (or substitute almost any affiliation, condition, or circumstance you can imagine—blacks, Hispanics, Italians, suburbanites, Democrats, born-again Christians, parents with children in the public schools, tax-paying couples without children)? On the one hand, members of a group are usually more knowledgeable about that group's goals and principles. They can bring insight and understanding to a story that an outsider could not. They also are less easily lied to and less likely to make major mistakes. On the other hand, members of a group are inevitably torn in their allegiances, even if they find themselves in a group to which they would rather not belong (such as people suffering from cancer). So long as the journalist is using his or her work to advance public understanding, rather than to simply advance his or her pet cause, the ethical problems can be avoided. In the case of Leroy Sievers, there was no question that his work for "My Cancer" adhered to the same high journalistic standards that he applied to his award-winning work years earlier for *Nightline.* The approach may have been different, and the format more personal, but the integrity of his journalism was not in question.

In the final analysis, it is the integrity, not the personal bias, of the journalist that makes for honest copy. As long as the journalist is fretting about bias, she or he is probably staying on the right side of the line.

Questions to Consider

1. First-person journalism such as "My Cancer" is not unheard of in daily journalism, but it is rare. What types of stories should be covered in such a fashion, and what types should not? Why?

2. Leroy Sievers was a prominent and well-connected American journalist, and as he and others noted openly, he had both the personal connections and the financial wherewithal to get access to arguably the best medical care available. As such, he was far from a typical cancer patient in the U.S. Does that in any way diminish the value of his insights and observations? Would it have been better for Sievers to perhaps find a willing person who was much more typical to produce content for "My Cancer" (and Sievers perhaps produce the project behind the scenes)? Why or why not?

3. What boundaries, if any, should there be regarding journalists who write about issues they are dealing with in their personal lives? Should gays and lesbians be allowed to cover GLBT issues (or, conversely, should GLBT issues only be covered by those directly involved)? What about issues regarding race and ethnicity? Religion? What does the news outlet gain by having members of particular groups cover their own groups, and what does it lose? If reporters cover their own groups, in what ways could that help or hinder their careers in journalism?

4. A major component of "My Cancer" was Sievers' blog and the comments posted to that blog by his readers. Unlike weekly columns or on-air commentaries, daily blogs generally require little or no original reporting, and often can be written right off the top of one's head. At what point does a blog become journalism and not just simply a diary of one's thoughts? What should be the minimum standards for a blog to be considered a work of journalism?

10 ▪ ▪ ▪

Fairness and Balance
The Hostile Interview: What Sets Real Journalism Apart from Fake News?

At the start of the twenty-first century, two of the biggest names in U.S. television were Bill O'Reilly of Fox News' *The O'Reilly Factor* and comedian Jon Stewart of Comedy Central's *The Daily Show*. Both are essentially entertainers who play at being journalists—O'Reilly is a blatantly biased polemicist who claims to be a journalist, and whose prime-time show on the Fox News Network is wildly popular among American conservatives; Stewart, who makes no claims to being anything other than a comedian, is host of a satirical news show that is often considered a legitimate source of news among young adults, especially liberals. Whether O'Reilly and Stewart are or are not journalists has been the subject of much debate (a debate the authors of this book engage in with the concluding chapter of this book, "What Is a Journalist?"), but for purposes of this chapter, we acknowledge that in the eyes of the public, both O'Reilly and Stewart are part of the broader journalistic landscape, and regardless of whether they are, in fact, journalists, what they do and how they do it does have a strong influence on public attitudes toward the professional news media. At minimum, the two, on occasion, do conduct interviews with newsworthy people that shed light on important issues. With that in mind, we consider in this chapter a pair of cases that exemplify the characteristics and importance of fairness and balance in both real journalism as well as in the fringes of the profession, where influential personalities such as O'Reilly and Stewart seem to operate.

Since the 1990s, O'Reilly's work has been defined by his bombastic and vitriolic attacks on those with whom he disagrees. One of the most memorable of such attacks occurred on February 4, 2003, when O'Reilly conducted an interview with Jeremy Matthew Glick, the son of Port Authority worker Barry Glick who was killed in the September 11, 2001, attack on New York City (now commonly referred to as 9/11). Glick had become a peace activist and a vocal critic of the wars launched by the United States after the attacks, and had signed his name to a newspaper advertisement opposing the U.S.-led war in Afghanistan. O'Reilly, an adamant supporter of the war effort and at the time a strong supporter of then-President George W. Bush, suggested that war opponents were unpatriotic and, in his words, "bad Americans."

As the interview began, O'Reilly introduced Glick as having "signed an anti-war advertisement that accused the USA itself of terrorism" and moments into the interview said, "I'm surprised you signed this ... and the reason I was surprised is that this ad equates the United States with the terrorists. And I was offended by that." Glick explained, in what appeared to be a rehearsed statement, why he thought the U.S. government bore some responsibility for the anti-American sentiments that led to the 9/11 attacks: "Our current president [George W. Bush] now inherited a legacy from his father and inherited a political legacy that's responsible for training militarily, economically, and situating geopolitically the parties involved in the alleged assassination and the murder of my father and countless of thousands of others."

O'Reilly's response was "All right. Now let me stop you here," and for the rest of the interview O'Reilly berated Glick, becoming increasingly combative and personally insulting with each passing minute, saying to Glick "I'm sure your beliefs are sincere, but what upsets me is I don't think your father would be approving of this" and "I don't really care what you think" and that Glick should "shut your mouth." O'Reilly appeared to become unhinged when Glick suggested, "You [O'Reilly] evoke 9/11 to rationalize everything from domestic plunder to imperialistic aggression worldwide." The interview fell apart from then on, as O'Reilly shouted at Glick to "Shut up! Shut up!," and then ended the interview with "I'm not going to dress you down anymore, out of respect for your father." O'Reilly told his stage crew to "cut his mic" and signaled for them to remove Glick from the studio, saying finally, "We're done." In the end, an interview that started with a degree of adversarial civility quickly degenerated into personal insults and ended with rude belligerence, all on one of the most-watched prime-time shows on U.S. television.

For comparison, consider the March 20, 2007, interview Jon Stewart conducted with the controversial former U.S. Ambassador to the United

Nations John Bolton. Again, we saw an openly biased interviewer (Stewart's liberalism is no secret) question somebody from the other end of the ideological spectrum (Bolton's strong right-wing positions and his dismissive attitudes toward the left is what made him such a controversial choice for ambassador). It was clear that the interview would be adversarial at best, and it largely was: Stewart and Bolton disagreed on the obligations of the U.S. presidency, the governing style of President Abraham Lincoln in the nineteenth century, and the controversy surrounding Bolton's appointment to the United Nations. However, what could have easily fallen into a belligerent farce actually unfolded as a thoughtful, civil, and mostly serious debate between the two.

Despite his strong disagreements with Bolton on several key points, and catcalling from the studio audience that appeared overwhelmingly dismissive and hostile toward Bolton, Stewart constantly maintained a civility and respect toward his interviewee. Stewart began the interview by shaking Bolton's hand and recognizing the hostile arena Bolton had entered, saying, "First of all, thank you very much for doing this, I really do appreciate it." Throughout the interview, Stewart would sincerely chuckle at Bolton's witticisms, and Bolton also would chuckle at Stewart's prods (such as when Stewart asked Bolton to "Tell us all the things that are said behind closed doors that they [the Bush administration] don't want the public to hear about their strategizing."). In that interview, Bolton suggested that President Bush, or any other president, has a primary obligation not to the entire nation, but to the people who elected him (or her) to office, a notion Stewart challenged strongly and incredulously but, again, with a degree of respect. The reverse also was true, as Bolton repeatedly said that Stewart's understanding of several issues was "wrong" and that some of his ideas were "a threat to democratic theory." Despite the contentious nature of the interview, Stewart ended the interview with a self-effacing joke and then, this: "I do appreciate your coming by and having this discussion with me about it, and I appreciate the difference of opinion, and thank you, sir, for coming on." Stewart encouraged the audience to applaud his guest, and then he enthusiastically shook Bolton's hand to conclude the segment.

A comparison of these two quasi-journalistic interviews—one in which a veteran talk-show host berated an angry and grieving son of a 9/11 victim, the other in which a comedian engaged a controversial and high-ranking bureaucrat in an informative discussion about democratic theory—sheds light on the importance (as well as the limitations) of journalistic fairness and balance. A lack of journalistic objectivity is clearly not an issue in these cases, as both O'Reilly and Stewart are open about their political and ideological biases and are popular because they are intentionally not objective (if the two shows are to be somehow classified as journalism, they surely are more like the opinion pages, not the news pages, of newspapers). Nevertheless, just because the very purpose of the shows are for the hosts to express their own views (whether to promote an ideology or to score laughs) does not mean they can't engage in a debate in a fair and balanced manner. As the fringes of what is journalism continue to expand, perhaps the one thing that sets true journalists apart from fake journalists is a deep, abiding respect for fairness and balance.

To begin, fairness can be achieved through simple civility and a display of respect toward the person being interviewed, whereas balance can be achieved by allowing the guest to express his or her opinions. Particularly in studio interviews that are recorded, when not just the content but also the tenor of the conversation is presented to the audience, a degree of civility and accommodation is important to establish and maintain journalistic credibility with the people being interviewed, the immediate audience, and the broader audience that will watch clips at a later time. It's important for journalists to remember that, in such situations, the interviewees are truly guests, people who are invited to appear on the program, and that the word host is not just a label for the journalists conducting the interview. A degree of hospitality is owed. Such one-on-one interviews, which are the stock and trade of radio and television journalism, also put the journalist in a power position, which can be intimidating and restrictive to even the most media-savvy of guests.

In that sense, it is no small irony that the award-winning journalist turned talk-show host, Bill O'Reilly, was largely (but not entirely) unfair and unbalanced toward his guest Jeremy Glick, whereas Jon Stewart (the comedian who repeatedly insists that he is not a journalist) demonstrated in his interview with Bolton a fairness and a balance that has impressed some of the most respected journalists of the day. Although both shows have been commercially successful, among serious journalists and journalism scholars, Jon Stewart is much more often sought out for his insights and opinions on the profession than is O'Reilly, who by the mid-2000s was largely viewed with disdain by the profession and academy. Some might attribute that to ideological bias, suggesting that journalists tend to be liberal and so, naturally, might gravitate toward a liberal comedian rather than a conservative newsperson. However, a more reasonable explanation is that, as in all other professions, journalists gravitate toward those who exemplify the highest ideals of the craft, and in Jon Stewart they find much to admire, and in O'Reilly they see much to scorn.

QUESTIONS TO CONSIDER

1. Is Bill O'Reilly a journalist? Is Jon Stewart? To what extent do you think that they and other point-of-view interviewers are obligated to adopt the ethical principles of journalism, particularly fairness and balance?

2. Beligerence on the part of journalists pops up often in recorded interviews, and is even expected and celebrated by some audiences. What are your thoughts about journalistic belligerence? When is it acceptable for a journalist to lose his or her temper and berate a guest on tape or even live?

3. Clips from both of these interviews are widely available on the Internet, and certainly can be obtained without much effort or expense. If you are able to view them, analyze in terms of both fairness and balance by keeping a list of instances in which you think the hosts are being fair or unfair and balanced or unbalanced.

4. Celebrity journalists such as O'Reilly and Stewart are often considered opinion leaders by their audiences, such that their behavior can be just as influential as their viewpoints. To what extent do you think journalists are responsible not just to seek truth and report it, but to behave in a manner that sets a good example for others? Could an argument be made that the title of journalist might be based more on how one behaves than on one's education and professional background (and, if so, what is that argument)?

11 ▪ ▪ ▪

Fairness and Balance
A Candidate's Past: News, Political Manipulation, or Mere Pandering?

Politics is too rarely fair and balanced within itself, and so it should be no surprise that journalists who cover politics are often dragged into dilemmas that challenge their own senses of what is fair and what is equitable. That is especially true in election years, when candidates start slinging mud and even the most expert journalists get splattered.

A timeless example of that is from June 1996, when three Republicans in the New England state of Maine were involved in a close race for their party's nomination for the U.S. Senate seat being vacated by retiring Senator William Cohen. The candidates were Susan Collins, the most politically moderate of the three (and the eventual winner); Robert A. G. Monks, a longtime conservative political operative in Maine Republican circles; and W. John Hathaway, a former poor boy who made a fortune in real estate in Huntsville, Alabama, during the go-go years of the 1980s. Hathaway, back in Maine after an abrupt departure from both politics and business dealings in Alabama, was running as the most socially conservative of the three in a New England state known for its political independence and ideological moderation. Collins enjoyed an early lead, but Hathaway stayed in the race, spending hundreds of thousands of dollars of his own money, stressing family values (opposing on moral grounds abortion, gay rights, extramarital sex, and other personal freedoms), and touting his close connection to conservative Christian organizations.

Then, in the final days before the June 11 primary, the *Boston Globe* got a tip about Hathaway's past that changed the race and quite probably inaugurated a new era in New England politics. The *Globe* was told that Hathaway had abruptly moved back to Maine from Alabama because of a sex scandal involving a twelve-year-old girl. The *Globe* sent its two-time Pulitzer Prize-winning reporter Stephen Kurkjian to Huntsville to investigate. In a day, Kurkjian had nailed down the story. On Wednesday, June 5, 1996, six days before the primary, Kurkjian had a front-page story outlining allegations of an eighteen-month sexual affair between Hathaway and the family baby-sitter, who was twelve when the affair started. The child was not identified, and no legal charges were ever filed, but local and state prosecutors from both political parties were quoted, by name and for the record, as saying that they had been thwarted in their efforts to prosecute the case as statutory rape only because the family of the girl had refused to allow the case to go forward. As the paper's assistant managing editor Walter V. Robinson explained later in a telephone interview, the girl's parents, who were well-heeled friends and business associates of Hathaway's, "did not want to put the girl through the ordeal of a trial and instead essentially drove the guy out of town."

When confronted with the accusation by *Globe* reporters, Hathaway would not acknowledge at first that there had ever been an investigation. Later, he called the charges groundless and said the girl "was in a mental institution" when she had accused him. Essentially, Hathaway "said the girl was crazy," Robinson explained. Hathaway later said he had misspoken in saying she had been in a mental institution. In fact, according to the *Globe*'s story, the girl had begun showing signs of increasingly serious emotional problems within months after she starting baby-sitting for the Hathaway children. Eventually, her parents moved her to a California school for emotionally troubled students. Five months later, according to the *Globe*'s story, the girl told a counselor at the California school of her affair with Hathaway, saying that she loved Hathaway.

Hathaway then accused his conservative opponent, Robert Monks, of being the source of the damning background data on him, a charge that was initially denied by a member of Monks' staff. However, Monks later acknowledged that he had hired a new breed of aggressive political consultant to conduct opposition research on Hathaway. The *Globe* did not say who had tipped the paper, and Robinson would not say unambiguously later, but the paper repeatedly noted, with such phrases as "widely held perception," that many believed Monks had put reporters onto Hathaway's past. The paper also noted that the opposition researcher whom Monks admitted hiring had looked into Hathaway's years in Alabama.

For the balance of the week, Hathaway and Monks traded insults, while Collins stayed out of the fray. Some of the slung mud apparently stuck, for Collins won the primary the following Tuesday and went on to win the general election in November.

This case raises a number of interesting questions for journalists who cover campaign politics. The first and most basic is whether the sex scandal in Alabama was a legitimate news story at all in Maine. The scandal had nothing to do with the concerns facing Maine voters, and it effectively brought to a halt any serious discussion of the real issues. By breaking the story, did the *Globe* raise the legitimate issue of the moral character of a candidate for high office, or was it just a "gotcha," albeit an especially powerful one, because the hypocrisy it exposes involves a candidate who was running as a Christian conservative on a family-values platform having had a long-standing sexual relationship with, not only a child, but his own baby-sitter and the daughter of a friend?

This story is not just about morals, although moral turpitude in a candidate is usually considered a legitimate area of voter concern. This story is also about a crime. One can argue that whether a candidate has an extramarital affair is a private matter and nobody's business beyond the people personally involved, but having sex with a twelve-year-old girl is statutory rape, which is a felony. It is hard to imagine building a case for an informed electorate, the foundation upon which democracy rests, which would exclude voters knowing about felonies in a candidate's past, especially the recent past. Robinson said that if Hathaway had been found to have had an affair with a twenty-five-year-old in Alabama, and all the other facts had been the same, "there would have been no story."

The second question raised is what if the story is not true? After all, no legal action was taken and no charges were filed. Yes, state and local prosecutors—the local district attorney and Alabama's attorney general—both went on the record saying they thought they had a case worth prosecuting, but an opinion is not a prosecution and a prosecution is not a conviction. The old truism about being presumed innocent until proven guilty is not true in the sense that it is often used,[1] but criminal charges were never even brought in this case. One purpose of a criminal trial is to give the state a chance to prove a suspect's guilt; another is to give the defendant a chance to establish innocence. The printing of the story did not put Hathaway in prison, but it may well have kept him out of the U.S. Senate.

Although no charges were ever filed, the *Globe* was convinced that the story was true, and prosecutors, both Democratic and Republican, in Alabama were willing to go on the record and say so. Robinson said, "There was lots of stuff our reporter knew but which we didn't publish," which convinced him and other editors at the *Globe* that the charges were true. "We were absolutely convinced, as were the prosecutors," he said.

The story's newsworthiness aside, the third question is whether its subject matter is simply too unseemly to discuss in a respectable publication. Robinson lamented what he called the "tabloidization of the entire culture. Everybody seems to be fair game." Keep in mind that in 1996, the Internet was just starting to become a significant mass medium, but even then, rumormongering on the Web was prevalent (the influential "Drudge Report" launched about two years earlier). Robinson noted that the *Globe* was "the responsible broadsheet in this town" but that not only newspapers, but "especially television, even the networks, have gone downmarket." Readers, "whether we like it or not, have more and more of an appetite for salacious stories. Societal values have changed about what ought to be put" up for public discussion, he said. And, especially given the increasingly intense competition for readers, Robinson added, "You and your readers are not in this hermetically sealed cocoon anymore." (Online media have aggravated that situation exponentially, adding to the competition untold millions of bloggers, amateur journalists, partisan hacks pretending to be average citizens, and so on.)

This shift is not entirely a degradation of culture and a decline in public taste. If it were, it would be easier to know what to do. The shifts Robinson described also reflect a healthy candor in discussing publicly—and thus condemning publicly—a great deal of hypocrisy and corruption that flourished in the secrecy of earlier times. Many topics that are now openly discussed in the media—calmly or breathlessly, for noble reasons or base—would not have been mentioned in polite company even a few years ago. At one time, tuberculosis was never mentioned as a cause of death in respectable circles, including the obituary pages of most major newspapers. Although this doubtlessly prevented discomfort to those who had been acculturated to find the mention of the disease embarrassing, the policy of not talking about the disease almost certainly contributed to the deaths of many people who could otherwise have been saved. So it was later with cancer and then AIDS, and so it is with a great many topics still. One of the functions of journalism, as Walter Lippmann pointed out more than eighty years ago, is to shine a searchlight on first one issue then another. Such illumination focuses attention on an issue and can generate the public interest to address it. On balance, the evidence seems strong that if the question is one of knowledge and discomfort or embarrassment on one side and ignorance and serious harm to either justice or health on the other, knowledge must win out. There was certainly nothing salacious about the content of the paper's reporting of the accusations against Hathaway in Alabama.

Fourth, there is a question of whether journalists are manipulated by politicians. Although it was never stated unequivocally that the leak came out of the Monks campaign, all the evidence suggests that it did. Even if it did not, it seems certain that the leak came from a political enemy of Hathaway's, someone with an agenda other than high-minded public service. Given that, was the *Globe* merely acting as the tool, witting or not, of a partisan in a political race? The answer lies in the adverb *merely*. Yes, there is almost no doubt that the story was initially leaked to the *Globe* to do Hathaway political harm. And, because he subsequently lost, there is little doubt that the story accomplished its intended purpose. However, no, that is not why the paper ran the story.

As Daniel Boorstin pointed out a generation ago in his foundational book *The Image*, very little news happens spontaneously. Sometimes planes crash and hurricanes blow, but most newsworthy events occur because someone, somewhere, makes them happen, and usually for the purpose of getting those events covered in the media. Effective protest organizers try to do or say something unusual enough, and often outlandish enough, so reporters will cover the event and then explain whatever more serious point the organizers want made. Similarly, the point of a ceremony in the Rose Garden at the White House or in the Great Hall of the People in China is for reporters to come and take notes and then spread the word about whatever policy the government wants promulgated. In this regard, the hard part for a journalist—but a critically important dimension of sound news judgment—lies not in making news decisions based on who wants what covered or ignored, but in making such judgments independently, apart from anyone else's agenda. In the Hathaway story, the responsible journalistic position is to assess the newsworthiness of the information about the events back in Alabama *without regard* to whether it sinks Hathaway's candidacy or revives that of one of his opponents.

Finally, the Hathaway story deals with a special journalistic form of promise keeping, that of keeping a confidential source confidential. From a legal standpoint, it is hard to pin down whether journalists have a legal right to keep the identities of sources confidential, and the rules change not just from nation to nation but from jurisdiction to jurisdiction (and those laws seem to be always in flux). However, even in restrictive legal situations, in which the journalist has little legal right to keep such secrets, the moral obligation of keeping promises has led many journalists to willingly go to jail, pay fines, and suffer personal injury to protect their sources. Even when there is no government pressure to reveal confidential sources, the social and professional pressure on journalists to out their informants can be great.

In the Hathaway case, Robinson faced just such a dilemma. On one hand, his paper had promised anonymity to the tipster who had first revealed the information about Hathaway. On the other, the identity of that tipster became part of the story. Robinson acknowledged that "we have an obligation to a source" not to reveal that source's identity if the promise of anonymity was made. Yet, he said, "We have a larger obligation not to mislead our readers." He would not like to burn a source, he said, but "there are higher moral obligations." Then, he said, "We will not allow a lie to appear in the *Boston Globe*." He said he had "a little bit of a problem" with the first-day story in the *Globe*, when Monks denied being the source of the leak, even though the evidence presented in the *Globe* in that story strongly suggested that Monks had been behind it. Then Monks admitted hiring an opposition research firm, and many Republicans in New England began accusing Monks of the leak. At that point, Robinson said, "we were off the hook."

Robinson kept his promise to his tipster—he did not identify him in the paper, nor would he name him later in telephone interviews—but he made it clear that rather than allow a lie to stand in the *Globe*, he would tell the source to figure out a way to stay anonymous, if possible, without the paper lying to protect the identity. What this case exemplifies perhaps more than anything is that a journalist's imperative to be fair and balanced does not only apply to the people who are in the news, but also to the people working behind the scenes to influence the news and, finally and most important of all, to the people reading the news.

QUESTIONS TO CONSIDER

1. If you had been the editor, how would you have handled the allegations against Hathaway so close to the election? How would you factor in the information that no formal charges had been filed? What about the identity of the girl—what would be the pros and cons of publishing her name?

2. Assume that the prosecutors had been willing to confirm the accusation but had not been willing to have their names used. In what way would that affect the credibility of the information in your mind? In the minds of your coworkers? Your readers? What if the prosecutors said they did not want their names used but would go public to testify for you if you were sued for libel and the case wound up in court?

3. Robinson said that if the accusations had involved a twenty-five-year-old woman instead of a twelve-year-old girl, he wouldn't have pursued the story. To what extent do you agree or disagree with Robinson, and why? Explain whether you think it matters or not if Hathaway campaigned as a family-values candidate (suggesting, among other things, that he would be opposed to adultery).

4. The evidence suggests, but does not confirm, that the tip about Hathaway's alleged crime came from the campaign of one of his opponents. How would you evaluate the political motivation as you decided whether to identify the tipster? Are there any situations in which you could see yourself breaking a promise of confidentiality? What long-term repercussions do you think breaking such a promise would do to your career?

Fairness and Balance
When a Journalist Balks at Talking about Journalism in Front of the Camera

The vast majority of journalists works in relative obscurity and may never gain much national or international acclaim. For every Sabine Christiansen and Seymore Hersh there are thousands of journalists who are only known locally, if at all. Journalism involves more than just reporters and photographers—there are copy editors, video editors, news directors, multimedia producers, page designers, fact checkers, and many more behind-the-scenes jobs that help package and distribute the news. As such, journalism, like any other profession, has its own star system, and within that system few taglines have more gravitas than "a Pulitzer Prize-winning reporter for *The New York Times*."

In 2007, one of the *Times'* Pulitzer winners was Linda Greenhouse, whose coverage of the U.S. Supreme Court had won many awards and widespread acclaim. Although often scorned by conservative ideologues for expressing her personal opinions on such issues as abortion laws (she opposes efforts to ban abortion), most serious observers can find little of that bias in Greenhouse's coverage of the courts, and few could argue that Greenhouse isn't one of the foremost authorities on the Supreme Court and the many issues the Court considers. As such, Greenhouse is often an invited speaker to various organizations interested in journalism and the courts in America, and it was one such appearance, in 2007, that triggered a minor media scandal with serious and complicated ethical implications related to fairness and balance.

In August of that year, the Association for Education in Journalism and Mass Communication (AEJMC) held its annual convention in Washington, D.C., where Greenhouse is based. The AEJMC has a large and diverse membership that includes not only journalism professors and professionals, but also scholars and professionals from other disciplines—public relations, advertising, political science, sociology, even entertainment studies. Even so, the organization that was founded as an organization for journalism teachers (many of whom are journalists themselves) maintains a strong focus on the journalism profession, and one of the marquee sessions scheduled for its 2007 session was a panel of prominent journalists who cover the U.S. Supreme Court. Greenhouse was one of the panelists.

Also at that convention were camera crews for C-SPAN, a cable and satellite television channel in the United States that provides continuous, unedited coverage of the U.S. Congress and special events related to government issues. A panel of Supreme Court reporters talking to journalism professors is exactly the kind of special event C-SPAN would cover, and so the network made last-minute arrangements with AEJMC to cover the panel, and the panel organizers (a small group of volunteers) sent e-mails to the panelists the day before the event, just to alert them to the coverage.

An AEJMC convention is a complicated and often chaotic affair, with more than a thousand people attending many different concurrent sessions in dozens of different rooms over the course of several days. The room for the Supreme Court panel was crowded, but still only a fraction of the conference attendees were there. What happened in that room was only observed by a relatively small number of people, but one of them was a student journalist who was covering the session for the conference newspaper. According to that student's report, Greenhouse arrived at the crowded Renaissance Hotel meeting room minutes before the session was to start, and when she saw the C-SPAN cameras, she balked, saying she had not received the e-mail the day before and had not prepared for a televised discussion.

In a telephone interview with one of this book's authors, Greenhouse said she was caught off guard when she arrived and saw the cameras, and felt that she had been done a disservice.

"Everybody likes to aggrandize themselves on C-SPAN," Greenhouse said, noting that she has appeared on the network dozens of times, and that the discussions that end up televised tend to be more constrained. "That completely changes the nature of the event," she said. "The reason I thought (the AEJMC panel) would be constrained is because I thought these professors would ask probing questions and would expect candid answers." However, Greenhouse insists that she didn't demand that C-SPAN leave, and would have participated in the discussion either way. "I didn't throw a fit or anything like that," she said. "What I said was that I personally would feel inhibited if C-SPAN were in the room. I would have stayed regardless."

The journalism professors who had organized the panel had to make a quick decision, and deferring to their star panelist and the crowd of scholars who had turned up to listen to Greenhouse and others, the panel organizers asked C-SPAN to leave. Insulted and outraged, the network's camera crew nonetheless packed up its gear and left the session under protest.

What followed generated much more rancorous discussion than anything Greenhouse would say in the panel session. There are few things that will get a group of American journalists enraged than a whiff of censorship and blocked access, and when many AEJMC members had learned that some of its own members had blocked access to C-SPAN, they became annoyed. When they learned that the request to remove C-SPAN may have come from a fellow journalist—and a Pulitzer winner at that—they became openly angry.

Of course, the panel organizers were in a difficult position. The lead organizer, Amy Gajda of the University of Illinois, told the *Columbia Journalism Review*: "We realized that it would leave a very big hole on the panel...and we decided to place a priority on our first constituency, the members at the conference." In a brief, private conversation at the convention, one of the other panel organizers, an expert on the relationship between the U.S. Supreme Court and the news media, explained to one of this book's authors (who was in attendance) that in the moments she and her colleagues had to decide, they gave the issue as much thought as they could, and certainly did consider the irony of journalism professors denying access to journalists. Even the staunchest critics of the decision had to concede that Gajda and her fellow panel organizers made what they thought to be the best ethical choice.

However, in the end, the decision did not sit well with most of the AEJMC membership. At the group's business meeting two days later, a resolution was introduced and unanimously adopted to make all sessions at AEJMC conventions open to the news media and to inform participants in those sessions of that open-door policy. Moreover, the membership asked outgoing AEJMC president Wayne Wanta of the University of Missouri to write a formal apology to C-SPAN, which Wanta gladly did. Even before that formal action, however, it was clear that the top leaders of AEJMC, the lead organizers of the whole conference, and the vast majority of the membership did not support the action to remove C-SPAN, regardless of the good intentions behind it and the difficulty with which the decision was made.

The incident resulted in some coverage in the national media, mostly focusing on the assumption that Greenhouse had demanded C-SPAN leave (again, Greenhouse made it clear she had not). In the interview for this book, Greenhouse expressed annoyance at the characterization that she may have thrown a fit, and that the criticism aimed against her was unfair and largely inaccurate. "The whole thing was just blown out of proportion in the blogosphere," she said. For example, the *Columbia Journalism Review*, which referred to Greenhouse as "the queen bee of Supreme Court reporters," noted that Greenhouse only objected to C-SPAN, and not other journalists in the room, and suggested, "At the very least, the public was denied the chance to listen in on what turned out to be an interesting discussion.

Nevertheless, it is important to consider that behind every split decision is a vast and complicated prologue. In the case of Linda Greenhouse, we have a high-profile reporter for one of the most influential newspapers in the world who is a constant target of criticism and ideological scorn (not to mention sophomoric plays on her name, i.e., "the Greenhouse effect"). She is absolutely correct in that there is a big difference between talking to a small group of journalism professors in an informal setting and having a more formal conversation on national television. Caught off guard by the cameras, Greenhouse's hesitation was amplified by the panel organizers, which rippled outward to the panel organizers, the AEJMC membership, and the broader public sphere. In the following days, Greenhouse explained her position, and it is one that on face value seems perfectly reasonable. And, the response by the panel organizers to accommodate her request also can be articulated in a manner that makes a great deal of sense; as can the outrage expressed by C-SPAN and by so many AEJMC members as word got around about what had transpired. Many people were treated unfairly that day despite good intentions.

The first and most difficult challenge of moral reasoning is to challenge gut reactions when they occur, and to resist rationalizing them after the fact. Given enough time and enough thought, even a hideous crime such as mass murder can be defended in a way that makes some sense. Journalists and journalism professors, as human beings, are as predisposed as anybody to make excuses, defend errors of judgment, and give in to emotions. That is why it is so important for journalists to study and think about the underlying principles of the profession, not so much to analyze what has already occurred, but more importantly, to be prepared for what is to come. The chain reaction that led, ultimately, to bad publicity for Greenhouse and AEJMC (and bad feelings from Greenhouse toward the organization—"I wouldn't lift a finger for them today," she told us) could have been avoided if emotions would have been checked a bit more, and reason given a little more preference.

Noted journalism scholar Dwight Teeter of the University of Tennessee, who introduced the resolution declaring that all AEJMC sessions should be open to the press, expressed his regret that he even had to raise the issue, that among a community of journalists and journalism scholars (including students), openness should be a given, an unspoken assumption. Nevertheless, this case reveals the problem with unspoken assumptions of principle: In the heat of the moment, they remain unspoken, and the assumption is no guarantee. In this case, the unspoken assumption, coupled with actions based on gut reactions, resulted in many different people feeling as if they were treated unfairly, and has strained relationships between professionals who all work in the same large arena of journalism.

QUESTIONS TO CONSIDER

1. Conferences and conventions are common in most professions, and some of those limit or even prohibit media coverage. Ignoring for a moment the irony that the conference in question was one of journalism scholars and professionals, what do you think are the moral arguments for and against allowing the media to cover sessions at professional conferences?

2. Not every member of AEJMC is a journalism professor or even interested in journalism. Many members work in and study cinema, informal personal communication, entertainment television, and other media forms. Others are strictly researchers of human behavior with no direct ties to the journalism profession and its principles. Should nonjournalists who belong to organizations dominated by journalists and journalism scholars be expected to embrace and follow the same ethical norms as their colleagues who work in journalism?

3. This case also raises many questions about the challenges of covering quasi-public events, in which the rights to access such events are unclear and speakers may feel inhibited to speak in front of journalists. What would the drawbacks be to having a blanket policy of open-access at such events? The benefits?

4. This case also shines a light on the ethics of an important part of the journalism profession—the teachers, researchers, and students involved in journalism education. To what extent should journalism professors adhere to the same professional values as the journalists they train and study?

13 ▪ ▪ ▪

Fairness and Balance
The Graffiti Artists: Turn 'Em In, Get the Story, or Both?

Graffiti is one of the oldest and most controversial forms of human expression. Dating back to antiquity and found around the globe, graffiti is often popular in countercultures and reviled by dominant society—as such, there is a perennial debate as to whether graffiti is art or vandalism. Archeologists have found graffiti used to make political statements in the ruins of ancient Rome and to advertise prostitution in the ruins of ancient Greece, and perhaps the most common use of graffiti throughout the ages is for couples to declare their love for one another. In modern times, graffiti is often used to express dissatisfaction with the powers that be or to show disrespect for the status quo—author and artist Tristan Marco suggests, for example, that the thriving graffiti culture in Sao Paolo, Brazil, is a form of expression against the stark social divide there between the wealthy and the poor; the graffiti covering the Berlin Wall was largely to express frustration and outrage at the oppressive politics that divided Germany (and Europe) for more than four decades. To government and civic leaders, however, graffiti is seen as a marker of urban and social decay. Governments the world over have taken varied approaches toward treating graffiti as a form of criminal vandalism, and have experimented with everything from providing spaces where graffiti is allowed and encouraged, to banning the sale and possession of spray paint, the most popular tool of the modern graffiti artist.

New York City in particular has a long-standing and persistent graffiti culture, and along with it a decades-long effort by city officials to combat what is commonly seen as an ugly and irritating plague of urban vandalism. The modern graffiti era in New York became especially publicized in 1970, when "Taki 183" began showing up on street signs, subway cars, bridge supports, and, eventually, almost any flat surface in the city. As it turned out, "Taki" was the nickname for a Greek-American teenager from Brooklyn named Demetrius (his last name is still not publicly known), and "183" was a shortened form of his street address. Taki's particular form of self-expression, called *tagging*, was quickly copied by others around the world who spray-painted their names, nicknames, and sometimes entire street scenes on any and every surface available.

For decades now, the city has been in a running war with the "taggers." New York City spends millions of dollars every year erasing and painting over graffiti and trying to develop new surfaces for the subways and other public spaces to make graffiti less likely to adhere and easier to clean off. The city even created a special police unit devoted just to dealing with graffiti.

In the fall of 1994, a new wave of defacement/announcement swept into the city. Hundreds, and then thousands, of paper fliers appeared all over the city, most bearing a single cryptic word, either *REVS* or *COST*, sometimes both. For months, more and more of the mini-posters showed up, stuck to almost any surface that would hold them. Occasionally, *REVS* and *COST* were also painted onto walls and the sides of buildings. The special police unit had declared whoever was behind the *REVS* and *COST* signs to be their most-wanted target, and police sought whoever was plastering the cryptic graffiti all over the city, but months went by and thousands of the fliers went up without an arrest. New Yorkers went about their business, but even in a city that seems to pride itself on a blasé tolerance of the latest urban nuisance, many eyebrows went up and many faces scrunched up quizzically at this bizarre new message, so obscure that it was impossible even to categorize it as either vandalism or political protest.

In late December of that year, the New York edition of *Newsday* ran a story about the rash of postings and an interview with those responsible: two young men who called themselves Revs and Cost. The *Newsday* reporter recounted meeting the two in a diner near the Queensboro Bridge, which connects Manhattan to Queens across the East River, and discussing their "artistry" and their philosophy. The story did not give their real names.

By the time the story ran, one of the two had been arrested and identified as Adam Cole of Queens. A warrant had been issued for the arrest of the other man, but he had not been caught and was not identified by the police.

Thus, the *New York Newsday* reporter, Julio Laboy, faced an interesting and common journalistic dilemma—whether to help the police catch the criminals or to protect the identity of criminals from the police. In reporting on criminal activity, there is perhaps no more common or difficult conflict of interest, or one that brings to bear more hand wringing over cultural relevance. The conflict, obviously, is between journalists' duty as citizens and journalists' duty as independent observers of government. The cultural relevance arises from the nature of the crime itself—graffiti is more of a nuisance than a serious crime, and far pettier than a crime of conscience. A reporter who interviews a murderer may feel considerably more pressure to cooperate with police; the reporter may feel little obligation at all to help police catch a peaceful dissident working to overthrow a violent and corrupt dictator. However, Laboy was not dealing with a Robin Hood, nor was he dealing with a Jack the Ripper. Instead, he was dealing with a couple of guys engaged in an obtuse form of agitprop.

Laboy had found out the whereabouts of the two wanted criminals and, according to his story, chatted with them in a diner before they were arrested. Was Laboy acting morally and responsibly when he interviewed the two wanted men without tipping off the police as to their whereabouts, or should he have told the police what he knew, which might well have led to the arrest of both men? Instead, the police spent several days trailing the pair and wound up arresting only one of them.

On the one hand, a journalist is a citizen and, like other citizens, has an obligation to uphold the law. In fact, it could well be that because reporters are far more interested and knowledgeable about public affairs than most citizens, and also do more to hold corrupt public officials accountable than others, the journalist-citizen has an even greater duty to the social contract. A journalist's most fundamental political role—the reason for constitutional press freedoms in the first place—is to help democratic self-government work (and privileging that over, say, any libertarian respect for freedom of expression). It seems that a journalist, in the role of citizen, would be obliged to help the police in any way possible. True, the journalist also has an obligation to monitor the role of the police, who, as public employees, report to the sovereign people, but in this case there was no hint of impropriety on the part of the police and no suggestion that the suspects were in any way victims of any miscarriage of justice. The general societal good that journalists take as their most basic raison d'être would seem to suggest that the reporter should tip the police about where to find the graffiti squad's most-wanted characters.

On the other hand, the journalist was able to provide his readers some understanding about who "Revs" and "Cost" were and why those two people wanted to plaster the city with their graffiti nicknames. The two do not appear in the *New York Newsday* story to be particularly insightful or profound, and the story is no great stirring example of urban insight; the two men are quoted as advocating a vague nihilism, a do-your-own-thing sort of anarchy. To the question: "What do all those *REVS* and *COST* signs mean?" the best answer, it turned out, was not very much. Still, the readers learned what there was to know—that the puzzling and widespread campaign fell into the category of graffiti vandalism rather than social protest.

By not notifying the police, the reporter did get an interesting but not very profound story, but the reporter failed in the obligation to help an orderly society function. There is, however, more to the problem of whether to turn in Revs and Cost, which has to do with the independence of the news media and—perhaps even more important—the public perception of that independence. Even in an age when the public is more critical of its press than perhaps ever before, journalists have a special motivation to earn and keep trust with their audiences and the broader community. That motivation for trust is not necessarily a stronger bond than many of the other bonds between the different parts of a society, but it is a powerful and an important one, and it is unique. It is not the same, say, as the relationship between the citizenry and its police force, or between the citizens and the judiciary. For the public to trust news organizations, the public must believe that journalists are bound to nothing but the truth and are not a secret, or not-so-secret, extension of law enforcement.

Under the best of circumstances, it is difficult to keep journalism independent of the police. The criminal justice system provides a large segment of our daily news diet, which is probably as it should be, and the police are far more helpful in providing information about crime than are the criminals. Reporters spend a lot of time with police officers and generally like them, often seeing them as natural allies, as in a sense they are as two different types of public servants.

Yet it is important to maintain journalistic independence, especially as it relates to monitoring the police force itself. In this case, the police had done nothing wrong, but there are many cases in which the police are also the criminals. The temptations of being a police officer are enormous. We give the police guns, sticks, and great latitude in their actions. We ask them to confront all kinds of danger and unpleasantness in our name and for our well-being. They are subject to bribes, intimidation, and a range of pressures, both physical and mental, yet we expect split-second judgment and flawless behavior. We have, and should have, high expectations of the police, and the best way to keep confidence in the police is to know what they are doing. The best way to have a scrupulously honest police department—which is in the best interest of an overwhelming majority of police officers as well as the rest of us—is to monitor police behavior closely. And the way to do that is to make the public know that journalists are independent agents, not an extension of law enforcement. On those rare occasions that someone in a police uniform does abuse the public trust, it is important for the citizenry to have someone to call whom they can trust. That is the subtext of the often-heard journalistic exclamation, "I'm not a cop."

Suppose that the reporter had arranged the meeting with the two vandals and then tipped the police, who then showed up at the diner and made the arrests. Several things would have happened, none of them good for journalism and none of them good for the principle of honesty.

First, the journalist would have been fundamentally dishonest in dealing with the graffiti vandals. Behaving dishonorably to anyone—good guy, bad guy or, like most of us, some combination of the two—is, on the face of it, the wrong thing to do. Other principles, such as saving a life, might sometimes be more important, but good journalists consider themselves obliged to be truthful and honest unless extraordinary circumstances warrant otherwise. The absolute core foundation of what they do is based upon the expectation that what they say and write will be as truthful as they can make it.

Second, at least two people, and probably a great many more before it was all over, would have learned that reporters are not to be trusted. In the case of Revs and Cost, this might or might not seem particularly important, but, as every investigative reporter knows, the journalist's reputation for independent integrity is very important. The chances of people telling journalists of abuses of power in the future are greatly diminished if it is known that reporters sometimes act as extensions of the police. The reporter who is tempted to set up Revs and Cost has to consider the harm that will be done to all reporters at all stations and newspapers.

Third, the police would learn that at least some reporters would lie on their behalf. That would inevitably lessen the deterrent value that comes from having police work—the public's business, after all—conducted under public scrutiny. A police officer who feels less likely to get caught is more likely to yield to the pressures and temptations that arise every day.

In this light, there was a great deal in favor of meeting with Revs and Cost without informing the police, and much less to recommend tipping off the police to their whereabouts. Another, less satisfactory course would have been to ignore the story altogether. That would have avoided the problem of deliberately refusing to help apprehend wanted men, which would be a plus, but it would have not fulfilled the journalistic obligation to tell the public (including the police) about the world around them. There are many different ways to manage an ethical dilemma, but doing nothing is not managing—it's quitting.

QUESTIONS TO CONSIDER

1. Would you agree to interview two criminals without telling the police who and where they are? Why or why not? Would the type of crime involved make any difference in your decision?

2. What would have been the obligation of the *New York Newsday* reporter if, during the interview, he had found out the vandals' plans for more graffiti? What about if he had found out that they were involved in crimes that were even more serious?

3. If a reporter at a crime scene spots physical evidence related to a crime, should that reporter notify the police?

4. Few would defend the morality of a journalist who poses as a police officer to get a story, but there seems to be less social objection to detectives who pose as reporters. Why do you think journalists protest so vehemently when those agencies allow their agents to pose as journalists?

14 ▪ ▪ ▪

Conflicts of Interest
When Your Own Newspaper Is in the News

A journalist's independence and objectivity become exceedingly difficult to maintain when the person in the news is a fellow journalist, and that becomes doubly true when that person is not just a fellow journalist, but a coworker and personal friend. Yet, the public nature of the news business, coupled with the many high-risk assignments some reporters pursue, makes covering your own a common dilemma for journalists. Often, such news involves outright wrongdoing or tragedy—a colleague is arrested for a crime, such as buying illegal drugs or purchasing child pornography, or is the victim of a fatal car accident or, more disturbingly, of murder. When a journalist is kidnapped in Lebanon, beaten in Mexico City, or shot down in cold blood in a California city (as was *Oakland Post* editor Chauncey Bailey in August 2007), the news value is obvious, and that journalists' coworkers must manage their emotions as they do their jobs of reporting on the incident. Less common, and therefore perhaps more difficult to manage, are situations in which a journalist's personal relationships come into conflict with her professional responsibilities, such that one's loyalty to family and friends supercedes loyalties to colleagues and peers.

The *New Castle News*, a small newspaper in western Pennsylvania, faced such a dilemma in summer 2007, when it was embroiled in a perfect storm of ethical quandary, a situation that involved ethical issues regarding journalistic deception, fairness to sources, privacy versus the public's right to know, and many levels of conflict of interest. The problem became news when local police arrived at the newspaper office with a search warrant and seized a reporter's computer. The grounds for the warrant were allegations that reporter Pat Litowitz had recorded telephone conversations with two local public officials without their consent, which could have been a violation of Pennsylvania's wiretapping laws. The story being reported was fairly routine—a basic article about a small public works project (specifically, a police firing range and training ground) that raised the objections of some residents. What made this situation complicated for the newspaper and its reporters is the fact that one of the interviewees was local police chief James B. Morris, whose officers seized the computer, and that Morris learned of the alleged wiretapping from his wife, Debbie Wachter Morris, a reporter at the *New Castle News*.

In an un-bylined article, the newspaper laid out the case in detail and announced the newspaper had filed a lawsuit against the police for, they claim, illegally seizing the computer.[1] In the article, the *News* presented arguments from both the newspaper's publisher and from local law enforcement, and also included comments from Litowitz and from Wachter Morris. In the article, Litowitz said he routinely taped interviews with public officials "to ensure the highest accuracy of my articles," and that he had clearly told both sources that he was a reporter working on a story. Wachter Morris explained in the story that she knew of Pennsylvania's wiretapping laws from her husband, and upon learning of the recordings she raised concerns with her managing editor and also with her husband, the chief of police. "I felt an obligation to both," she said in the article. "I felt (that) if my husband was the victim of an alleged crime, and I was seeing it happen, I felt obligated to bring it to the attention of my employer and my husband as the victim."

Such relationships between reporters and public officials are not unheard of, particularly in smaller towns. Research by one of this book's authors found that some small-newspaper editors in the United States considered the most common type of conflict of interest they dealt with to be situations in which reporters' family members were in the news.[2] Generally, such situations are managed with the conflicted journalists not getting involved in coverage of their family members and full disclosure of the potential conflict of interest. Informally, of course, such relationships can also benefit the newsroom and the general public, because reporters can get tips and inside information about public wrongdoing at the dinner table, or a casual phone call from a second cousin who works in city hall. The reverse also is certainly true, as journalists complain about problems in their workplace with close friends and family as would any other professional, and those complaints can spread around the community to harm the reputation of the newspaper or station.

Nevertheless, journalists are in the truth-telling business, which means that they often feel a professional obligation to make public the dirty laundry of their own workplace. At a basic level, with situations in which a news organization is itself in the news, the moral principle with the most primacy is loyalty, and the ability of the reporters writing about the conflict to keep their emotions in check as they gather and present information to the public.

When those loyalties are unbalanced, the credibility of the news organization suffers at many levels. Within the community, particularly a small town such as New Castle, Pennsylvania, the incident will certainly be known to the public through word-of-mouth and lunch-counter gossip, so not reporting on the incident harms the newspaper's external credibility. Yet, it is not unusual for editors and publishers to be fairly secretive about problems in the newsroom—many journalists have encountered situations in which editors have killed stories or publishers have prohibited publication of information that would put the newspaper or television station in a bad light. Within the newsroom, of course, such situations can be disruptive and demoralizing, and can undermine the trust and camaraderie that is so essential to any professional news organization. And, within the professional community, such situations involve both internal and external credibility, as other journalists manage professional relationships with their colleagues through state press associations, national professional groups, journalism awards banquets, and the like. A journalist who has the misfortune of working at a news outlet during a time of internal scandal may suffer the consequences as she looks for another job, even if she was in no way involved in the situation.

If there is one person upon whom such a dilemma hangs the heaviest, it would be the top official of the company—the newspaper publisher or station manager, the person who is the primary steward of the institution. A newspaper publisher who is more concerned about profits than journalistic integrity might be tempted (and willing) to simply ignore such a situation and let it pass, or to micromanage coverage to ensure it portrays the newspaper only in a positive light. A publisher who takes no action could lose the respect of his employees as easily as a publisher who jumps to conclusions and rushes to punish the employees involved. The publisher, as a member of the local business community, also must maintain the respect of other local business leaders to ensure the newspaper remains successful and influential.

The way the *News* handled coverage of its internal struggle is, perhaps, a textbook example of how it should be done: It published a basic article about the dilemma, one that was well balanced and fair to all of those involved. It not only embraced the ideal of journalistic objectivity, but also minimized the emotional aspects of the story. The newspaper framed the situation as little more than a workplace disagreement that needs to be worked out, rather than as a breech of ethics that needs to result in punishment. It delineated the root cause of the problem—ambiguities in the state's laws regarding the taping of interviews by journalists—from the ancillary issue of Wachter Morris being a reporter at the paper and the wife of the local chief of police. All parties involved are given an opportunity to have their say, and the resulting information reveals the merits on many sides of the complex argument. Rather than allow the situation to be framed in simplistic terms (i.e., a classic antagonism between the press and government, or a clear-cut case of conflict of interest in the newsroom), the newspaper presented an article that laid out the complexity of an issue as if the *News* was just another business in the community and the publisher just another business spokesperson. It affirms that the issue of whether Litowitz broke the law is best reserved for the courts to decide, and the concerns about conflict of interest in the newsroom is best left up for the newspaper staff to wrangle. Finally, it preemptively defangs other businesses in the community that might want to accuse the *News* of covering them more rigorously than it covers itself.

Perhaps ironically, the most ethical solution to a very complicated journalistic dilemma was for the *News* to fall back on the most basic procedures of journalism: Publish what you know about a newsworthy situation, and let members of the public decide who is right or wrong.

QUESTIONS TO CONSIDER

1. If you were in a situation in which your personal life conflicted with your professional life, how would you balance your loyalties? What is your opinion on the way Wachter Morris handled the situation, and would you have handled it differently?

2. If you were the police reporter and one of your coworkers was married to a police officer, how would you manage your professional relationship with that coworker? What if the two of you became friends outside of the newsroom?

3. The publisher of the *News* tried to balance his responsibilities to maintain the journalistic independence of the newspaper, to be a lawful business leader in the community, and to be an effective manager of employees. Based on what you have read about the situation, how well do you think the publisher managed to balance those responsibilities? Would you have done anything differently?

4. If you had a professional disagreement with a coworker that resulted in a public debate, how would you manage your emotions when you interact with that coworker in the newsroom?

5. We all develop biases through our personal relationships—for example, a journalist who is the child of a rabbi may be more sympathetic to anti-Semitism than a journalist who is deacon at a Catholic church, or an editor whose spouse works in construction might be more sympathetic to pro-development policies than an editor whose parents' farm is threatened by suburban sprawl. To what degree do you think Wachter Morris was able to balance her personal biases toward law enforcement against her colleagues' biases toward journalistic freedom?

15 ▪ ▪ ▪

Conflicts of Interest
Primary Authorship: Can You Lie about Your Day Job?

The vast majority of journalists in the world have fairly simple careers, focusing on their primary duties and, at the end of the day, going home to their private lives. They may do good work, but their careers don't define who they are as people. However, for a very small minority of journalists in the most elite positions of the profession—the journalists who are also celebrities—the primary job is not the only job, and many moonlight as authors of journalistic books, guests on late-night talk shows and Sunday-morning analysis programs, with side projects such as newspaper or magazine columns, and the lecture circuit (where they often command sizable honoraria). Many of those side projects do not conflict in any way with the primary job—for example: *Sports Illustrated* senior contributor Frank DeFord has also been a correspondent for HBO's *Real Sports with Bryant Gumble*, a weekly commentator on sports issues for National Public Radio's Morning Edition, and even the author of several critically acclaimed books (including a few works of fiction about the sports industry). The late political commentator Molly Ivins was as famous for her books as for her newspaper columns (even though most of her books were collections of those very same columns), and she was a popular public speaker for her wry wit and famously coarse language. In addition, Sudanese journalist Hassan Ibrahim, although a longtime BBC correspondent from the Middle East, didn't achieve widespread fame until he began working for

Al Jazeera and was featured in the award-winning documentary *Control Room*.

Most of those types of arrangements tend to be above board and out in the open—the journalists have the blessings of their primary employers (who benefit from the added publicity of their star reporters) and are un-ambiguous about authorship. However, in the mid-1990s, one high-profile journalist crossed a line that many of his contemporaries thought went much too far.

For most of the first half of the presidential election year of 1996, the strange world of political Washington—part trivia, part gossip, and part deadly serious politics—was abuzz over a new novel called *Primary Colors*, a thinly disguised *roman à clef* of Bill Clinton's 1992 presidential campaign. The buzz was not just over how much was literally true and how much was literary license, but also over who had written it. For in the book, published by Random House, the author was listed as Anonymous.

The book was a spectacular success, spending twenty weeks on the *New York Times* best-seller list, the United States' most credible list of book sales. For nine weeks it was number one, the best-selling fiction book in the country. It sold more than one million copies and fueled a fascinating game of sleuth played inside the Washington beltway and among political junkies beyond.[1]

The mystery was a publisher's delight, for speculation about the author's identity prompted talk of the book, and when books are hot topics of conversation, people buy them, if only to see what the fuss is about. Plus, the mere presence of a mystery suggested that someone high inside the Clinton administration might have written the book. The political intrigue was as high as it had been since Deep Throat kept Bob Woodward and Carl Bernstein on the trail during the Watergate investigation. The book was so successful that film director Mike Nichols bought the movie rights for more than $1.5 million, according to published reports, and cast major Hollywood stars for the leading roles (John Travolta played the lead role).

Periodically, speculation centered on Joe Klein, then a prominent Washington political columnist for *Newsweek* magazine, as the author.[2] Klein denied it—vehemently, categorically, and unequivocally. He denied it when asked by friends and competitors in the press corps, and he denied it when asked by CBS, where he moonlighted as a political consultant. He denied it in February 1996, when *New York Magazine* reported that a Vassar professor with a computer program that analyzes writing styles had identified Klein as the author. And he denied it when a *Washington Post* staffer asked him if he would stake his journalistic reputation on his denial. Each time, the questioning went elsewhere—toward a mole in the White House or a one-time speechwriter for Mario Cuomo, the former governor of New York.

As it turned out, Klein's denials were lies. He had written the book, a fact that emerged only when the *Post* took off after the story again later that summer, that time hiring a handwriting expert who compared the handwriting on an early draft of the manuscript with several submitted writing samples and concluded, without question, that Klein was the writer.

Random House held a news conference to fess up and say, Oh, by the way, the book will be out in paperback in a couple of months. The initial press run: another 1.5 million copies.

Klein wrote his *Newsweek* column on the matter the next week, repeatedly referring to his "little white lies" and "fibs" and maintaining that he had been "almost relieved" when he had been found out. He wrote that he had figured that nobody would believe his initial denials and that the charade would be quickly over.

However, journalists in Washington and elsewhere were outraged, not amused, at Klein's duplicity. The *Philadelphia Inquirer* said he should be fired along with *Newsweek*'s editor, Maynard Parker, who knew that Klein was the author but kept the secret. Parker even ran several short pieces in the magazine that directed speculation on the identity of Anonymous toward various other people. CBS dropped Klein immediately, and *Newsweek* gave him a few weeks off to let things cool down.

So what? Is this a serious breach of ethics, or is the anger directed at Klein by his friends in the press corps just grousing that he tricked them—even gave them bald-faced lies—even though what he did was essentially harmless? Klein describes the matter as a little joke that got out of hand so quickly that he had seen no graceful way to get out of the deceit he had begun. He said he had been caught between "two ethical systems—book publishing and journalism." He said he regretted having been so categorical in his denials, rather than dodging the questions, but he noted, by way of explanation, "I was on the spot and Von Drehle [from the *Washington Post*] wouldn't let go."

It was, he said, just a novel, a work of fiction, and, therefore, not important, and he complained about the attention his unmasking received. "This is the kind of overzealous, bloodthirsty, witless pursuit, over a very trivial matter, that does far more damage to journalists than anything I've done," he said in a published interview.

Besides, he said, his agent at Random House insisted that he keep his commitment to them to remain anonymous. And no wonder. Although there may be some credence to Klein's argument that he had initially wanted to write anonymously so his book's harsh portraits of the Clintons would not affect his subsequent White House coverage, it is doubtless true that Random House's marketing people realized full well that mystery in Washington translates into news copy, which translates into sales.

Klein has something of a point when he describes the Washington press corps as highly aggressive. The primary focus of journalism is politics, and as Washington is the political capital of the nation, so Washington is the epicenter of political reporting. Journalism's strengths and weaknesses stand out in starkest relief in Washington. The "feeding frenzy," as one popular book of press criticism called it,[3] is at its fiercest in Washington, but so are the political efforts to use journalists for partisan ends. The latter has perhaps not been so well illustrated as the widespread failure of the Washington press corps to challenge the faulty intelligence used by the Bush administration to justify the 2003 invasion of Iraq, and to not heed the few journalists in their midst who were skeptical until years later. The stakes are at their highest in the capital and so are the egos, the salaries, and the perquisites of both journalists and politicians.

Doubtless, some of the reporters who gave Klein a hard time at his confessional news conference were personally angered—and may even have felt betrayed—at having been lied to, especially by a friend and colleague. Nevertheless, there is a good deal more at work here than personal pique. What gets serious journalists in a lather more than almost anything else is hypocrisy.

As a journalist, Klein's primary job is to tell the truth as well as he knows it and to make those he covers do the same. Journalists should not issue a free pass to those who say that the story is not important, as in: "It's only a multimillion-dollar book-and-movie deal." It is important, and terribly so. Although it may not have been a life-or-death issue, there could have been any number of harmful outcomes as the speculation ran wild: a White House staffer falsely accused of being Anonymous would certainly have lost her or his credibility and reputation for loyalty; a respected and well-connected White House reporter under the same scrutiny would have lost the trust of sources as well as coworkers. The book showed keen insight and great familiarity with the 1992 presidential campaign. If it had not been written by a member of the press corps, then it almost had to have been written by a member of the campaign staff. And, given the unflattering portrait painted of Clinton, such a staff member, if discovered, would have had her or his reputation essentially destroyed.

Both Klein and Random House made millions from the book's popularity, which was greatly enhanced by the guessing game and the suspicions that this was an inside job. Reporters who called for sanctions against Klein and his magazine saw his categorical denials as a betrayal of the most sacred trust in journalism: to tell the truth.

For Klein to excuse his dishonesty by saying that the *Washington Post* reporter "wouldn't let go" is dissembling in the extreme. A reporter is supposed to get at the truth and not take evasive answers. Klein is good at his craft and knows the rules. Once the *Post* reporter made it clear that Klein was staking his journalistic reputation on his answer, he could be taken at his word. A reporter, whose core principle should be telling the truth, instead first got rich by evading the truth (when he published anonymously) and then got richer by lying about it, even when others' reputations stood to be seriously harmed by being mistaken as the book's writer. In addition, Klein's editor went along with the ruse, to the point of putting several stories in the magazine that he knew were not true.

Klein was a highly paid and well-connected member of the journalism establishment's inner circle. He was reaching for no literary device. In *Primary Colors*, Klein had no particularly important story to tell (although, on balance, it is an entertaining story). And, the deception he undertook for half a year, lying with indignant vehemence to friend and colleague alike, served no purpose beyond personal enrichment.

Philip E. Meyer, professor of journalism at the University of North Carolina at Chapel Hill, posted a message on the Internet that sums up Klein's case admirably. "'Anonymous' was a clever marketing ploy to make the book seem more authentic, i.e., more of an inside job, than it really was," Meyer wrote. "You have to admire that. But it also means that the lie was much more than a white lie; it was created for the purpose of enriching the liar, and it did so with spectacular effect—at the expense of all those who bought the book thinking they were getting the inside scoop." Meyer's conclusion was, "Anyone who lies to enrich himself at the expense of others should not be in journalism or any other form of public service."

It is perhaps telling, then—and a bit damning of the upper echelon of American journalism—to note the postscript to the Anonymous affair. Later that very same year, Klein left *Newsweek* and began writing a regular column on Washington politics for *The New Yorker*. In 2000, after Clinton left office, Klein wrote a sequel to *Primary Colors* (under his own name that time) called *The Running Mate*, and two years later a work of nonfiction, *The Natural: Bill Clinton's Misunderstood Presidency*. In 2003, Klein was hired to be a Washington columnist for *Time* Magazine, which held the top spot over *Newsweek* in the U.S. news-magazine market. Over the years, he has also contributed to such notable publications as *The New Republic, The New York Times*, and *Rolling Stone*.

Unlike many other journalists who have paid a high price for their deception—from Janet Cooke to Stephen Glass[4]—Klein managed to shed the scandal and quickly move on to even more journalistic success. Perhaps he has redeemed himself (his commentaries have been and continue to be quite good), but there will always be the question: Where would Joe Klein be now if *Primary Colors* had not been so profitable?

QUESTIONS TO CONSIDER

1. Some might argue that *Primary Colors* had nothing to do with Klein as a journalist and that it should have no effect on his reputation as a journalist. Do you think it was related? Why or why not?

2. *Primary Colors* is considered a *roman à clef*, or a work of fiction that is actually a thinly veiled account of real events. If there had been no deception involved about the authorship of the book, what ethical issues would *Primary Colors* have raised for a journalist who covers national politics?

3. Journalists hold politicians to a high standard in their personal lives. Should journalists have to meet those same high standards? Under what circumstances should journalists make public their investments, speaking fees, or any other factors that could be seen as a conflict of interest for them in covering certain stories or beats?

4. If you accept the premise that journalists should be personally honorable to be worthy of public trust, does that mean they should be drummed out of the profession if they cheat on their taxes? Engage in activities that some might consider immoral? Just what kind of standard of behavior do journalists need to meet?

5. Klein wrote a book of fiction and lied about writing it. Janet Cooke and Stephen Glass tried to pass fiction off as nonfiction. Do you see one as more of a transgression than the other? Why or why not?

Privacy vs. the Public's Right to Know
Private Citizens in the Courts: When to Name Names

The democratic ideal is that the administration of justice be conducted in a fully open manner, so that the cases of the accuser and the accused can be stated before the entire public and the performance of court officials held to public scrutiny. However, as stated in the first part of this book, innocent until proven guilty, jury of one's peers, and other principles of the judicial systems are ideals that we are far from achieving. Many times, the mere accusation of a crime, even if based on no evidence and resulting in acquittal, can ruin the defendant's life. In some cases, innocent people are jailed for crimes they did not commit. Consider the work of The Innocence Project at Yeshiva University, which has exonerated more than two hundred convicted felons of sexual assault and murder in the United States over the past fifteen years (from 1992 to this writing). Or consider the British case of Sally Clark, a lawyer convicted in 1999 of killing her two infant sons based on testimony of pediatrician Samuel Roy Meadows; after several different trials in which Meadows' testimony was deemed erroneous, Clark was exonerated and released from prison in 2003; she died in March 2007, at the age of forty-two, her family saying she never fully recovered from her wrongful imprisonment. The judicial systems of the free nations of the world have demonstrable flaws, and the damage done to the wrongfully accused is the most egregious. Even those accused of lesser crimes, such as petty theft, can face far greater penalties from the court of public opinion than from the court of law. And those who stand in judgment—the juries made up of private citizens—can also suffer the consequences of having their names made public.

This chapter explores the issue of balancing privacy against the public's right to know by focusing on two cases that occurred in two different nations (the United States and Great Britain), at two different levels of journalism (a major urban newspaper and a small-town newspaper), and involving two different sides of the legal system (a jury in a highly publicized child-murder case and a cancer-suffering defendant in a petty theft case). Both cases illustrate starkly how the legal right to publish information does not necessarily equate with the moral obligation to do so.

The first case involves a small newspaper in Congleton, a small town south of Manchester in central England, and the theft of about £600 (about U.S. $1,200) by a volunteer at the charity from which the money was stolen in early 2007. According to news reports, the volunteer was suffering from cancer at the time of the theft; the person was arrested and, having no previous convictions, was let off with a warning from police after returning the stolen funds.

Jeremy Condliffe, editor of the *Congleton Chronicle*, was facing a dilemma that is well known to journalists in small towns but would likely be overlooked by journalists in larger markets: Should the news article about the crime include the name of the offender?

Such a question is rarely asked in the metropolitan and international newsrooms of the world. In such newsrooms, the more pressing question would be whether such a relatively small incident was worth an article at all—there certainly is nothing unusual about a volunteer at a charity succumbing to the temptation to take a jar full of donations. Yet, if the decision were made that such an item was worth some coverage, running the name of the accused would be a matter or course—it's in the police report, so it's fair game. More importantly, there are issues of truthfulness and social responsibility. The fact that somebody is accused of a crime should be documented in some form. And if the social responsibility of the press is to foster civic life, then publishing the names of criminals could serve as a deterrent to crime. (In fact, Condliffe noted that leaders of the charity in question insisted that he run the name of the thief to shame the person publicly.)

However, the ethical considerations are weighed differently in a small town, where even a small crime can be big news, and where naming names in a crime story can not only embarrass the accused, but also the accused's family, friends, coworkers, and children. In such cases, the moral imperatives to seek truth and report it are often challenged by the combination of human empathy and the intimate nature of living in a small, tight-knit community. The decision there is not so matter of fact; it will have real consequences on real people who the journalist is very likely to meet personally (if she or he hasn't already), and will likely see in town for years to come. It is easy to ignore the consequences to a single soul in a sea of millions; it is much less so to ignore the consequences to the woman you'll someday bump into at the local grocery store.

It is with that gravity in mind that Condliffe consulted his peers in the International Society of Weekly Newspaper Editors, a small but active organization whose membership is largely made up of editors of small newspapers in rural communities. In an editorial published February 22, 2007, Condliffe stated that the feedback he received from his fellow small-town editors was largely supportive of his inclination to not publish the story at all, with or without the name: "[W]e had to balance the fact that this person had stolen money from a charity, money that belonged to ordinary people, against the fact that the person was of previous good character and that the [prosecutor] had decided not to prosecute. In the end, I decided that we could not assume superiority over the justice system and we would not report the story, apart from discussing it here."

Condliffe described other situations in which his newspaper had dealt with similar dilemmas—including one case in which he had published the name of a teacher accused of sexual misconduct: "We once reported a preliminary court hearing of a well-respected teacher accused of buggery— the father of a friend of mine—which got to Crown Court only for the complainant to admit he'd made it all up. By then it was too late; mud sticks and the poor man had been forced to move house." The editor also acknowledged a case in which he had withheld the name of a person who claimed to be falsely accused of having sex with a prostitute, only to learn later that the person admitted to the crime in court.

Condliffe concluded his editorial with a request for feedback from the community: "So what do readers think? Is naming and shaming a duty of a newspaper? If you're from the charity, what do you think should have happened? Do you work for another charity where the same thing happened? If you're the thief, what do you think? Was it an out-of-character action? You can write in anonymously. Or do you know the thief and know more than we do—has the *Chronicle* let someone off the hook? Most of all: have we made the right decision?"

That same week, across the Atlantic Ocean in the United States, the editor of the largest newspaper in metropolitan Cincinnati, Ohio, the *Enquirer* was facing a very different dilemma related to the identity of people in the judicial system. In an editorial published February 26, 2007, which began with the simple sentence, "I apologize," Tom Callinan explained the circumstances under which his late-night staffers had, a few days earlier, published the names of the nine jurors who had rendered a guilty verdict on a woman accused of a heinous act of child murder.

The woman in question had just been convicted of tying up her three-year-old foster child, abandoning him, and then incinerating the body in a chimney. It was an infamous case throughout Ohio and the rest of the nation, and even before it was resolved had prompted a statewide review of the foster-care system. The trial, of course, was covered heavily by regional and national media. As the hometown newspaper, the *Enquirer* was pressured to be the definitive source for information about the case and its trial. As Callinan has said both in print and in person, the news staff had been caught up in the drama and attention of the case.

Each state in the United States has slightly different rules regarding public records, but in most states, including Ohio, the names of jurors are a matter of public record. As Callinan said in his column, "[T]here's good reason for that. We want a system that allows us to know who is judging us. We want a system that allows us to watch out for age, gender, or racial bias. It is interesting and not irrelevant that a power company lineman, restaurant server, and psychiatric nurse are among those entrusted such an awesome and important responsibility. Certainly, jurors bring those life experiences to the process. But it's not necessary to publish their names."

Callinan noted that it is a different matter when the jurors agree to be interviewed—"It is not unusual for us to quote jurors who are willing to talk with us when a trial ends. Their voices give us insights into their world"—and he also noted that under some circumstances, the right thing to do is to publish the names of jurors. However, in such a high-profile and horrific case, in which the jurors endured hours of gruesome testimony and heart-wrenching deliberation, he said publishing such names could result in harm for the jurors, for the judicial process that relies on citizens willing to serve as jurors, and for the reputation of the newspaper itself.

The decision to publish the jurors' names was made in the heat of the moment on the cusp of a deadline, but Callinan made no excuses. "It was a late-night, deadline decision that simply was wrong," he wrote.

These two cases exemplify very clearly the difference between law and ethics. In both cases, the journalists had every legal right to publish the names because, indeed, the names were a matter of public record, meaning any citizen could access them for any reason. And, in both cases, the dilemma was caused by the much more human dimensions of the issue— just because something *can* be legally done doesn't mean it *should* be done.

They also exemplify the very powerful influence of cultural norms on journalists. In Cincinnati, it was a situation in which a newspaper's staff made a perfectly legal decision, perhaps in an effort to be objective and unemotional reporters, that would not sit well with the general public. In the case of Condliffe and the *Congleton Chronicle*, it was a recognition by an editor that even the guilty have certain rights, even if the public thinks not.

In the end, it is perhaps best to neither celebrate nor castigate the journalists who made these difficult decisions to publish (or not publish) names, nor the responses of the editors either supporting or condemning those actions. When the futures of unique individuals are at stake, it is perhaps best to treat the situation itself as unique.

QUESTIONS TO CONSIDER

1. To what extent, if at all, do you think journalists in small towns must approach ethics from a different perspective than journalists in large cities? What difference should it make that a journalist is much more likely to personally meet the friends and family of somebody accused of a crime?

2. Does the severity of the crime change the ways journalists should consider whether to print the name of the accused? What arguments can be made for always publishing the names of the accused, regardless of how serious or petty the crime is?

3. What are the possible social benefits of publishing the names of jurors? What are the possible negative ramifications?

4. To what degree do you think journalists should defer to the values of their community in deciding whether to publish the names of people accused of crimes? In what circumstances do you think journalists should resist those values?

5. What role should journalists play in the administration of justice in terms of reporting criminal proceedings? At what point do you think journalists are obligated to publish the names of the accused as well as the victims? Under what circumstances do you think the names of neither the accused nor the alleged victims should be published?

17 ▪ ▪ ▪

Privacy vs. the Public's Right to Know
Sex in an Elevator: Legitimate News or Sophomoric Titillation?

College newspapers tend to be a breed of their own in the journalism business—they generally blend elements of serious, mainstream news coverage with quirky alternative press-style attitudes. The personalities of campus newspapers change dramatically over very short periods of time, given the unavoidable change in staff and leadership in a student-run program. However, in the end, most campus newspapers are community newspapers, more often reflecting the attitudes of the local student community than of any hierarchical standards of journalism. For example, student journalists who produce campus newspapers tend to be much less concerned about the repercussions of what they publish, just as college-aged students generally are less concerned about the consequences of their late-night behaviors.

So it was on a Monday morning in November 1993, after a big home football weekend at The Pennsylvania State University, that students reading the student newspaper, the *Daily Collegian*, found this item leading the daily police report:

> A man and a woman were charged with disorderly conduct Saturday night after police found them having sex in an elevator.
>
> The State College Police Department was called to Park Hill Apartments, 478 E. Beaver Ave., because an elevator was stuck between floors.

When the doors were opened, a gust of hot wind was emitted and two people...were found partially dressed having sexual intercourse. The officer reported the couple was practicing safe sex by using a condom.

The ellipsis in the third paragraph represents where the two students' names were printed in the newspaper story. Although the *Collegian* felt comfortable using the students' names, the authors of this book do not, even these many years later.

At the time, Amy Zurzola Quinn was a journalism student who was the midlevel editor at the paper responsible for both running the item and using the names of the two students. Shortly after her graduation, she insisted that she did the right thing by printing the names, although she did not see the incident as particularly important.

"This was not anything major—this was not a big deal," she said at the time. "It was funny. If you are going to have sex in an elevator, then you'd better be prepared to take whatever happens....On a Sunday after a big football weekend, strange things happen. People pick up the *Collegian* on a Monday after a football weekend and go directly to the police log. They know they are going to find stuff like this. We did one where a guy was dressed in a cow suit, standing in the middle of College Avenue making obscene gestures with the udders, things like that. And the reporters know this when they go off to look for things like that because it's interesting stuff."

Today, after full-time stints as a reporter for the *Asbury Park* (N.J.) *Press* and then the *Philadelphia Inquirer*, Quinn is a freelance journalist and publisher of the *Citizen Mom* blog. She noted in an e-mail that her attitude back in the 1990s was representative of her "too-cool collegiate glory," but maintains that she still would have published the names: "In truth, now that I'm older and wiser, I probably would have run the names but I would have thought about it longer and not been so flippant about it."

Part of Quinn's new perspective on the case is based on experience and maturity, but another part is the reaction she gets from today's students when she guest-lectures in journalism classes. "I have lectured college and high school journalists on ethics and always give them that story, about the elevator sex, as a case study, and they almost without fail say they would have published the names."

Audience attitudes can be a powerful influence on journalists trying to make ethical choices. If the community has strong attitudes against certain kinds of information—such as the use of profanity in news stories, or pictures of dead people—journalists can be swayed against publishing such things even if they are highly newsworthy. The reverse is also true: An audience that is generally tolerant of (and even demanding of) embarrassing information about individuals in their midst may give journalists a sense of license to publish such information. When the audience is a college campus that expects to read about "interesting stuff" the Monday after a big party weekend, the student journalists who produce the campus media may have no moral qualms whatsoever to publish the names of foolish people caught in compromising positions.

Whether the elevator-sex incident is newsworthy at all is, of course, a big part of this debate. Just because something is "interesting stuff" doesn't mean it is "important stuff." That distinction has been a real and important one for centuries, and both kinds of "stuff" have been staples of journalism since at least the beginning of mass-market newspapers in the 1830s. The profile—a long, supposedly revealing article about a single person—was essentially invented by James Gordon Bennett in 1835, when his *New York Herald*, then a brassy new paper, ran a profile of a madam whose brothel had been the scene of an especially titillating murder. Today, much of the content of news media is devoted to such things, from pictures of topless women on page two to fluff pieces on the evening news to whole magazines and Web sites devoted to little more than gossip about the personal lives of famous people.

In reporting a case of sex in an apartment-house elevator, the story has little importance. It is an entertaining story—albeit collegiate humor at the expense of the students involved, at least one of whom was deeply embarrassed by the report. Although the possibility of embarrassing a newsmaker does not usually warrant leaving a name out of the paper, the people in this story were not newsmakers in the ordinary sense. There are many more arguments against the news value of the story itself than there are arguments in favor of publication—in retrospect, the dilemma might have best been resolved by simply not publishing the item at all.

The only real crime in this situation was that two people couldn't keep their passion in check long enough to get off the public elevator and into the privacy of an apartment. That intense sexual desire can lead people to make bad choices is the oldest story on Earth; it was hardly news in State College, Pennsylvania. Granted, publishing the story could have, as Quinn pointed out, alerted other hormone-driven students on the campus that having sex in an elevator could result in a police citation—in that regard, the story served a valid informational purpose, especially in the college community. Yet, that is something of a reach. For one thing, if the goal was to alert the community that elevator romance is a petty crime, there was no pressing need to identify the perpetrators by name. However, this police story was published primarily because people like to read them. Although there is nothing inherently wrong with a news outlet publishing items that its readers, listeners, or viewers want (as opposed to things they need), a story without significant news value should be much easier to knock out of the story lineup when other issues against publication arise.

The immediate and long-term embarrassment to the students also is a significant factor weighing against running the story. The students involved certainly had friends, classmates, and teachers in the community, and had friends and family elsewhere. It is worth noting that the young woman involved in the incident withdrew from the university immediately afterward without finishing the academic semester. It is impossible to tease apart fully the embarrassment of being caught in the elevator and the mortification of having the story appear in the paper, but the publicity almost certainly played some part in her decision to drop out of college. Such a trivial little story could have serious, long-lasting, and harmful repercussions on the mental and emotional state of the people involved, as well as on their relationships with others, whether romantic, familial, or professional. Serious news might justify such embarrassment; trivia is less likely to.

The authors of this book have concluded, for example, that even though the students' names have already been published, there is little added value in repeating their names here, certainly not enough to get past the threshold of the potential extra embarrassment to those people and their families. Because the question of reprinting information arises in journalism all the time, it is worth noting that the relative significance of the questions related to publication changes over time. The argument for identifying the two students in a news story in November 1993 in State College, Pennsylvania, is different, and greater, than the reason that could be given for identifying them in a retelling of the story many years later.

These questions take on new importance when factoring in the Internet. As many news media have now been archiving their online content for nearly two decades, an embarrassing news story from 1993 does not disappear when the next day's newspaper arrives. Employers routinely run Web searches for the names of potential hires as an informal background check, and increasingly they are discovering all manner of personal information about their job candidates that is less than flattering, whether they are news reports of crimes or sophomoric postings to Facebook and MySpace. One can never know when a particularly embarrassing incident from the past can resurface years later, causing a whole new wave of repercussions and opening old wounds. The publication of such a story could very much impose a life sentence upon people who had long ago paid for their misdemeanor. Again, it is these kinds of long-term repercussions that so rarely enter into many decisions made by college students, whether it's to have a passionate tryst in a public elevator or to decide whether to publish their names in the next edition of the student newspaper.

QUESTIONS TO CONSIDER

1. Would you have run the item in the police log? Why or why not? If you would have run it, would you have used the names?

2. In making your decision, how much consideration would you give to the embarrassment caused to the students? What if the embarrassment was likely to be significant enough to cause some harm to one or both of the students?

3. Should a newspaper police log carry all items handled by the police? If it usually does, should some items be withheld at times, when circumstances seem to justify it?

4. The decision on whether to use the item was made by a student journalist. (It might have been made by a student in any discipline because journalism training is not necessary to work on a college newspaper—or in any other area of journalism.) Moreover, the decision had serious consequences, at least for one student. Should college student newspapers have some sort of supervision, by faculty or professional journalists, to handle these kinds of questions? What about high school newspapers? Should some kind of training or proficiency—in ethics and libel law, for example—be required for student or professional journalists, given the potential for harm?

5. How much should a news outlet's audience affect its decisions on propriety? Should student-produced media have different standards than the news produced by professionals?

18 ▪ ▪ ▪

Privacy vs. the Public's Right to Know
Suicide: Important News or a Grotesque Invasion of Privacy?

Suicide presents journalists with a number of ethical problems. Northwestern University journalism professor Loren Ghiglione, formerly the editor and publisher of one of the most thoughtful small newspapers in the United States, the *News* of Southbridge, Massachusetts, wrote this column in the *News* about journalists' conflicting responsibilities concerning the coverage of suicide. In it, he raises a number of important questions that remain as true today as when he first wrote the column.

SHOULD SUICIDES BE REPORTED?[1]

The day after Thanksgiving, Bonnie Mataras, a funeral director at the F. A. Sansoucy & Son Funeral Home, telephoned *News* reporter Michele Morse with an obituary about a 24-year-old Sturbridge man.

Morse, who had gone to high school with the man, asked Mataras the cause of death. She replied, "Just say that he died."

"As soon as she said that," Morse recalls, "I knew that it was a suicide." Though a medical examiner ruled a self-inflicted gunshot the cause of death, *The News* reported only that the young man had "died early yesterday morning."

"People always lie about suicide," a newspaper editor instructs the cub reporter in novelist Benjamin Cheever's *The Plagiarist*. "The family lies. The police lie. Even the medical examiner will lie if he has to."

The newspaper, too, lies. Or it unquestioningly reports the lie or dissemblance of the victim's funeral home.

A review of death certificates from area towns for the past 15 years reveals that medical examiners have ruled almost 100 of the region's deaths to be suicide. But, with few exceptions, those self-inflicted deaths have not been described by *The News* as suicides.

News obituaries, based on information provided by funeral homes, often have misled readers. A 65-year-old Southbridge man who shot himself in the head with a .22 caliber rifle, *The News* reported, "died today in his home." A 79-year-old Southbridge man who hanged himself, the newspaper wrote, "died Saturday afternoon in Harrington Memorial Hospital."

In other instances, *The News* has hinted at suicide but has failed to report the medical examiner's ruling. A Charlton man, 26, was "found dead in his car near his home." A 20-year-old Woodstock man "died of carbon monoxide poisoning at his home."

Debate rages over press coverage of suicide. "It should not be reported," says Robert W. Bullard, director of Bullard's Funeral Home. "Word gets around. It doesn't have to be printed for the archive. The family doesn't have to pick up a clipping 10 years from now and read that somebody blew his head off."

"When it's suicide, I refrain" from telling reporters, says Elaine Sansoucy, owner of F. A. Sansoucy & Son Funeral Home. "It's for the survivors—if it is 10 people that don't know about the suicide, that's 10 less people they have to deal with."

But Stanton C. Kessler, acting chief medical examiner for the Commonwealth of Massachusetts, believes accurate disclosure—not grisly, gory reporting—"is really important. I would report fully. The more the news gets out, the better things are. How can you not report suicides?"

What should a small-town newspaper—any newspaper—do about reporting suicides? The local standard has changed over the last century. In 1888, when the weekly *Southbridge Journal* deemed Sylvanus Davis' purchase of two cows newsworthy, a suicide guaranteed front-page coverage.

The *Journal* detailed the suicide of a Charlton farmer who stood on an old chair and hanged himself in his barn. "When found the chair was turned over and his palmleaf hat, with a red bandanna handkerchief in it, was lying near the chair," noted the *Journal*.

Suicide began to be reported more discreetly at the beginning of the 20th century. The humiliation felt by surviving family members, the false belief that suicide runs in the family, the religious attitude of condemnation—all worked to encourage understatement, if not nonstatement.

George Grant, owner of the weekly *Southbridge Press* between 1891 and 1938, never reported suicide. "He ignored it because he was an old-fashioned type who didn't believe in a certain kind of news," recalled Andrew Tully, who got his start in journalism as a $7-a-week *Journal* sportswriter and proofreader. "Of course, everybody loved him."

The News, founded in 1923 and published by Virgil McNitt and Frank McNitt between 1931 and 1969, downplayed suicide. A suicide at home was "left up to the readers," Tully said. In 1957, a 64-year-old optical worker hanged himself. *The News* merely noted that he "died at his home yesterday morning."

A prominent person's suicide in a public place might result in a tiny article, recalled George A. Anderson, *News* managing editor during 1945–50 and 1964–69. In 1953, an automobile dealer, missing for six days, was found dead in his car on a cart path off Eastford Road.

The News kept the word suicide out of both the headline and the lead of the two-paragraph news brief. However, the second paragraph listed the medical examiner's finding and concluded, "A hose had been run from the exhaust pipe of the car into a rear window."

The News in 1976, by then under ownership of this editor, announced a policy change in reporting suicide: The newspaper would describe the medical examiner's finding—for example, "suicide by carbon monoxide asphyxiation"—even if its reporters could not learn that finding until after publication of the victim's obituary.

To remain silent, *The News* editorialized, threatens the newspaper's credibility and "risks making suicide into an invisible death." Suicide patterns that deserve public scrutiny, the newspaper warned, would otherwise go undetected and undiscussed.

The new policy failed on four fronts.

First, more than three-fourths of suicides still went unreported. Of deaths termed self-inflicted by medical examiners in the next four years, 1977–1980, *The News* reported only four as suicides. Medical examiners and funeral directors often had kept the cause of death from *The News*.

Second, the ethics of the newspaper, which spoke of its duty to try to tell the truth, ran into the ethics of readers. Some attacked the new policy as, in the words of Sally Kalis, a 1980 letter-to-the-editor writer, "tasteless and totally lacking compassion." Others criticized it as an invasion of privacy that threatened a victim's right to a Christian burial.

The harder *The News* tried to track the cause of death, the louder readers protested. In 1982, *The News* reported that a 17-year-old student had died "in Worcester City Hospital." The funeral director and medical examiner refused to tell *The News* the cause of death. *The News* spent two weeks locating the death certificate, which confirmed suicide.

Without mentioning the student's name, *The News* editorialized about the need to provide the facts that would encourage readers' understanding of adolescent suicide locally. "A newspaper shouldn't seek to sensationalize suicide," *The News* said, "but it should at least report the truth."

A letter signed by three residents of the victim's hometown sided with the medical examiner and funeral director: "They realize the family involved has to live with hurt every day of their lives. After weeks have gone by, you just had to let your readers know the truth about [the young woman's] unpleasant death. For what purpose?"

Third, *The News* began to worry about the impact of reporting suicide on those who might themselves be considering suicide. Dr. Richard L. Fowler, the medical examiner for the region, said, "I personally would prefer that suicides wouldn't be reported. When a prominent person commits suicide, usually two or three others follow. Apparently it stirs people thinking of something of that sort."

The notion of an account of one suicide causing—through suggestion or imitation—another suicide dates from at least 1774. Johann Wolfgang von Goethe, inspired by a diplomat's suicide, wrote a novel, *The Sorrows of Young Werther*. Goethe declined to discourage reports, since refuted, that his novel's publication led to a wave of suicides. In studies between 1974 and 1979, sociologist David P. Phillips found what he called the Werther effect: Newspapers' suicide stories were followed by statistically relevant "excess suicides."

Fourth, the manner in which an understaffed newsroom tried to carry out *News* policy encouraged the newspaper, like most media, to focus its feature reporting on certain suicide patterns while ignoring others.

If a young person's cause of death was not made available, the *News* staff, logically, pushed for the cause. But the death of a 70-year-old failed to attract as much staff attention. Aware of teenagers killing themselves, *The News* devoted lengthy articles to local teenage suicides and the response of the health establishment.

Suicides of older people, however, went unreported. A review of local death certificates suggests *The News* missed an important story. Of the region's 21 suicide victims between 1976 and 1980, for example, none was a teenager. But 11—more than 52 percent—were men between the ages of 60 and 79.

Since 1985, *The News* has returned to reporting the cause of death as provided by the person's family or funeral home. In effect, suicides have gone unreported for the past seven years: Of 11 Southbridge deaths that medical examiners have ruled self-inflicted, not one has been reported by *The News* as a suicide.

Reporting policies by New England's major metropolitan newspapers provide no simple answer to what the policy of *The News* should have been or should be. Newspapers everywhere find it virtually impossible to report suicides evenhandedly. Some families, doctors, and undertakers go beyond hiding the truth.

Daniel Warner, editor of the *Lawrence Eagle-Tribune*, caught a police captain—aided by a coroner—falsifying the death certificate of his father-in-law, a suicide victim. Edward Patenaude, veteran Webster reporter for the *Worcester Telegram & Gazette*, remembers a millworker's obituary submitted by undertaker Bernard Shaw. "Shaw said the man 'died after a short illness.' He had hanged himself."

But reporting of suicide by *The News* and other media suggests a "do" and "don't" list:

1. Don't report suicide as entertainment, glamorizing or glorifying suicide as the ultimate flight from life, the great getaway for eternity.

   If Shakespeare had his Romeo and Juliet, newspapers and magazines have their leaping suicides. The *Worcester Telegram & Gazette* publishes a large photo atop page one of a man in Toledo, Ohio, swinging from a 200-foot-high bridge girder, threatening to jump. *New York Magazine* features Theodora Sklovar, "a remarkable woman" who sees her solution to life's problems as a leap to her death from a ninth-floor midtown Manhattan apartment.

   A *New York Times* profile of the 900th suicide off the Golden Gate Bridge romanticizes the jump from "the beautiful span that is San Francisco's signature." The article ends with a quote from the sister of the dead man, Ron R. Berst. Berst's leap from the bridge, she says, "has eloquence to it, and maybe that's what he wanted to say."

2. In a society fixated on the young, don't suggest by the frequency and quantity of prominent coverage that suicide almost exclusively befalls people—especially bright people—in their teens and twenties.

   Suicide "epidemics" and "copycat suicides" among the young are staples of press coverage. Even the staid *New York Times* gives page-one tabloid treatment to adolescent suicides: "4 Jersey Teen-Agers Kill Themselves in Death Pact."

Reporters, who often are young and who often see themselves as brilliant, write there-but-for-the-grace-of-God-go-I profiles of young, brilliant suicide victims: Frank Aller, Bill Clinton's "brilliant" roommate at Oxford; Emily Ann Fisher, "a brilliant" Harvard Phi Beta Kappa; James Dallas Egbert III, a "brilliant" computer student who entered Michigan State University at age 16; Paul Leahy, one of the "most brilliant students" at Conestoga High, Berwyn, Pennsylvania, and Eddie Seidel Jr., "a sometimes brilliant boy" from St. Paul who jumped 200 feet to his death.

3. In reporting the news of suicide, don't appear to sell the so-called rational suicide or assisted suicide as ultimate civil rights appropriate for all.

Headlines like the *New York Times'* "In Matters of Life and Death, The Dying Take Control" may suggest suicide is a simple, rational act. Media attention focuses on Derek Humphrey's best-selling suicide manual, *Final Exit*, on Dr. Jack Kevorkian, the Michigan doctor who has helped eight people commit suicide, and on initiatives in California and Washington state that would have authorized doctors to assist in suicides.

But most suicides, say psychiatrists, are far from rational. They are desperate, often irrational acts of depressed, despairing people. The hopelessness that leads to those suicides often can be reversed through medication, hospitalization, therapy, and support. But, in a statistic that the press should take to heart, two of three Americans with serious depression will not seek help. They do not see treatment, which receives little coverage, as a choice.

4. Do demand that vital sources of information about suicides—autopsies and the state's annual cause-of-death survey—are continued and be sure to study them.

Budget cuts and staff reductions statewide threaten the compilation and publication of death data. Dr. Kullikki K. Steen, the area's primary medical examiner for the past eight years, warns, "for one and a half years [1990–91] we were not autopsying all suicide cases." When asked about annual Massachusetts reports on causes of death, Kessler, the state's acting chief medical examiner, says, "We haven't been doing them."

Of significance locally, perhaps, a federal survey last year showed that suicides among the elderly, which dropped between 1950 and 1980, have risen in recent years. Indeed, the rate of suicide for people ages 75 to 84 is almost double the rate among young people—in 1990, 26.1 suicides per 100,000 versus 13.6 per 100,000 for people ages 15 to 24.

Kessler reinforces the data's message by repeating an acronym he uses when lecturing medical students about suicides—MA'S

SALAD. The letters, he says, stand for middle-aged and older people with previous suicide attempts, males who are single, alcohol users and abusers—lonely, alone, and divorced.

5. In reporting suicides, do put the emphasis on the living—on those who might be able to help a suicidal person, or on the bereaved who are trying to cope with their loss.

Two articles earlier this year by Jane E. Brody of the *New York Times*—"Suicide Myths Cloud Efforts to Save Children" and "Recognizing and Rescuing Suicidal Youths"—deftly described signs of depression, suicidal triggers, and overlooked hints to recognize the seriously suicidal. Such reporting is all too rare.

The media need to make the public aware of sources of help....

6. Do acknowledge the possibility that reports of suicide—possibly even this column—may encourage people at risk to question their shaky hold on life.

Caution should push newspapers to question photos, extensive page-one coverage, headlines that use the word suicide, detailed accounts that suggest suicide is easy, and intimate, romanticized reconstructions that invite readers to identify with heroic victims eulogized by their communities.

However hard-nosed the self-image that journalists wish to perpetuate, they need to recognize the emotion—the anger, even terror—that surrounds suicide. It symbolizes society's failure. Parents, ministers, counselors, and other safety nets have not worked. That "frightens the horses in the street," as Virginia Woolf wrote before killing herself.

Painful for survivors, suicide nevertheless remains newsworthy. It should not be allowed to disappear, slipping silently back into the community's closet. But it may be most usefully as well as most sensitively reported not in a details-and-drama profile about a victim. And not in a medical examiner's one-sentence finding or in an obituary code phrase like "died suddenly."

It may be best reported in an annual review of the region's suicides that, without identifying victims by name, draws attention to patterns and issues that should concern us.

So this scribbler will add one item to his list of New Year's resolutions: To report at the end of each year on those in the area who killed themselves. Perhaps those who died can provide a lesson or two for those who live.

More than fifteen years have passed since Ghiglione wrote this column, and as this book is being written, he has just finished writing a biography of CBS correspondent Don Hollenbeck, who killed himself.

Ghiglione says he has a deeper understanding today of what leads to death by suicide. In his essay, he wrote about "the false belief that suicide 'runs in the family.'" However, Hollenbeck's death by suicide, which followed his mother's death by suicide decades earlier, led Ghiglione to take a harder look at family histories. In his biography of Hollenbeck, he wrote: "Increasingly, experts associate suicide with the convergence of as many as seventy-five behavioral factors—from aggression to impulsivity—and such genetic factors as brain-related abnormalities and the impact on serotonin, a neurotransmitter that affects mood. Hollenbeck said that he, like his mother, considered suicide when hit by 'a good haymaker to the emotional midriff.'" So now Ghiglione feels death by suicide can, indeed, "run in the family."

In considering how to cover suicides, if at all, Ghiglione raises a point that is easy to overlook from the classroom, but that every successful professional knows well: You must, absolutely must, know your readers or viewers. What is acceptable as good journalism in New York or London may not be considered good journalism in small towns just sixty miles away. The responsible journalist for example, might give more weight to the potential for a family's embarrassment in a small town than in a metropolis. Some details of a story might lend themselves to a written description but be too gory for television footage.

The strongest reason for covering suicides is the newspaper's obligation to cover the community it serves—in this case, to inform the sovereign citizens of that part of the Commonwealth of Massachusetts of events and patterns of events going on around them so that they may be able to make informed decisions about how to govern their own lives. It is important to note that this coverage is, in Ghiglione's mind and in the mind of most thoughtful journalists, not a mere right, but a positive obligation. That was Ghiglione's point when he announced in 1976 that the *News* would henceforth cover suicides.

However, as time went on, he discovered that his policy was difficult to carry out. The first problem he encountered was that despite his and his staff's best efforts, he could not find out about most area suicides to report them. Funeral home directors and others in the community would not tell the newspaper about suicides. True, the cause of death is a public record, which means that the cause of death can eventually be reported, but certainly not in a timely enough fashion to include in a news story about the death. That raises a fundamental question of fairness. A policy, however high-minded, is seriously flawed and unfair if it is uneven in its application.

The unevenness of the coverage was Ghiglione's first problem. It was also the fourth in his list, although as he describes this further flaw in his policy, it stemmed from an inevitable unevenness resulting from making editorial decisions about marshalling scarce resources to cover the news.

That meant that some suicides, young people's in his example, were covered, whereas an important element of the story, suicides among the elderly, were not being covered.

Ghiglione's ethical "duty to tell the truth" clashed with the ethical sense of the readers who wanted the newspaper to respect the privacy and taste of the families and friends of suicide victims. Readers are not required to buy and read a newspaper. Ghiglione could not fulfill his primary obligation of conveying information to his readers if he chased them all away from his paper with repeated violations of their sense of probity and good taste.

The other thing Ghiglione mentions as a reason for not covering suicides is the fear of generating copycat behavior, prompting disturbed people to follow suit. That could certainly amount to doing harm needlessly.

Many newspaper publishers would have given up at that point, and part of what set Ghiglione apart is that he did not. In his judgment, the obligation to cover his community is a powerful one that is worth finding a way to accommodate. The solution he found is not perfect—by definition, a compromise never is. Ghiglione no longer covers a suicide as breaking news, which robs it of timeliness, a significant dimension of news by anyone's definition. Yet he has found a way to cover the issue still, which is a clear plus. His new policy, of covering suicides as part of a year-end wrap-up, is farther from the journalistic ideal of full disclosure than the old one, but that old policy did not work. Hence Ghiglione's attempt to fulfill his responsibilities as a journalist while respecting the feelings of the community he served. One can ask no more of a journalist.

QUESTIONS TO CONSIDER

1. Why would we want to report suicide as the cause of death anyway? What is the point?

2. Was Ghiglione's policy on suicides the best you can envision for small newspapers or broadcast outlets? Why or why not? Does your assessment of the policy change when you consider it for metropolitan or national news outlets? Why or why not?

3. If the policy in your newsroom was to report suicides and there was a string of suicides by teenagers in your coverage area, would you change that policy? Why or why not? What if it was your policy *not* to report suicides and there was a string of suicides by teenagers in your area?

4. How should the issue of assisted suicide be reported? Is it possible to report on this issue without encouraging more assisted suicides? Do we have an obligation to make this information available so more people can avail themselves of suicide assistance?

5. What did Ghiglione mean by this statement: "Do acknowledge the possibility that reports of suicide—possibly even this column—may encourage people at risk to question their shaky hold on life"? What good does it do to acknowledge that?

Sensitivity vs. Responsibility to Inform
Offensive Cartoons: Inciting Anger or Inspiring Serious Debate?

The opinion section is one of the oldest fixtures of the news media, and the tradition of using the media as a forum for opinion, analysis, and commentary goes back to the Enlightenment period at the earliest. Today, those sections are fairly uniform across the media—each will feature one or more editorials expressing the opinions of the editors of the publication, some pieces by staff or syndicated columnists, a handful of letters to the editor, and an editorial cartoon or two. Although the word cartoon tends to be used to describe illustrations meant to amuse, editorial cartoons do the additional work of making a statement about a serious issue. It is the mixture of humor and biting commentary that often makes editorial cartoons the most controversial items on an opinion page, because they usually include unflattering caricatures of powerful and influential people, depicted in demeaning and insulting situations.

The power of editorial cartoons is not to be underestimated—in late eighteenth-century New York City, the *Harper's Weekly* caricaturist Thomas Nast launched a crusade against the corrupt city politician William "Boss" Tweed, and Nast's cartoons of Tweed are largely credited with Tweed's eventual arrest and prosecution. Nearly a century and a quarter later, a series of cartoons depicting the prophet Mohammad were published in the Danish newspaper *Jyllands-Posten*, eventually circulating throughout the Muslim world and resulting in large and sometimes

What Would Mohammed Drive?

The late political cartoonist Doug Marlette drew this cartoon in December 2002, to satirize religious zealotry, but the cartoon drew considerable condemnation (and several threats of violence) from Muslims who were offended by the cartoon. Marlette had previously drawn cartoons that speared other religions that are used by zealots to justify violence—including many cartoons ridiculing radical Christians and anti-Palestinian Jews (a gallery of such cartoons can be seen online at www.dougmarlette.com). Cartoon used by permission, courtesy of Melinda Marlette.

violent protests, including attacks on European embassies and properties in Syria and Gaza City.

Several years before the infamous Danish Mohammad cartoons incident, another depiction of Muhammad in a cartoon caused a big controversy for a relatively small American newspaper, the *Tallahassee Democrat* in the state capital of Florida. It was late December 2002, just over a year after the September 11 terrorist attacks, when tensions between Muslims and non-Muslims were still raw in the United States. At the time, the late Pulitzer Prize-winning cartoonist Doug Marlette was the staff cartoonist for the *Democrat*, and he was known for his hard-hitting depictions of cultural and political absurdity. The cartoon in question depicted a Ryder moving van with a nuclear missile in the back and a man wearing an Arabic headdress in the driver's seat, and above it the question, "What Would Mohammad Drive?" There are some important cultural contexts that gave the cartoon its power: the post-9/11 fear of Muslim extremism, hypersensitivity to negative portrayals of Muslims by mainstream Islamic groups; the depiction of the Ryder truck (a reference to the 1995 bombing of the Murrah Federal Building in Oklahoma City, in which American Timothy

McVeigh filled a Ryder truck with homemade explosives and attacked the building as a protest against the U.S. government); and the punch line, which was a rip on the catch phrase of environmentally conscious Evangelical Christians, "What Would Jesus Drive?" (suggesting gas-guzzling vehicles were antithetical to Christian teachings).

Marlette didn't work in the Tallahassee newsroom, but rather from his home in North Carolina, and his cartoons were automatically posted to the newspaper's Web site for consideration to be published in the print edition. In this case, the cartoon was never printed in the newspaper, and then-editor John Winn Miller said he would have never allowed the cartoon to be published by his newspaper. The cartoon was only on the Web site for a short period of time before Miller saw it and ordered it to be removed, knowing how offensive it would be to Muslims in his community.

As it turned out, the cartoon didn't have to be online for very long to create a firestorm of protest from mainstream Muslim groups, particularly the Council of Islamic-American Relations, which demanded an apology for the cartoon. Marlette and the *Democrat* received thousands of angry e-mails, including death threats, calls to violence, and e-mail traffic so heavy that the newspaper's servers crashed. Editorial page editor Mary Ann Lindley recalled, "John Winn Miller and Doug and I were all bombarded with e-mails — I got more than 10,000 to my e-mail address alone, and it truly bogged the entire newspaper e-mail system to a near stopping point. It was a nightmare." Other staffers at the *Democrat* received hostile e-mails stemming from the cartoon; one senior reporter was suspended without pay for one week after responding to one of those e-mails with his own vitriolic response. In a November 2003 essay for the *Columbia Journalism Review* (CJR), Marlette quoted some of the e-mails he received, including one that read, "I will cut your fingers and put them in your mother's ass," and another that read, "What you did, Mr. Dog, will cost you your life. Soon you will join the dogs...hahaha in hell." There were many complaints asking the newspaper to apologize for allowing the cartoon to be posted on its Web site.

Marlette was unapologetic for the cartoon, and was actually unhappy that it hadn't been published by the newspaper. He wrote a response for the *Democrat* titled, "With All Due Respect, an Apology is Not in Order," in which he defended the cartoon, the merits of publishing it, and the important issues behind the imagery. As he explained in his CJR essay a year later:

"I reminded readers that my 'What Would Mohammad Drive?' drawing was an assault not upon Islam but on the distortion of the Muslim religion by murderous fanatics—the followers of Mohammad who flew those planes into our buildings, to be sure, but also the Taliban killers of noncompliant women and destroyers of great art, the true believers who decapitated an American reporter, the young Palestinian suicide bombers

taking out patrons of pizza parlors in the name of the Prophet Mohammad. . . .

"Free speech is the linchpin of our republic. All other freedoms flow
from it. After all, we don't need a First Amendment to allow us to run boring, inoffensive cartoons. We need constitutional protection for our right
to express unpopular views. If we can't discuss the great issues of the day
on the pages of our newspapers fearlessly, and without apology, where
can we discuss them? In the streets with guns? In cafes with strapped-on
bombs?"

In a December 24, 2002, column in the paper, Miller explained that he,
too, was offended by the cartoon, but also felt no need to apologize. "I
frankly am uneasy about making fun of religious icons in the *Democrat*,"
Miller wrote. "There were some cartoons that we did not run because we
thought they crossed the line of good taste. Different editors draw that line
in different places. . . . However, I defend Doug's right to ridicule anyone.
This is an honored American tradition. Granted, good comedy like his
often depends on exaggerations. But he does have some fair basis for satire
in this case. . . . While the vast majority of Muslims are a peaceful people
and preach a peaceful religion, there are some who have subverted the
message of the prophet Mohammad for their own violent purposes."

What both Marlette and Miller were arguing is an old and time-tested
argument about why editorial cartoons are more about journalism than
they are about making people laugh. In his 1949 textbook *Editorial
Cartooning*, Dick Spencer III of Iowa State University wrote, "An editorial
cartoon is, first of all, an editorial. . . . The leaders in the field are news
analysts. They are trained to study an event, or series of events, and give
the reader a clear, tailor-made, easily assimilable interpretation." The
purpose of an editorial cartoon is not about making people laugh, but
rather about making them think.

By extension, the purpose of an editorial cartoon is also to get people to
react, generally in the form of debating the opinions expressed in the cartoon via letters to the publication. Although much of the e-mail received
by Marlette and the *Democrat* was hostile and poorly written, the *Democrat*'s editorial page editor Mary Ann Lindley did find a few letters to publish that expanded the debate over the very points Marlette was trying to
make, and offered more reasoned argument for and against the publication of the cartoon and, more importantly, the message of the opinion.

One of the most pressing modern problems facing editorial cartoonists
is the sensitivity of their editors toward not offending readers. Cartoonists
often lament the pressures they are put under to tone down their commentaries. Marlette put it this way in his *CJR* essay: "Ignorance and bigotry
[are] reinventing themselves . . . by dressing up as 'sensitivity' and mas-
querading as a public virtue that may be as destructive to our rights as
religious zealotry." It is important to recognize that while sensitivity to

the feelings and concerns of the community are important, it is sometimes necessary to raise issues and air views that some will not like. There are times when offending people can serve a greater and more noble purpose.

By many measures, non-Muslim Americans were known to be largely ignorant of the Islamic faith and the practices of its followers prior to September 11, 2001; after those attacks, and revelations that many innocent, peaceful Muslim citizens had been attacked and harassed by bigots seeking revenge, a national dialogue started about one of the world's most important and influential religious faiths, and how that faith fits into the various cultures of the world. The angry responses to Marlette's cartoon revealed that there are many Muslims who do believe violence—or at least the threat of violence—is justified by their religious views. Yet responses to the responses revealed a greater and more important truth—that Muslims on the whole value peace and tolerance, and are fully capable of confronting an offensive opinion in the media with civility and reason, and getting beyond death threats and name-calling to engage the serious issues of the day—even when the prompt for that discussion is a cartoon.

QUESTIONS TO CONSIDER

1. What topics, if any, do you think should be off limits to editorial cartoonists? If you think there are topics that should be off limits, why?

2. One of the many complaints against the "What Would Mohammad Drive?" cartoon was the stereotypical depiction of the driver of the van in Arab attire. Cartoonists often use stereotypes to depict certain types of people—should they? What other options are available to cartoonists to effectively illustrate a particular culture?

3. If you were the editor in this situation, would you have published the cartoon in the newspaper? Why or why not? To what degree would you balance your sensitivity toward your audience (i.e., not wanting to offend people) against your professional obligation to inform people and to spark debate on serious issues?

4. What differences, if any, are there between publishing an offensive cartoon on the Internet versus publishing it in the print edition of a newspaper or magazine? In what ways (if any) does the medium change the ethical considerations? Why or why not?

20 ▪ ▪ ▪

Sensitivity vs. Responsibility to Inform
When Journalists Put Themselves in Harm's Way

Within the relatively small world of professional journalism, those afforded the status of heroes tend to be the journalists who openly defy death and danger to keep the public informed of government corruption, organized crime, and the horrors of war. For such journalists, their duty to keep the public informed is often given primacy over their own personal safety and well-being. Such luminaries include Ernie Pyle, the American journalist who traveled with the troops during World War II; Kate Webb, the late Australian war correspondent for United Press International who was captured by North Vietnamese troops in Cambodia in 1971 and presumed dead until her release twenty-four days later; and Anna Politkovskaya, the Russian investigative journalist for the newspaper *Novaya Gazeta*, who was murdered in 2006 in the elevator of her Moscow apartment building (it is believed that the murder was arranged by corrupt police and government officers). In Iraq alone, from March 2003 through August 2007, an estimated 112 journalists had been killed, and so had another 40 support workers, according to the Committee to Protect Journalists; of the journalists, about 90 of those were Iraqi journalists and more than 70 deaths were results not of cross fire, but outright murder.

One of the most dangerous places for journalists in the early twenty-first century has been war-ravaged Somalia and, in particular, its capital city of Mogadishu. A prolonged civil war between religious extremists and

Ethiopian-backed government troops has made the Horn of Africa one of the deadliest civil-war zones in the world, and, in 2007 alone, at least six journalists were killed in that country, making it the second-deadliest nation for journalists that year after Iraq. Through September 2007, the Committee to Protect Journalists listed more than thirty incidents of attacks on journalists in Somalia, including police raids of newsrooms, arrests and detention of journalists covering police and government activities, beatings of journalists by police, and ambushes by armed militia.

One of the journalists who barely survived that milieu was Sahal Abdulle, who, in 2006, left the relative security of his home and family in Toronto to return to his native Somalia. Abdulle was raised in Mogadishu, but his family moved to North America in the 1980s. He returned to Somalia in the 1990s to cover the violence that erupted there in 1991, then returned to Canada and eventually started graduate studies in photojournalism in the United States. After completing his coursework in 2006, Abdulle returned to Mogadishu to work as a reporter for Reuters Africa, and, in 2007, he moved his wife and young son to Kenya so he could visit with them while off duty. As a reporter for Reuters, Abdulle was often on the front lines of the violence, but in his off hours he used his family's Mogadishu home as a refuge for his fellow journalists. Many of the journalists who were detained, threatened, beaten, and killed in Somalia in those months were his friends.

One of those friends was Mahad Ahmed Elmi, a popular talk-show host and commentator for Horn Afrik radio, the independent news organization in Mogadishu known for being equally critical of the Somali government and the Islamist insurgents. On August 11, 2007, Elmi was assassinated as he was entering the radio station—witnesses told Abdulle that four armed men jumped Elmi and shot him in the head several times. Abdulle wrote the story of his friend's murder for Reuters, and quoted another of his close friends, Horn Afrik cofounder Ali Iman Sharmarke.

Hours after filing the news story about Elmi's murder, Abdulle and Sharmarke attended their colleague's funeral. On the drive back from the funeral, a roadside explosive erupted under their vehicle, killing Sharmarke and injuring Abdulle.

Abdulle recalled the attack in a piece for Reuters:

I am in a car full of journalists driving from the funeral of a colleague murdered hours earlier in Mogadishu for doing his job. We don't get far. An explosion throws our vehicle up and fills it with excruciating heat. Black smoke billows about us. I can feel the pressure rushing up inside my clothes, my neck splits open.

Climbing from the smoking wreck, blood spits through the fingers I clamp to my throat.

It was a remotely detonated bomb. Death is often random in Mogadishu, but in this case we were the target.

After the attack, Abdulle returned to Toronto to recover. In published essays, as well as telephone and e-mail conversations with us, he detailed how his physical wounds were healing, but the emotional damage was harder to handle. It wasn't just the murder of Elmi and the fatal attack on Sharmarke's vehicle, but also the endless and grotesque violence ravaging his native land. "I saw countless burned bodies in hollowed-out houses, the corpses of 90-year-olds and infants ripped to pieces," he wrote in the Reuters article. "I watched colleagues die trying to get the Somali story out to a world already jaded by wars in Iraq, Darfur, and Afghanistan.... My colleagues and I in Somalia often talked about why we did the job. Some of us had left lives and families in the West. Mine was in Canada. Ali and I asked each other that question many times. He, too, had a Canadian passport. Ali believed until the end that he was giving Somalis a voice and, like me, kept coming back."

Of course, one of the most difficult ethical dilemmas such journalists must deal with is balancing their close personal connections with sources, translators, and other journalists against their responsibility to tell the truth about what is happening. Abdulle said he was constantly balancing concerns for his own safety, and the safety of those around him, against pursuing dangerous stories.

"One example," Abdulle wrote in an e-mail, "would be the stories of security personnel detaining hundreds of people illegally, and then forcing their families and loved ones to buy them out before they transfer them to the main jail and indict them with highly cooked charges. I researched the story and collected names of who was responsible for those abuses. But at the end, I stayed away from it out of fear. Ethically, I was duty-bound to report this story, but at what cost?"

Those close personal connections with colleagues become especially difficult to manage when the news is about colleagues who are kidnapped, injured, or killed. Abdulle said that writing the article about Mahad Ahmed Elmi's assassination was "one of my hardest stories to cover.... When I was covering it, I treated it as any other news story that I would cover, and for Mahad's and my sake I wanted to know what happened and to report it as objectively as humanly possible. People were accusing this-and-that group for carrying out Mahad's assassination, but at the end I wrote the story without exactly saying any group had carried out this assassination because I didn't have tangible proof that group so-and-so had committed it."

Abdulle had also interviewed his close friend Ali Iman Sharmarke (the two were so close that Abdulle's young son referred to Sharmarke as "uncle") for the story. That interview raised in Abdulle's mind concerns about both conflicts of interest and concerns for his friend's safety. "I did find that to be somewhat of a conflict of interest," Abdulle explained, "but regardless of Mr. Sharmarke being a friend, he was the only named source for this story who I could get because colleagues who were with Mahad that day were not willing to go on record for fear of being the next victims, and I understood them clearly for their hesitation. My counterparts at the AP had interviewed Ali as well. Up to this day, I wonder if Ali was assassinated for what he said in those quotes that we used, or whether we had endangered the man because of using his quotes, which certainly pointed fingers at certain people.

Another difficulty Abdulle and his colleagues faced was trying to balance their understanding of journalism ethics (largely derived from their studies in the relative safety of Western democracies) against their realization that such ideals are not always feasible in a war-torn, impoverished region. "In working in Somalia, you quickly learn that the norms of the job are different here than, say, in North America," he explained. "Working here, you are amazed by the bountiful stories, and how much of them you can cover without stepping on somebody's toes. In this region of the world, people tend to personalize stories more so than in any other region I have experienced. By covering certain stories, such as the forgery of money and related corruption, my colleagues or I will pay a very high price. But at the end of the day, how do you live with yourself for shying away from reporting those stories, which matter both to my countrymen and to the world, because of fear? One way that I dealt with the dilemma was to give the [story idea and leads] to colleagues who are outside of the country, knowing that the stories might see the light of the day without endangering someone's life."

Perhaps the most difficult part of the assignment for Abdulle, on a professional level, was watching as some of his fellow journalists succumbed to the moral corruption they were trying to reveal to the world. "One example that I witnessed was, one day a group of us were taken to another town by [a member] of the ruling party, and on our way back to Mogadishu this high official offered and gave $5 telephone credit cards to everyone in the car, and most of the journalists in the car took it. Even though $5 doesn't seem like that much money in North America, by Somali standards, it is big deal, because with that kind of card one can make about 50 minutes' worth of telephone calls. I found it to be ethically wrong to receive that gift, and it clearly looked to me as a bribe."

"A second example," Abdulle continued, "was one day when we were covering a rally against the TFG-Ethiopians [the Ethiopian-backed Transitional Federal Government]. One Somali radio reporter working for one of the international radio services was conducting an interview, and she started coaching the source on the questions that she would be asking before she rolled her tape."

Although troubled by such behavior among his peers in front of officials, Abdulle was particularly concerned about what he saw as unethical behaviors by journalists who interacted with the innocent victims of the struggles in Somalia. "The local photojournalists were being intrusive in a local hospital," he offered as an example. "They would just run into the emergency room and stick their cameras in the faces of the people who are suffering greatly, without any care whatsoever. They would act like paparazzi chasing celebrities. In the end it gave us all a bad name, and some of us were barred from entering the hospital."

For his part, Abdulle said he chastised the offending photographers, remembering that one of the moral imperatives of professional journalists is to police their own ranks for moral conduct. He told them that someday it might be them on the hospital bed needing care and compassion from the very people they intruded upon. "I earned a lot of goodwill from the hospital staff that day, and was welcome there afterward," he said.

To Abdulle's credit, and the credit of many of his colleagues around the world who risk their lives to keep the public informed, striking a balance between being a brave and tough reporter and a compassionate, thoughtful human being is not all that difficult, even (or perhaps especially) in a milieu as dangerous and seemingly inhumane as the violent streets of Mogadishu.

QUESTIONS TO CONSIDER

1. If you were asked by an editor or news director if you would be willing to cover breaking news in a dangerous locale, would you accept the assignment? Why or why not? What ethical arguments would you make in favor of, or against, your taking the assignment?

2. What ethical dilemmas do you see in journalists who become close personal friends with other journalists working for competing media? At what point do you think personal feelings toward friends would have to be set aside in favor of revealing truths about their questionable tactics and behaviors?

3. Abdulle mentioned that the culture of Somalia is much different from the cultures of North America and Western Europe, where journalists can work in relative safety. To what extent should a journalist in a high-risk environment balance sensitivity toward cultural differences against the basic principles of ethical journalism?

4. Many news agencies only have one reporter assigned to cover dangerous locales, and so when a story breaks and the reporter faces a conflict of interest, assigning the story to somebody else isn't a viable option. In the case in which Abdulle wrote the article about a friend getting assassinated, and quoting another friend in the story, how do you think you would have performed? Would your close personal ties to the people involved inhibit your ability to report the story with fairness and balance? Why or why not?

21 ▪ ▪ ▪

Sensitivity vs. Responsibility to Inform
The Grisly War Photo: Powerful Information, but What about Taste?

This case also is about the long-standing violence in Somalia, but goes back nearly fifteen years before the incident discussed in Chapter 20. On Monday, October 4, 1993, photo editors and news executives all over the country were faced with a grisly dilemma—whether to publish a ghastly photograph that had just moved over the picture wire. A pair of images from Somalia showed a street mob cheering wildly as the body of a dead U.S. soldier, stripped and trussed up with ropes, was dragged through Mogadishu's dusty streets. In one picture, a person swings a stick at the body as it passes; in the other, a member of the crowd kicks at it.

The photos, taken by the *Toronto Star*'s Paul Watson, carried the warning to editors that the body had not been identified and that the dead man's family might not have been notified.

The images prompted ethical debates all over the country, but no consensus emerged. A group of journalists who happened to be attending an ethics seminar at the Poynter Institute in St. Petersburg, Florida, grappled with the question and split every way imaginable. Some said they would have run the picture on the front page, and in color. Others chose black and white, to make the photograph less offensive, but agreed on the front-page placement. Some said they would have run it on an inside page; a few would not have run it at all; some could not decide. Journalists at work that day split in similar ways. A *Minneapolis Star-Tribune* survey of thirty-four major dailies found eleven that had used the picture on the front page. Fifteen used it inside, and eight did not run it at all.

Editors all over the country face this sort of problem almost every day: How graphic is too graphic? At community papers, it comes up when there has been a traffic fatality, and at the big metro dailies, it arises when particularly gruesome images move over the photo wire from Israel, Bosnia, Africa, or any of the world's trouble spots. Is there a clear line between providing useful visual information to readers and viewers even if that information is horrific, and pandering to morbid curiosity, which is forbidden by both decency and the Society of Professional Journalists' Code of Ethics? No. Conscientious people of goodwill can and do disagree over which items should weigh how much in the decision.

Nobody had a tougher call to make than the late Cole C. Campbell, then the editor of the *Virginian-Pilot*, whose readership drew heavily from military families at Fort Eustis and Norfolk Naval Air Station. The photograph was powerful and compelling, an instant symbol of an American humanitarian mission to a starving, war-torn African nation gone horribly wrong. Yet, Campbell said in an interview, war pictures in a military town must be handled with special care. "There is a real strong sense that in a military community, we have a different standard to protect the sensibilities of our readership."

Campbell passed the photo around the editors' story conference, the mid-afternoon meeting held at most newspapers to decide which stories deserve to go on page one, which pictures to use, and so on. (It is a remarkable measure of journalists' continuing concern for ethics that somewhere between eight and two dozen top editors at major papers routinely spend about 10 percent of the workday, often more, deciding the most appropriate use of the precious news hole to best inform their readers, just as television and radio executives meet to allocate their airtime. Some discussions concern practical and logistical matters, of course, but the great bulk of story conferences everywhere is taken up with the *should* dimension of journalism. It is hard to think of another major industry whose chief executives spend so much of their time on ethical issues.)

The editors at the *Virginian-Pilot* split evenly over whether to run the picture or not, so Campbell adjourned the story conference out into the newsroom, where the picture could be called up on a computer screen and adjusted so the editors could see how the photo would look on the page in various layouts, crops, and sizes. "Lots of people gathered around, and we asked each person when they came up what they would do. So we had a whole lot of staff discussion and deliberation on this," Campbell said.

Eventually, it was Campbell's call, and he decided to use the picture, in color, beginning above the fold, with the soldier's body below the fold, accompanied by a story and the headline, "Cheering Mob Drags Body of Soldier through Streets."

Toronto Star correspondent Paul Watson won a Pulitzer Prize for capturing Somalis dragging the body of a slain American soldier through the streets of Mogadishu, Somalia, in the fall of 1993. The graphic nature of this image upset many who saw it, particularly those with connections or sympathies to the U.S. armed forces, but it also showed a brutal reality about one of the most violent and dangerous cities on the planet. Photo used by permission, Toronto Star Newspapers Limited.

With the story's continuation inside the paper, on what is called the jump page, Campbell offered this note to his readers:

Today's *Virginian-Pilot* includes a photograph of jubilant Somalis dragging the body of a U.S. soldier killed in action Monday. The photograph is difficult to look at. It was difficult for us to publish. We decided to do so only after long discussion involving many voices in our newsroom. There was no unanimity. There was no consensus.

It is painful to publish this photograph in a community in which so many people are connected to the military. More than 125 troops from Fort Eustis are in Somalia, although none of them was among those injured Monday. We can see in this fallen soldier members of our own families. We worry that the indignity imposed by the Somalis is compounded by publication of the photograph.

In the end, this photograph portrays an outrage against a U.S. soldier in a powerful, profound way that words alone cannot convey. In an era of instant, worldwide visual communications, images such as this one shape the reaction of policymakers as well as the public. We could not deny people so closely linked to events so far away the fullest understanding of what is happening and what others are seeing and reacting to.

In an interview after the picture ran, Campbell said, "In the final analysis, this was a question of whether this was a picture that was going to change the course of United States policy, one way or the other, either to intensify our involvement or to limit our involvement. And we decided that it was. Did our readership need to see that? And we decided that it did."

Whereas the *Virginian-Pilot*, like many newspapers, generally does not put pictures of dead bodies on the front page, Campbell said, the picture's news value overrode the usual ban. Campbell saw in that photograph a symbol of an age, an image that transcended the particulars of the moment. Comparable images include the picture taken by AP photographer Eddie Adams of South Vietnamese Brigadier General Nguyen Ngoc Loan executing a Vietcong suspect point blank; or the photograph taken by a Kent State University student, John Filo, of Mary Ann Vecchio kneeling in agony over the body of a student shot on that campus during an antiwar rally in 1971.

So far in this analysis, we have seen that the questions concerning the use of this photograph are fairly straightforward, even if there is no consensus on the answers. That is, we recognize the basic elements to be weighed in making such a decision, although there may be disagreements about how much relative weight each element should have.

The picture has great news value, which is the primary reason to publish it. As a straightforward news photograph, it has important elements of newsworthiness: timeliness, impact, conflict, and human interest. (And for papers like Campbell's, which serve large military areas, it also had a kind of proximity that increased its news value, but which, at the same time, raised the question of whether it would hit too close to home. Generally, the farther away a gruesome event occurs, the less objectionable pictures or footage of that event will be perceived to be.) The Somalia picture seemed likely to have a serious impact on American foreign policy. Campbell argued that the importance of the situation increased his obligation to show readers something that was likely to cause the Pentagon and the State Department to rethink their policies.

On the other hand, the picture is grisly and extremely distasteful, which is the primary reason not to run it. Different editors put different weights on those two dimensions. Some opted for running it in black and white rather than in color or for playing it inside instead of on the front page in an effort to make it appear less grisly and less startling, thereby tipping the decision toward publishing. Other editors believed that there was no way to tip the balance, and they wanted to not publish it at all.

However, this is more than just a case of a grisly picture. It involves both a dead body and national humiliation. Some editors make it a policy not to run pictures of corpses at all on the grounds of taste. Others might shy away from this picture on some sort of nationalist grounds. In it, a dead body of a representative of the greatest military power on Earth is being deliberately desecrated by third-world nationals with crude sticks and big grins.

There are other dimensions to the photograph, quite apart from its enormous news value, its grisly image, and, in some eyes, its extremely poor taste. One complex and vexing problem is hinted at in the editor's note from Campbell: "We worry that the indignity imposed by the Somalis is compounded by publication of the photograph." The people in the photograph, like the people in so many events reported on by journalists, did not just happen to behave the way they did spontaneously. Many of the people in the photograph were looking directly at the camera. Much of what they were doing was done at least in part *because* journalists were there to record their actions.

That is a problem for journalists for which there is no fully satisfactory answer. Journalists, especially photographers and television crews, are occasionally accused of staging events. When that happens, there are cries of outrage from the journalistic community and from readers and viewers. That is probably as it should be. Yet, at the most basic level, it is undeniable that people behave differently when they know they are being watched, and more so when they know their actions are being recorded for mass distribution. There is a journalistic version of the Heisenberg uncertainty principle, which maintains that the very act of measuring something changes it. In journalism, it may be said that the very act of reporting on events changes them. It is impossible for a journalist to become invisible and thus not affect events at all. If it were possible to blend into the background, would that not raise equally valid questions about reporters using deceptive tactics to do their work?

If, to any degree at all, those Somalis who dragged the body of the serviceman through the streets of Mogadishu were doing so because of the embarrassment and humiliation it would cause the United States and its allies, is the journalist aiding and abetting that embarrassment by photographing that event? Media manipulation has always been a serious problem for journalists, particularly the modern public relations industry that came of age after World War I, but the problem goes far beyond slick politicians and captains of industry with their high-priced spinmeisters. Nobody in Watson's photograph needed public-relations counsel to advise them on how best to humiliate the United States.

In one sense, the job of journalists is to report on real occurrences, not those orchestrated for their eyes, microphones, and cameras. The problem of the made-for-coverage "pseudo-event" is brilliantly explored by Daniel J. Boorstin, the former Librarian of Congress, in his 1961 book *The Image*.[1] Yet could anyone truly argue that an event is not newsworthy just because it was set up in whole or in part for the convenience of journalists? Examples abound. Take the arrest of a wanted criminal: The arrest is clearly news; does it become *not* news just because the police chief calls a press conference to make the announcement? Or is the picture of the suspect less newsworthy because the suspect has been paraded by the authorities for the benefit of photographers and camera crews in the so-called perp walk? In the case of the Mogadishu picture, one can argue that it is in such bad taste that it should not have been run, but can anyone argue that it was not news?

Everyone from politicians to protesters tries to manipulate reporters all the time, feeding them information that will serve their own interests yet still meet the journalists' standard of newsworthiness. It is tempting to resist being taken in by the manipulators by refusing to photograph or write about anything created or staged for the convenience of reporters. If the event is legitimate news, it needs to be covered. Although it would be irresponsible to swallow whole every line fed to a reporter, it would be just as irresponsible to refuse to report at all on legitimate news that serves some other interest.

The Mogadishu picture raises another question: Who was this soldier, and had his family been notified of his death? Whose son, brother, husband, or boyfriend was he? The dead soldier was not identified, then or later, and many publications have it as one of the most inviolable of newsroom policies to not identify victims until close relatives have been notified. They consider that the news value of the victim's identity is more than offset by the shock and dismay it would cause a reader or viewer to learn first of a family tragedy through as impersonal a medium as a news story. (The rule is far from perfect. Journalists generally agree to wait until a victim's next of kin has been told of the death, but such a standard assumes the universality of a nuclear family, which is not the case. Take a child of divorced parents, for example. Is it appropriate to wait until both parents hear of the child's death through other means before identifying the child in a story, or just until the parent the child was living with has been notified? What about children brought up by other relatives—aunts and uncles, say, or grandparents? What if the child is grown or married? Or has a live-in friend or lover?)

The Pentagon knew which of its soldiers had gone on that mission and who was unaccounted for, so it was able to inform the missing soldiers' next of kin. What the Pentagon could not do for the families was say whose body was being desecrated so grotesquely by the Somalis. The Pentagon called Mary Cleveland of Portsmouth, Virginia, and told her that her stepson, Staff Sergeant William Cleveland, thirty-four, was among the missing, so when she saw the *Virginian-Pilot* the next day, she was spared some of the horror when she thought she recognized the body as that of her stepson. (However, other members of the Cleveland family did not have their shock cushioned by a call from the Pentagon. They saw the picture first.) So the Cleveland family "sat by the phone all day, waiting to hear from the Pentagon," Campbell said. "They didn't hear anything, so the next day they called us and said, 'We think this may be our stepson, but we can't get anything from the Pentagon. Maybe you'll help us.' They actually turned to us for help." Campbell said the paper's military reporters had tried to get identification from the Pentagon, but were not successful.

Campbell stressed that immediately after the picture was published, the Cleveland family saw the paper as a source of information, not as a ghoulish invader of their privacy. "At that stage, there wasn't any anger or hostility on the family's part," Campbell said. However, as days passed and the list of possible soldiers in the picture narrowed—eventually to just five men killed in Somalia—the Cleveland family was besieged by reporters, Campbell said. "By the end of the experience, they were very hostile toward the news media," he said. "They decided it was not appropriate for a newspaper to have run this picture."

Sergeant Cleveland's birth mother, Nada Morford, also turned to, not away from, journalists in trying to sort out the horror of the picture.

After Mary Cleveland told the newspaper she thought she recognized the man in the photograph, Morford protested and said it was not, could not be, her son. "I want him to rest in peace," she said then.

However, Morford had not yet studied the picture carefully, and the possibility that the photograph was that of her son's body gnawed at her, according to published accounts. She went to the town library to make photocopies of pictures in a *Time* magazine article. Then she asked a reporter for the photograph from Somalia.

She broke down as she described how she pored over the pictures, how she found contours that seemed so familiar, but not enough for her to say with certainty that the soldier in the photograph was her son.

"My son had black eyebrows and eyelashes," Morford said. "He [the soldier in the picture] had light hair, black eyebrows." Then, she said, she noticed that the legs and feet resembled her son's. "I would hate to say this is positively my son and have it be somebody else's," she said. Then, she began to cry, according to published accounts.

Campbell said he conscientiously tries to be sensitive to the individuals and families who might be especially affected by the publication of a story or a picture, but added, "I begin with the strong presumption that we're here to publish the news." Privacy or respect for the grieving might outweigh that obligation to publish, Campbell said, but publishing news "is what the newspaper is all about, to say what are the issues of the day that people need to be aware of."

If the paper knew the identity of a photo subject such as the dead soldier, Campbell said, "We would probably contact the family before we published it and tell them that it was our intention to publish it." He also said he would allow the family to see the picture before it appeared in the paper.

The body in the photograph has still not been identified and may never be. The military knows it has to be one of five men who were killed that day in Somalia and whose bodies were temporarily held by the Somalis, but is making no effort to determine for sure which one it was. Several months after the incident, a Pentagon spokesperson told reporters, "They were American soldiers. That in itself is jarring enough. You don't need an individual's name to express horror at the treatment of the bodies."

One thing is quite certain. This was not a case of ghoulish editors yielding to tawdry sensationalism to sell more papers. Thousands of readers called and wrote their local newspapers the next day, the vast majority of them to object to the picture's publication, and many canceled their subscriptions in protest. In this instance, the editors who chose to run the picture were printing not what they knew their readers wanted, but what they thought their readers needed to know.

QUESTIONS TO CONSIDER

1. War is grisly, and so are the images that come out of it. To what extent should journalists depict the horrors of war in photographs, video, and multimedia?

2. Journalists all have home nations, and many times their coverage of war portrays their home nations in negative lights. To what degree should

journalists balance their patriotism with their obligations to share the truth, even if that truth is unflattering to their own countries?

3. Military families are particularly sensitive to the ways negative images can affect support for war efforts on the home front, as well as morale on the front lines. What kinds of ethical dilemmas do you think the news media in military communities face that are different from those faced by other news outlets?

4. Compare this case study with the one in the previous chapter (Chapter 20). Both discuss different perspectives on journalism ethics from Somalia and its capital city of Mogadishu. What, in your opinion, are the ethical obligations of editors in relatively "safe" communities to present information prepared by journalists in danger zones?

22 ▪ ▪ ▪

Verification and Attribution
Memogate: The Reporting Scandal that Trumped the Real Story

In political scandals, it is often said, "It isn't the crime. It's the cover-up," meaning that attempts to hide the truth of wrongdoing often are greater crimes than the original offenses (such as, for example, a president lying about an affair under oath and getting impeached for perjury). In journalism ethics, there is a parallel aphorism—many times, what sinks a big story isn't that the information is wrong, but that the methods by which the information was obtained were flawed. When shoddy reporting becomes the basis for a big story, the result is a double-whammy—the story itself becomes inherently tainted, and the public's trust in the journalists who brought the issue to light is deeply shaken. *The New York Times* suffered such a sting when one of its young journalists, Jayson Blair, was revealed to be a habitual plagiarist and fabricator; the same thing happened to *The New Republic* when the plagiarism and fabrications of Stephen Glass were revealed. That is why many journalists consider the process of verifying the accuracy of information, and attributing that information to sources, to be more than just a basic display of professional competency. Verification and attribution also are moral obligations for serious journalists.

In the first decade of the twenty-first century, one of the most infamous examples of such a moral lapse was the CBS News Memogate incident of 2004, in which one of the most respected television news magazines in the

United States—*60 Minutes*—suffered deep embarrassment. In its wake, several of CBS's most important and influential journalists were either fired or resigned as a result, most notably the anchor of CBS Evening News Dan Rather (hence the other nickname for the incident, Rathergate—both "-gate" terms obviously referring to the Watergate political scandal of the 1970s).

The underlying claim of the story actually was not new: It was about the dubious nature of the Vietnam War-era military service of George W. Bush, the two-term Texas governor and U.S. president, whose military service was an issue in all of his campaigns for office. Bush's family has a long history of political clout in Washington, D.C.: his great-grandfather was a railroad and steel executive who served as a federal official during World War I; his grandfather was an influential U.S. senator from Connecticut; and his father (who would later be vice-president to Ronald Reagan and a one-term president himself) was a Texas congressman in the late 1960s when George W. Bush reached the draft age. The allegations are that his family's political connections not only resulted in preferential treatment that allowed Bush to avoid combat duty in Vietnam, but that his domestic service in the Texas Air National Guard was not entirely fulfilled. At issue were several gaps in Bush's military records regarding why he lost his flight status in 1972—many media reports indicated that Bush had not obtained the necessary physical examinations, had not reported for several required duty assignments, shirked his duties to work on a senate campaign in Alabama, and had been discharged about seven months earlier than the full six years he committed to. Those allegations were raised by critics of Bush during his two campaigns for the Texas governorship in the 1990s and again in the 2000 and 2004 presidential campaigns. Military records about those matters have been deemed either incomplete or misplaced, and several organizations—most notably the Associated Press—sued the federal government to release all documents about Bush's military service.

During the summer of 2004 and in the midst of a bitter presidential campaign season, CBS News and USA TODAY both received some documents that appeared to answer the questions about the quality of Bush's service in the Texas Air National Guard.[1] The papers were said to be from the personal files of the late Jerry Killian, the lieutenant colonel who was Bush's commander in Texas. At CBS, they were obtained via fax by veteran news producer Mary Mapes from Lieutenant Colonel Bill Burkett, who had been an officer in the Texas Air National Guard. The documents appeared to have been produced by typewriter (computer word processors were rare in the early 1970s), and the content of the memos expressed concerns about both Bush's qualifications to retain his flight status and his personal reasons for wanting a transfer to Alabama. One unsigned memo outlined a telephone conversation with Bush stating he was "working on another campaign for his dad" and wanted special accommodations to continue to do so.[2] Another memo that appeared to be signed by Killian stated, "On this date I ordered that 1st Lt. Bush be suspended from flight status due to failure to perfor [sic] to USAF/TexANG standards and failure to meet annual physical examination (flight) as ordered."[3] It was the proverbial smoking gun—hard evidence that Bush had not fulfilled his military obligations and was seeking preferential treatment.

Mapes and others at CBS immediately began to validate the information in the memos, and they hired some experts in document forensics to determine the authenticity of the letters. Their reporting through August 2004 involved interviews with people who may have been familiar with the documents and the situation they described, most notably Robert Strong, who had worked in the administration of the Texas Air National Guard and was a friend of Killian's. On September 8, 2004, the segment titled "For the Record" aired on the *60 Minutes Wednesday* news magazine, with Rather as the anchor, and it featured images of the memos and interviews with Strong and others. In the interview, Strong did not validate the memos themselves, but did say that such information was "compatible with the way business was done at the time." The segment led with an on-camera interview with Ben Barnes, the former speaker of the Texas House of Representatives and former lieutenant governor of Texas, who said he had pulled some strings in 1968 to attempt to get Bush into the Air National Guard so the young man and son of a congressman could avoid being drafted and sent to Vietnam.

Within hours of the September 2004 broadcast, the segment came under intense criticism on right-wing blogs, with much attention focused on the dubious authenticity of the memos upon which the report was based. In particular, critics focused on the use of a superscript "th" in some of the memos, a typographical option that was not available on most typewriters in the early 1970s, but is a common function of computer word processors (Microsoft Word, for example, automatically changes "th" to superscript as a default setting). By the next day, questions about the validity of the memos was being reported in the mainstream news media, causing CBS News in general, and Rather in particular, to use their own and other media outlets to defend the integrity of the story and the memos, dismissing criticisms as little more than sour grapes and petty partisan politics.

Within a week, however, the charges of shoddy verification on the part of Mapes, Rather, and others at CBS News were starting to stick. On September 15, 2004, one of the forensic document experts CBS had retained in August, Emily Will, publicly stated that she had expressed doubts to Mapes about the authenticity of the memos, and another, Marcel Matley, also said he told CBS that he was unable to ascertain the authenticity of the memos. By that time CBS had tracked down Killian's assistant when the memos were allegedly written, Marian Carr Knox, who said she did not recall typing the memos, although the information in them was consistent with what she knew about the situation.

On September 20, less than two weeks after the segment aired, CBS News president Andrew Heyward conceded that the memos were of dubious value and that reliance on them for the segment had been a mistake. Dan Rather also publicly stated that had he known at the time the concerns expressed about the authenticity of the memos, that he would not have used them.

CBS later retained former U.S. Attorney General Dick Thornburg (who served in that role under Bush's father, President George H.W. Bush) and Louis Boccardi, retired president and executive editor of The Associated Press, to conduct an independent review of the reporting practices of the CBS News staff related to the "For the Record" segment. Their report, issued in early January 2005, found multiple lapses in CBS News' verification of both the memos and the information they contained, including overlooking or ignoring multiple concerns raised by experts prior to the airing of the story. They also criticized CBS News for not sufficiently vetting the integrity of the source of the documents, Colonel Bill Burkett, who eventually admitted to lying about from whom he had obtained the documents and claiming to have burned the originals (if they ever existed). The validity of the memos themselves, and of the information they contained, was not part of the investigation, and as of this writing it is unclear as to whether the information in the dubious memos is true or not.

After the report, CBS fired Mapes and demanded the resignations of three other top news executives. Rather himself resigned from CBS News later that year under intense political and professional pressure stemming from the Memogate story (although Rather at the time said the incident was not the reason he resigned; in a 2007 lawsuit against CBS, he argued that he was made to be a scapegoat in the incident). The problems with the story were reported in major news media around the globe, and the case has been referred to repeatedly in trade publications, professional journalism conferences, and, of course, the classrooms of journalism schools. Rumors persist about why the story was pursued and aired with such zeal, considering the many red flags that were waved as the segment was being put together. Conservatives accused Mapes, Rather, and other CBS journalists of anti-Bush bias, alleging that the story was an attempt to influence Bush's reelection campaign against U.S. Senator John Kerry; some liberals have built a conspiracy theory around the issue, arguing that the memos were created by pro-Bush operatives in an elaborate scheme to discredit the mainstream news media just prior to the election.

This case certainly is worth studying simply as a cautionary tale about the process of verification and attribution, and the Thornburg-Boccardi report should be required reading in newsrooms and journalism classrooms everywhere to remind journalists why great care should be taken when reporting a big story. Hindsight is 20/20, certainly, and, in retrospect, it is easy to find much fault in how the story was pursued, reported, and presented. Certainly, Mapes, Rather, and the rest of their team had every right and obligation to pursue the story itself. If we believe that the public has the right—in fact, the need—to know about the background of their leaders, then CBS would have been irresponsible to not pursue the story told in the memos. The fact that the military service of the candidates was a significant factor in the 2004 presidential campaign only amplifies that fact. Nevertheless, pursuing a story and running it are two very different things, and the latter shouldn't happen until the information has been carefully scrutinized and verified.

Even in this age of shrinking newsrooms and timid news executives, the political arguments for ethical journalism stands, and getting to the truth about allegedly corrupt politicians—especially when the incidents in question happened decades earlier—is important work. Unfortunately, incidents such as Memogate can have a chilling effect on such journalism, as journalists become leery of being too aggressive lest they make serious errors, and newsroom managers shy away from pursuing big stories for fear of wasting time and resources chasing after unsubstantiated rumors and possible dead ends. The hypercritical responses from the blogosphere can be an aggravating factor to that chilling effect, although on a philosophical level there is considerable value to the public having more tools to police and critique the work of journalists who make mistakes.

From an ethics standpoint, perhaps the greatest lesson from Memogate is not so much what CBS News journalists did wrong, but how the story behind the story came to overshadow the story itself. Very little has come from the allegations that Bush was given preferential treatment because of his family's political connections, and that the record of those accommodations may have been tampered with to obfuscate his questionable service to the military—he was narrowly reelected to the presidency in 2004, and afterward his political foes turned their attention to Bush's performance as president rather than his wayward youth. However, the fallout at CBS and, in big-time journalism in general, has been much more damaging to the public good. Even though CBS went to great effort to find out the truth behind what happened in its own newsroom, expending great amounts of time and money to essentially give itself a black eye, the end result is that the public trust in one of the most important news organizations in the United States was severely and perhaps irretrievably damaged. Perhaps every future investigation by CBS and its staff will be tainted with the stains of Memogate, and the journalists who follow Mapes and Rather and the rest will be branded, to some degree, with the folly of their predecessors. The incident gives the unfair and venomous critics of the so-called mainstream media another high-profile example to trot out every time they want to undermine reports that are vitally important and impeccably verified, and it gives politicians of questionable character a straw man to attack whenever their own dalliances and misdeeds are revealed in the popular press.

The connection between accuracy and integrity in journalism could not be clearer. As a profession that holds as its paramount objective to seek truth and report it, making sure what is reported is true, as much as is humanly and reasonably possible, could not be more important, and the consequences of cutting corners could not be more dire. The key to "accuracy, accuracy, accuracy" is "verification, verification, verification."

QUESTIONS TO CONSIDER

1. Under what circumstances are the military records of politicians important for the public to know? When those records are provided by former military officers, how much (or little) trust should journalists have for those former officers?

2. In an age when technology makes it very easy to forge official-looking documents, and when politicians have the means to hide, destroy, or obfuscate actual documents, how much verification is too much? What should journalists do if they can verify the information in such documents, even if the documents themselves might be forgeries?

3. CBS journalists interviewed several people who may have known about the alleged accommodations made to the young George W. Bush in late 1960s and early 1970s. As the incidents happened nearly thirty years before the report, how much effort should CBS have put into checking out the claims of people relying on distant memory so much?

4. CBS, USA TODAY, and other news outlets have posted images of the questionable memos on their Web sites, so that the public can review them themselves. To what extent might publishing such memos be ethically questionable? Are there ethical boundaries to the publication of original-source documents, even if those documents are at the center of the controversy?

5. CBS News stuck by its report, and its journalists, for only a few days; within a few months, CBS executives had fired or forced the resignations of several top staffers. To what degree do you think news executives should stand behind the work of their journalists, even if those journalists make big mistakes? Should journalists with long, distinguished careers be fired for a single lapse in judgment that results in a story that is still, for the most part, verified and attributed properly? Should political pressure influence the way news executives handle such situations? Why or why not?

23 ■ ■ ■

Verification and Attribution
Anonymous Sources: From Deep Throat to the Clinton–Lewinski Affair

Few characters in the history of journalism have as much cultural recognition as that of Deep Throat, the anonymous source who, in the early 1970s, fed important information to two young reporters at *The Washington Post* as they detailed the petty crime of political high jinks that ultimately led to the first-ever resignation of a sitting U.S. president, Richard M. Nixon. The Watergate scandal and the series of investigative stories written by Bob Woodward and Carl Bernstein is the stuff of legend, and the true identity of Deep Throat was one of the best-kept (and most discussed) secrets in Washington for more than thirty years. Woodward and Bernstein promised not to identify Deep Throat until he either died or chose to go public. Those journalists kept their secret until 2005, when former FBI deputy director William Mark Felt admitted to *Vanity Fair* magazine that he had been the secret source. Woodward, Bernstein, and the former editor of the *Post*, Benjamin Bradlee, all confirmed Felt's claim shortly thereafter, thus ending more than three decades of speculation by scholars, journalists, and political operatives, some of whom had long suspected that Felt was Deep Throat. A few months later in 2005, Woodward published the book he had been writing about Deep Throat, called *The Secret Man*, in which he provided more details about how he had met Felt, cultivated a rapport with the man, and used information provided by Felt to reveal connections between the Nixon administration and the 1972 break-ins at the Democratic National Committee office in Washington's Watergate Hotel.

The Deep Throat–Watergate case is perhaps one of the most discussed in modern journalism because it centers around one of the more controversial common practices of journalism: the use of unnamed sources in news reports. Although a long-standing practice in journalism, using unnamed sources has, since Watergate, become a fixture of investigative reporting, and has led reporters to uncover corruption at all levels of government, from small-town mayors' offices and rural townships to the White House and 10 Downing Street. The concept is simple—well-placed officials who have the information the public needs to know would not remain well placed for long if they were caught leaking secret information to the press. Even though most democratic nations have some legal mechanisms to protect such whistleblowers, the hard truth is that a government official who gives up insidious secrets about his superiors is risking political and professional suicide. Caught between loyalties to the public and to the people one works for, a would-be whistleblower likely will only talk to reporters on the condition that his or her identity be kept a secret.

For journalists, such deals can be extremely tempting. Especially in the competitive, high-stakes arena of investigative reporting, journalists are always looking for their own Deep Throat. Oftentimes, a long, in-depth investigative piece needs just one or two key pieces of information to make the story solid enough for publication, and an anonymous source may be the only person with that information. Many journalists argue that it is only in such last-resort scenarios that anonymity be granted to key sources. However, in reality, the use of anonymous sources is fairly routine, particularly in coverage of the highest public offices of national governments. More often than not, when a journalist uses information from "a high-ranking government official who spoke on condition of anonymity," the anonymous attribution is just a shortcut to quickly get information that could, with more time and effort, be obtained from other sources who would be willing to go on the record. In fact, in Washington especially, using unnamed sources is almost business as usual for daily reporting on the mundane activities of the U.S. federal government.

The use of anonymous sources is not exclusive to watchdog journalists, as the practice can also be used to reveal serious issues not directly related to government activities. A newspaper investigation about drug abuse in local schools may be built on interviews with teenage drug users whose names are changed or dropped entirely in the final report; a BBC radio reporter in Baghdad may interview a witness of a suicide bombing who "would only give his first name"; in Japan, television journalists routinely interview eyewitnesses with the camera focused only on their torsos, so that their faces cannot be seen and their identities are obscured. An argument could be made that the less important and influential the source of information, the less important is his or her identity to the public—as most listeners to BBC Radio World News are unlikely to know anybody in Baghdad, the name of an eyewitness to a suicide bombing there is unlikely to have any significant meaning whatsoever. Moreover, if the witness were to be identified by his full name, he might be put in danger of retaliation or attacks from terrorists who hear the report. In the places of the world where people truly can be punished for what they say to the press—whether in the streets of Baghdad, the jungle villages of Colombia, or the halls of a public high school in Chicago—the granting of anonymity very well could be the only way reporters can get information from knowledgeable sources. Media scholar William Blankenburg made the argument this way: "Anonymous attribution seems to be widespread, and it fluctuates with the sensitivity of its associated information. It is integral to newsgathering in a variety of settings and vital in some circumstances. Prohibitions fail because anonymity works."[1]

Anonymous attribution may work, but it can undermine the credibility of journalism. Much of that loss of public trust results from situations in which anonymous attribution is misused. One commonly cited example stems from the early 1980s, when *Washington Post* reporter Janet Cooke was stripped of a Pulitzer Prize when it was revealed that her heart-wrenching story about an anonymous child drug addict was fictitious.[2] The much-discussed case of Cooke's "Jimmy's World" is often used as a cautionary tale against journalistic fabrication and a warning against reporters becoming so focused on telling a good story that they fictionalize their reports. However, the case also is a cautionary tale to editors about being more careful about allowing reporters to use unnamed sources.

One of the most significant government scandals in recent U.S. history—the investigation and impeachment of former U.S. President Bill Clinton—offers a more complicated example of the problems with anonymous sources. Normally in the United States, criminal investigators are careful about what information they release to the press lest the investigation and ensuing trials are compromised. However, there were many leaks to the media from unnamed aides to U.S. Independent Counsel Kenneth Starr, who was in charge of the years-long, open-ended investigation into allegations of wrongdoing by Clinton. Clinton, a Democrat, was largely reviled by Republicans who controlled the Congress, and one of the Republican efforts was to appoint an independent counsel (Starr) to find evidence of corruption against Clinton. Starr's investigation started as a probe of an alleged real-estate scandal from the 1970s and 1980s involving Clinton and his wife Hillary Rodham Clinton. In the end, no evidence was found to connect the Clintons to the Whitewater scandal. Starr's investigation went on to probe other alleged Clinton scandals, eventually focusing on widespread rumors that the Arkansas governor-turned-U.S.

president had a history of extramarital affairs, including one in the White House with intern Monica Lewinski in the mid-1990s.

Details of the investigation, and of Clinton's defense strategies, were widely covered in the news media well before any charges were brought against Clinton and the U.S. Congress began legal proceedings, and public opinion about the case was largely solidified before any official action was ever taken against Clinton by the Congress. The story broke in January 1998; Starr's report to Congress did not arrive until September of that year. It was a clear example of a case being tried in the court of public opinion, and the evidence presented to the public over more than eight months was mostly provided by unnamed sources in the news media.

Scholar Steven Esposito, in a study published in 1999, found that 72 percent of more than a thousand prime-time television news stories about the Lewinski scandal included anonymous sources, and that anonymous sources accounted for nearly one-half of all sources in those stories.[3] Among those sources, Esposito found nearly five times as many were from the Clinton staff than were from within Kenneth Starr's staff. However, the numbers alone may have been less important than what was being said. From Starr's side, reporters received many tips about specific details about the affair and the evidence of it (i.e., the infamous blue dress that provided DNA evidence implicating Clinton in the affair). The anonymous sources from Clinton's camp, meanwhile, attacked Lewinski's credibility and mental state, trying to frame Clinton's encounters with her as "innocent"; at the same time, they accused Kenneth Starr of being a Republican hack on a political vendetta, and they argued that the investigation was little more than an out-of-control political witch-hunt. Those very arguments seemed to permeate public opinion, as during the Lewinski investigation in 1998, Clinton enjoyed very high job-approval ratings, even after Clinton finally admitted to having sex with Lewinski in his office and apologized for lying to the public about it. Clinton was impeached by the U.S. House of Representatives, and the U.S. Senate narrowly acquitted Clinton; he finished out his elected term as one of the most popular, but controversial, U.S. presidents of the twentieth century.

For journalists in the national news media, the Clinton–Lewinski sex scandal was a case of anonymous sourcing run amok. It started, ironically, with an anonymous leak to the Drudge Report news aggregator Web site that a more mainstream publication, the weekly news magazine *Newsweek*, was working on a story by investigative reporter Michael Isikoff about the Lewinski–Clinton affair. Drudge Report editor Matt Drudge published an unattributed article that Isikoff's story was being held by *Newsweek* (which later said it held the story until it could substantiate some of the evidence). From that point on, the national news media seemed to be in a feeding frenzy for any and all information about the investigation, many times bending the established norms of good journalism, and sometimes breaking with those norms altogether in the drive to scoop one another, no matter how trivial (or flat-out wrong) the information. Deborah Potter of the Poynter Institute, a journalism think-tank and training organization, lamented the rush to publish stories about the Lewinsky–Clinton affair in early 1998:

> Competition on a story this big is inevitably intense, but today's technology amplifies the pressure. In the 1970s, during Watergate, deadlines generally came twice a day, for the morning newspapers and the evening network newscasts. . . . We held stories because they were exclusive. But because we held them, we had time to confirm and reconfirm every angle, to be thoughtful and reflective about the consequences of our reporting. Today, the deadlines come every minute, with all-news cable networks and the Internet reporting developments instantaneously. Instead of holding exclusives, the networks run with them, knowing they won't have a story alone for long. Newspapers post stories to their Web sites, wire services pick up those stories, and they are broadcast within minutes. As the Clinton story spread at warp speed, many news organizations jumped aboard, leaving behind the standards of sourcing and confirmation that caused *Newsweek* to hold the story in the first place.[4]

In the years since the Lewinsky–Clinton scandal, many major news outlets have set down stricter guidelines for when, and whether, they will rely on unnamed sources. A 2005 survey of 419 newspaper editors in the United States, conducted by the Associated Press Managing Editors organization, found that about three-fourths of those editors would be willing to allow reporters to use anonymous sources, but most said they would only do so if the information was very important and only if it couldn't be obtained any other way.[5] Many editors reported that they had implemented, or were in the process of implementing, strict protocols for deciding whether and when to use anonymous sources.

The profession has seen such efforts before, however. In the early 1970s, for example, Ben Bagdikian was a junior editor at *The Washington Post*. He recalled how just shortly before the story of the Watergate scandal was uncovered by his colleagues Woodward and Bernstein, *Post* editor Ben Bradlee had issued a moratorium on the use of unnamed sources by his reporters. Although a fierce competitor who hated getting scooped by other news organizations, Bradlee was frustrated with the sheer volume of information coming from the Nixon administration that was arguably untrue and almost always published without attribution. Bradlee's position was meant to crack down on such abuses by public officials, but it quickly served only to hinder his reporters in their reporting, particularly of the Nixon administration. After getting scooped by competing national newspapers, Bradlee reluctantly relented—his moral stand quickly succumbed to the practicalities of reporting on the White House. "The experiment ended after two days," Bagdikian wrote.[6]

Anonymous sources probably will always be a necessary evil of journalism, but as we have seen time and time again, journalists seeking scoops may overlook the potential abuses of the courtesy by unnamed sources, and may assume anonymity is necessary even when it isn't.

QUESTIONS TO CONSIDER

1. What are the political arguments for and against granting anonymity to government sources? What are the reasons other than "anonymity works" to justify the practice? What are the reasons other than "it undermines credibility" to reject the practice?

2. Are there other ways journalists can attribute information to sources that provides more credibility to the information without naming the individual? When do you think "a high-ranking official" is not enough of a description of the source's credibility?

3. Many times, journalists offer anonymity to the most powerful people in society (such as government officials or corporate executives) while not offering anonymity to everyday people (such as eyewitnesses of a house fire, or people commenting on a proposed tax increase). What problems do you see with that double standard?

4. When a government official offers information to a journalist in exchange for anonymity, what kinds of counteroffers do you think journalists can make to get the official to go "on the record" with the claims?

Verification and Attribution
Anonymity in Feedback from the Public: How Open Should Forums Be?

Journalists may use anonymous sources in their reporting, but that doesn't mean they have much love for anonymity itself. As professionals who regularly put their names to their work, and then put that work out for public scrutiny, many journalists understandably have very low regard for people who want to speak their minds but not reveal their identities, even if those people have good reasons to want to remain anonymous. On the issue of anonymity, there is clear tension between the values of journalism and the values of the public, and that tension has long been behind professional debates regarding whether, and how, to publish anonymous feedback from the public. And as journalists embrace new technology and try new things, those tensions sometimes rise again to the surface.

As the Internet became a more ubiquitous delivery medium for traditional news organizations, those tensions arose often and in different ways. One example of that can be seen in the case of *The Times* newspaper of Shreveport, Louisiana, a relatively large newspaper in the Deep South of the United States, which, in 2004, ended a long-standing anonymous call-in forum and within two years launched multiple online forums that accommodated anonymous commentary.

Published regularly for about twenty-five years, "Tell the Times" was a typical anonymous call-in forum started at many newspapers in the 1980s with the implementation of sophisticated phone-message systems. The forums published short comments that were called in to a voice-mail box by a newspaper's readers, transcribed by newspaper staff, and ran in the print edition. Seen as a hybrid between letters to the editor and talk radio, the forums were largely derided in professional circles as promoting mean-spirited attacks and irresponsible, sometimes slanderous sniping. However, some editors defended the forums as living up to the spirit of the First Amendment to the U.S. Constitution, in which freedom of speech was to be largely unfettered. One such editor was Jim Sachetti of the daily *Press-Enterprise* in Bloomsburg, Pennsylvania, who in 1997, defending his newspaper's popular "30 Seconds" call-in forum, said in an interview, "We caught a lot of hell about it, especially from the powers that be, like the local chamber of commerce and elected officials. And then I realized that, if anything, this gives a voice to people traditionally cut out of the loop in any community." (Research has since shown that most people in the United States who write signed letters to newspapers, and get them published, are college-educated, middle-class, middle-aged, and White, and many women, minorities, young adults, senior citizens, and lower-income people would write letters if their names would not be published.[1])

Although "Tell the Times" was a popular feature among many Shreveport readers for years, *Times* editor Alan English announced via a column in the September 5, 2004, edition that the forum would be ended. His argument was strongly based on moral grounds. "I have long held the belief that 'Tell the Times' does more harm than good," English wrote. "(The) column is divisive on most days and recent postings confirm this. Also, the unsubstantiated accusations from anonymous callers often belittle and berate members of our community for what they do and for their points of view. ... Now, 'Tell the Times' is meeting its demise. It is time for our community to move away from a debate injected with anonymous, mean-spirited lobs and on to a more credible, responsible forum." The headline on English's column made the moral stance clear: "A Mark for Credibility: Bell Tolls for Tell the Times."

Three years later, English said that his decision at the time was not strictly one of curbing irresponsible commentary offered by anonymous readers. There also was a strategic aspect—after years of trying to invest staff time and energy into policing harmful submissions to 'Tell the Times,' English decided that he could put those resources to better use in the newsroom. Nevertheless, his underlying belief in the problem of anonymity remains strong: "There is no better, credible conversation than the one that comes with names attached."

In a telephone interview,[2] English recalled that it took him many years to consider and reach the decision to kill "Tell the Times," and that in the years before he ended the feature, he and his editors had tried to rehabilitate the forum to encourage more considered, thoughtful comments.

However, in the end, he decided that "Tell the Times" had run its course. Reactions to the decision were mixed, both in the community and in the newsroom. In the community, some people wrote signed letters lamenting the loss because (as one letter put it) "'Tell the Times' is usually good for a laugh or two. We need something to laugh about to start our day. Don't you agree?"[3] Others commended English for the change. The mayor of Shreveport at the time, Keith Hightower, wrote a letter in which he described "Tell the Times" as "a pit bull with distemper" and "the journalistic equivalent of a drive-by shooting," and suggested that "(T)he much bigger issue for our community is that 'Tell the Times' dragged us down. It put the worst face on issues and people, not the best.... There were so many things going right in our cities, but if you read TTT every day it seemed things were only going wrong."[4]

Feelings also were mixed within the newsroom of *The Times*. "Some people enjoyed the humor," English recalled. "Some lamented the loss, because the feature brought them some lighter fare. One of the editorial writers told me he got great ideas from 'Tell the Times.' But the majority of people in the newsroom were glad to see it go."

About two years later, however, English and his staff were grappling with the same old conundrum in a brand new package. *The Times'* Web site began offering readers an opportunity to respond online to news and opinion articles, and also to discuss other issues via online forums provided on www.shreveporttimes.com. English was keenly aware of the apparent change of heart he displayed by launching new anonymous forums so soon after closing "Tell the Times" on moral grounds. "In one way, I know I was facing claims of hypocrisy, because we had just got (anonymous comments) out of the newspaper and now we were publishing them online," English said. "But it's a new world. The growth of the Internet means things are not the same."

That new world includes a seemingly infinite number of online forums where anonymity is the norm, but it also includes many technological advances that make managing such forums faster and easier than the old call-in forums. English said that in the online realm, "Anonymity isn't purely anonymous. Users of our forum have to register. We can track down an IP [Internet protocol] address of a computer used to post a comment. Users have to include their e-mail addresses, which may not be their real names, but does give us a means to track them and contact them. If people abuse the forums, we have mechanisms to cut them off, and there are new tools appearing almost every day that can help us counsel and guide the conversations."

Concerns about anonymous feedback from the public is a fairly recent development in professional journalism. For centuries, letters to the editor were common in newspapers and magazines, and many of those were published without the names of the writers. Aside from giving people a means to comment on what they read, letters columns also gave the citizenry a means to express opinions on all manner of political, social, and cultural issues; to share news and information they felt the newspapers did not provide; and ultimately to participate in public life. Woven inextricably into that tradition was the tradition of anonymity. For example, the storied 1735 trial and acquittal of printer John Peter Zenger in New York—held up as an early victory for freedom of the press—was essentially an effort by colonial governor William Cosby to discover (and silence) those who wrote criticisms of his government for Zenger's *New York Weekly Journal*. The right to anonymous speech also was very much part of debates regarding the U.S. Constitution itself, as evidenced in a thread of letters published in several Northeastern U.S. newspapers in 1787 debating whether newspapers should reveal the names of letter writers. Most letter writers argued that anonymity was an important civil liberty—for example, in the November 8, 1787, *Providence United States Chronicle*, "Argus" wrote: "The Liberty of the Press, or the Liberty which every Person in the United States at present enjoys...is a Privilege of infinite importance," and argued that efforts to suppress anonymous speech by "our aristocratical Gentry, to have every Person's Name published who should write against the proposed Federal Constitution, has given many of us a just Alarm."[5]

The very first letter to the editor appearing in *The New York Times* was printed on September 23, 1851, five days after the fledgling newspaper began publication. It was a lengthy note regarding the *Times'* "just rebuke" to the civic leaders of Philadelphia printed earlier that week, and was ostensibly written by a Philadelphia native who agreed that the city played "second fiddle" to the economic and cultural might of New York City. The letter was signed, simply, "Visitor." In the decades that followed, the *Times* would publish many letters under either fanciful pseudonyms ("Then and Now," "Zouve") or simply the writer's initials (i.e., "J. S.").

Such pseudonymous letters have not appeared regularly in *The New York Times* for many decades. The newspaper largely stopped the practice sometime in the 1940s, although evidence of such letters continued into the early 1970s—the *Times'* letters-editor at the time, the late Kalman Seigel, wrote in a collected volume of letters that "Anonymous letters are ignored....Letters signed with pseudonyms are considered, but rarely used. (If the quality of the letter is high and the reason to protect the writer's identity good, the letter will be considered for publication.)"[6] *The New York Times* was not alone in the practice—in fact, letters signed under pseudonyms were published in the *Chicago Tribune*, the *Los Angeles Times*, and many other major U.S. newspapers well into the twentieth century. *The Times of London* also published such letters into the twentieth century; in his 1976 collection of letters, Kenneth Gregory noted in the introduction that "Letters signed pseudonymously—generally Viator,

Senex, Public School Man or Disgusted—continued to intrigue readers of *The Times* until the Second World War...."[7]

It was in the years during and after that war that editors began to debate the pros and cons of publishing letters without the authors' names. The issue was broached many times in the 1950s and 1960s via essays in *The Masthead*, the magazine of the National Conference of Editorial Writers, a U.S.-focused organization of opinion-page editors and writers. Some of those essays presented moral arguments for stopping the practice; others seemed more interested in rejecting anonymous letters simply to stream-line the process of selecting and editing letters for publication. Yet, the language in those essays revealed a clear disdain journalists of the day had toward those who submitted anonymous letters—one editor argued in 1968 that his newspaper's recent ban on unsigned letters kept "haters and hollerers from cluttering up the column and scaring off other writers.... We became convinced that anonymity was their principal defense, so we stopped printing any letters that did not carry the author's name and address. The new rule worked."[8] By the mid-1990s, virtually all newspapers would only consider signed letters, and the vast majority refused to withhold the names of letter writers for any reason.[9] Some newspapers provided anonymous forums such as "Tell the Times" in Shreveport, but the practice never gained wide acceptance and was largely derided by most journalists, and like *The Times*, many suspended the practice altogether.

With the advent of online discussion forums on the Web sites of traditional newspapers, the debate seems to have come full circle. As in the early days of journalism in the West, the public is demanding, and expects, forums to accommodate anonymous speech, much to the chagrin of the powerful and the intellectual elite. And many journalists are once again making impassioned pleas against such commentary, expressing doubts as to the value of commentary submitted anonymously and the questionable ethics of publishing such commentary within the pages, or Web sites, of professional newspapers. For example, newspaper reporter Andy Schotz, 2007 chair of the Ethics Committee of the Society of Professional Journalists, contended in the August 2007 issue of *Quill*: "We let people hide behind a screen name and hurl insults, which we may or may not scrub from the Web site, depending on whether someone has noticed or complained. The result is a lower level of discourse. Amusement and rants replace reasoned debate. And, by setting up this process, we solicit and encourage anonymous nonsense and barbs. We're responsible."

The Internet undeniably has allowed the free marketplace of ideas to again become as rough and tumble today as it was in the revolutionary eighteenth century, perhaps even rougher, and certainly with millions of more participants from all walks of life, including walks Enlightenment-era thinkers couldn't possibly have imagined. As professional journalists balance their personal views on anonymity against the public's demand (and, arguably, need) for it, it is important for us all to recognize the risks of throwing up too many barriers to public commentary, even if those barriers are couched as professional standards.

English, who clearly has strong and valid concerns about the tone and content of many anonymous posts, also recognizes that one of his obligations as an editor is to facilitate public discourse. "Even if it's not on our site, it'll be out there anyway," he said. "And I want to harness that somehow." English sees the online forums as places where his reporters can find news tips, where editors can engage in conversations with the community, where journalists can post questions to gather comments via what is commonly called crowd-sourcing. "It's part and parcel of being online," he said. "I am seeing the forums evolving into a place where the public can collaborate with my staff in the news-gathering process. . . . It gives us information to consider, and I think that can help the reports." And, perhaps ironically, English has again created a space in his printed newspaper for anonymous commentary, in which particularly interesting postings to *The Times'* online forums are printed in the newspaper's "Conversations" section. "So some of those comments are back in print," English said. "We are basically reinventing 'Tell the Times.'"

Editors who provide anonymous forums should be concerned about the lack of civility and accountability in what English, and many others, call "the Wild West of the Internet." However, thoughtful editors should also see in those forums the spirit of speech- and press-freedoms that were hard won in stable democracies and are still being fought for in the oppressed nations of the world. Anonymous forums may be abused by cowards and people of questionable morality, and may include comments that do much harm and little good, but those forums also can be inviting to the fearful, the downtrodden, and the oppressed—people who for many decades had no place to have their voices heard in the mainstream press.

QUESTIONS TO CONSIDER

1. What standards, if any, should editors impose upon postings to the online forums they provide? To what extent should such postings be held to the same standards as signed letters to the editor? Are they comparable forums? Why or why not?

2. Spend some time reading comments on an online forum provided by a major news organization. If you were an editor, which comments would you take down, and why? Which comments would you hold up as good examples, and why? Are there comments that you, personally, disagree with (or even find offensive), but would still publish? Why or why not?

3. Anonymity is historically tied to freedom of speech and of the press. Yet times change, and so do professional and public standards. What do you see as the positive aspects of anonymous speech in the Internet age? What do you see as the negative aspects?

4. Journalists are ultimately responsible for what they present to the public, even if it's commentary from anonymous members of the public. Should editors, as some argue, exert much more control over their anonymous online forums? Should they be less concerned with control or more with allowing the free flow of ideas to sort itself out? How would those goals be accomplished while still upholding the journalistic principles of verification and attribution?

25 ▪ ▪ ▪

Avoid Deception
The Casting Couch: Is Entrapping a Libidinous Actor Serious News or Simply a Ratings Stunt?[1]

The so-called casting couch is a well-known phenomenon in which aspiring actors—most often women—will have sex with established actors, producers, and others in exchange for favorable consideration in getting roles in films and television. The ethics of the casting couch itself is worth discussion in a more general media ethics context, but for purposes of this book, the main question is whether such behavior between consenting adults, behind closed doors, is at all newsworthy.

That was the dilemma considered by Indian journalists Jaya Shroff and Mansi Tiwari when they were working on their master's degrees in journalism in the United States. At this writing, Shroff was a senior correspondent with the *Hindustan Times* and Tiwari was a senior correspondent for the *Economic Times*, both in New Delhi. What follows is an abbreviated version of a case study they presented in August 2006, in San Francisco, California, at that year's convention of the Association for Educators in Journalism and Mass Communication.[2]

"Hidden Cameras" in Bollywood: Indian Responses to the Journalistic Ethics of Undercover Reporting of Celebrities

By Jaya Shroff and Mansi Tiwari

India TV launched in 2004 as an edgy new alternative channel to India's airwaves. It garnered considerable attention in the spring of 2005 when it broadcast an exposé in which a popular Bollywood actor was depicted soliciting sex from a reporter posing as an aspiring actress. The report, aired on March 13, 2005, showed Shakti Kapoor, a popular "bad guy" in Hindi movies, meeting a young aspiring actress in her New Delhi hotel room. Kapoor was shown promising that his secretary would introduce the "actress" to movie producers and directors in exchange for granting him sexual favors. The report showed Kapoor making advances toward the "actress," but when she hesitated and did not respond to his overtures, he returned to his seat and did not persist. But he was shown saying that anyone who hoped to make it in Bollywood is "expected to sleep around."

After the broadcast, the actor held a press conference and said that the reporter, in her role as the actress, had been pursuing him for a few months prior to the incident depicted in the report, and that only after she threatened to commit suicide did he decide to meet with her. In news reports, Kapoor was quoted as saying, "I have been framed. The tapes have been doctored. I am totally shattered by this incident and don't know what to do. They haven't shown my face, and in segments where they have shown it's very hazy. They had everything planned out. Two and a half months ago, I went to meet her because she threatened that she would commit suicide if I didn't meet her."[3]

In response, India TV stated that it wanted to expose the casting couch phenomenon in the Indian film industry, in which aspiring actors are expected to have sex with established actors, directors, producers, etc. "Everybody knew that there is a casting couch in Bollywood, but the film industry refused to accept it. We merely showed them the mirror," said Rajat Sharma, one of the owners of the channel, in an interview by Rama Lakshmi published in the April 19, 2005 edition of *The Washington Post*.

Even as the debate was gaining momentum, and just four days after the episode, the channel broadcast another exposé, that one featuring a popular television actor, Aman Verma. The same journalist had apparently also met Verma, and he was shown on camera leading her to his bedroom. The footage showed that he stopped at the bathroom and she took the opportunity to open the front door of the apartment, where a camera crew was waiting. They barged inside and demanded comment from the actor.

However, India TV's exposés did not bring the acclaim that the channel might have sought. Instead, the reports led to considerable public and professional criticism. *Deccan Herald*, an English newspaper in India, reported that the channel was likely to drop its further casting couch exposés following adverse reaction and publicity its sting operations got from the media and public. While India TV's goal of increasing its ratings appeared to have been fulfilled, Sharma did not appear too pleased with the bad publicity his station got from the reports. "I really don't want to focus so much on Bollywood exposés. I think we've proven our point and cautioned wannabe stars about the casting couch," he was quoted as saying in the *Deccan Herald* on March 20, 2005.

One question that India TV's undercover exposés raised was whether it was a form of journalistic entrapment that employed an unjustified form of journalistic deception. It also raised the question in India of whether it is right for a television channel to broadcast what a public figure does in his or her private life, even if those activities might be considered immoral by some.

The case generated debate not only in the entertainment industry, which came under direct scrutiny when the news was broadcast, but also led to an uproar in the broader Indian media industry, with many journalists criticizing the actions of India TV. Lakshmi wrote in *The Washington Post*: "The Indian public expressed outrage, not at public figures implicated but at India TV, the upstart channel that implicated them. Stars from Bollywood, as the Indian film industry is known, have denounced the reporting. So have government regulators. Newspapers have called the channel's exposés 'a new low in journalism' and 'televised entrapment,' accusing its employees of being 'peeping Toms.'"

One interesting aspect of this case is how it seems to bring into sharp focus the conflicting cultural norms of India's Western model of journalism and its Eastern attitudes toward privacy. That conflict between professional norms and cultural ideals is exacerbated by the fact that the TV news market in India is changing fast. Since private broadcasters were first allowed in India in 1991, the number of channels available on TV screens has gone from 1 to 129, and some media analysts see cutthroat competition leading the entire industry into developing some possibly bad habits.

But of much more significance is that India TV used deceptive practices to invade the privacy of a Bollywood star to reveal to the public something that was hardly a secret—that the casting couch is a part of the culture of Bollywood. Amrita Shah, a columnist with the *Indian Express*, wrote on December 26, 2005, that the exposé had come a decade or two too late to be considered news—"There is not much skepticism about the probability of there being a casting couch in Bollywood. 'A reality,' 'a cliché,' are the kind of words being used to describe the mythical couch."

India's watchdog organization for journalistic ethics, The Press Council of India (PCI), does not have a mandate to handle complaints about broadcasting and internet journalism, only newspapers. Still, PCI has laid down certain guidelines that journalists are expected to abide. For example, former PCI chairman R. S. Sarkaria wrote in 1995, in *A Guide to Journalistic Ethics*, that "Journalists should not tape-record anyone's conversation without that person's knowledge or consent, except where the recording is necessary to protect the journalist in legal action or for other compelling good reasons" (p. 22). The PCI also laid down three elements integral to investigative reporting: first, it has to be the work of the reporter and not of others; second, the subject should be of public importance for the reader to know; and, third, the private life of an individual, even of a public figure, is his or her own. Exposition or invasion of privacy or private life is not acceptable to the PCI unless there is clear evidence that the wrongdoings in question involve a misuse of a public office or adversely affects the public, Sarkaria wrote. In terms of undercover reports, the PCI's guidelines are quite clear, Sarkaria explained: "The investigative journalist should resist the temptation of quickies or quick gains conjured up from half-baked, incomplete, doubtful facts, not fully checked up and verified from authentic sources by the reporter himself" (p. 23).

Even assuming that there was no other means of reporting on the casting couch story, one important concern that arises is whether the use of hidden cameras was fair and within ethical bounds. Other media outlets in India decried the exposé as little more than a publicity stunt. Vir Sanghvi, editor of the *Hindustan Times*, argued in a March 2005 editorial that the channel did so to gain publicity: "I do know that it is among the least-watched Hindi news channels in the country and I am aware that Shakti Kapoor has suggested that the exposé emerges out of its desperation to find an audience: when news fails to attract viewers, why not try sleaze and sensationalism?"

Rajat Sharma, editor-in-chief of India TV, in a March 17, 2005, interview with Rediff news, denied the charges of doing it to gain viewership. But in the same interview, he argued that all TV news outlets use exposés to gain "Television Rating Points," or "TRPs." (The TRP system was launched as a panel system and it has now become the dominant ratings system in India.) "When people say we are doing it for TRPs, I'm certainly not apologetic," Sharma said in the interview. "If I don't work for the ratings of my channel, who will? Everyone does exposé for TRPs. Everything on television is for that."

Hindustan Times editor Sanghvi focused his criticism of India TV on the reporting tactics it used. "The objection that many journalists have to the Shakti Kapoor story is that it takes methods (hidden cameras, stings, etc.) that most of us would use reluctantly and only when there was no other way of exposing corruption, and applies them to areas that are not in the public domain, solely as a means of generating sensational footage and creating a scandal. In the process, it demeans the very basis of sting journalism and transforms it into a Peeping Tom approach to cheap thrills" (Sanghvi, 2005).

Bahwana Somaaya, editor of the *Indian Express*'s film magazine *Screen*, in a March 16, 2005, column, also condemned the deception by India TV's journalists. The actor was constantly contacted by the reporter under disguise, Somaaya wrote, and that changed the whole situation: "It is not as if the camera crew followed Shakti Kapoor on one of his pursuits. If that were the case, perhaps, the story would justify being categorized as a 'scoop.' But to use an undercover journalist posing as a film aspirant is messing up with the ethics of investigative reporting. What the channel describes as 'breaking news' is more salacious than investigative."

In the end, the arguments against India TV's tactics are much stronger than arguments in favor. Although there might be some public interest in revealing the casting couch, the public already had an idea that such a phenomenon existed; the activity involved consensual sex between adults, or, at worst, a form of sexual harassment; and India TV did not attempt other, more accepted journalistic tactics before resorting to deception and invasion of privacy.

But journalistic ethical norms are by no means binding. Unlike other professionals, whose ethical obligations often are more clearly defined, journalists have been left to work out their roles and determine their ethics themselves, such that the "rightness" or "wrongness" of a journalist's action often can be debated vigorously. But there are some ideals to which all journalists should aspire, and among them are the avoidance of deception and the respect of personal privacy.

There are times when deception can be justified. If the information obtained is of profound importance and all the other means of getting it have been tried and failed, then deception can be acceptable. Deception should never be used as a shortcut. It should never be used as the first option or the easy route but only when other, more ethically sound tactics fail. What India TV did was seen by many as a shortcut to gain publicity.

Still, condemning India TV completely may be shortsighted. The casting couch syndrome has been part of the Indian film industry for some time and is a serious problem. There is no question that the proverbial casting couch is a dirty fact that both the media and public have to come to terms with. Perhaps for the first time, the problem had been recorded on tape and made public, and the India TV exposé did result in considerable discussion of the problem. However, there are some alternate actions that the channel could have taken, such as finding cases in which a victim was ready to disclose her or his personal experiences, or cases in which people have actually reported instances of such abuse. Of course, actors and actresses might not agree to disclose such bitter realities in front of the public. Then again, there are tactics that would be more ethical than outright deception, such as partial disclosure—presenting a story without the victim himself or by using another voice or by simply relating the event and bringing about an awareness.

In the end, India TV may have had the public interest in mind, but its rush to use the sensational hidden camera to invade the seedy private lives of actors negates such good intentions.

In the conclusion of their essay, Shroff and Tiwari note that there is some moral justification for the deceptive practices India TV used to expose the casting-couch problem in India's entertainment industry. That is often the case with most controversies in journalism ethics; even the most widely reviled action may have a hint of silver lining to it. However, as the authors point out, the justifications for the entrapment are not as strong as the arguments against it.

Beyond illustrating the ethical dilemmas of deception, this case also demonstrates how much of a balancing act ethical journalism can be. In those nations that provide broad freedoms to journalists, arguments can be made in favor of nearly any tactic in the name of exposing truth to the public. When those tactics involve lying, however, the truth revealed is of dubious credibility, and can do more harm than good not only to the public, but also to the journalism profession itself.

QUESTIONS TO CONSIDER

1. Celebrity entertainers rely on publicity for their careers, but should the public, in turn, have any ethical claim to knowing about celebrities' private lives? Why or why not?

2. Under what circumstances do you believe it would be morally acceptable to use deceptive reporting practices to investigate and reveal aspects of the seedier side of the entertainment industry?

3. In this case, a reporter not only pretended to be somebody she was not, but also allegedly made false threats of committing suicide if the actor in question did not meet with her. When undercover reporting is undertaken, should there be limits on the extent of the lies a reporter should tell to get at the information being sought? What should some of those limits be, and why?

4. This case also illustrates the pressures, especially on television journalists, to present news that achieves higher ratings and, by extension, more advertising revenue. Recalling the economic justifications for journalism ethics, was India TV somehow vindicated by the higher ratings it achieved? Why or why not?

26

Avoid Deception
The Exploding Truck: If It Doesn't
Have Pictures, It's Not Good TV

Today, most consumers of television news are well acquainted with televised news magazines. For years, CBS's *60 Minutes* had the field largely to itself, and the show has been a huge success, both with viewers, who have consistently made the program among the top-rated shows, and with critics, who have praised its solid investigations and dedication to accuracy and journalistic integrity (despite the occasional scandal, as discussed in Chapter 22).

Then came cable and a proliferation of news shows like *Inside Edition* and *Hard Copy*, which are electronic versions of the supermarket tabloids—not the mostly fiction tabloids, such as the *Weekly World News* (with its stories of alien abductions and Elvis sightings), but the modern yellow journals, such as the *National Star* and the *National Enquirer*, with their emphasis on sex and violence and celebrity gossip. The response from the networks was roughly this: If (relatively) staid old *60 Minutes* worked—that is, drew enough viewers to draw enough advertisers to make a good profit—and if the television tabloids worked, then there must be room for more news magazines with lighter formats than *60 Minutes*. CBS added *Eye to Eye* and *48 Hours*; ABC had *20/20* and *Prime Time Live*. NBC's entry was called *Dateline: NBC*. It was broadcast for the first time on March 31, 1992. The aim was to produce a show to rival *20/20*, but for a younger audience.

For six months, the show went well. However, in November 1992, *Dateline* broadcast a segment on pickup-truck safety that cast a pall over the whole industry. Producers and executives involved with the segment were fired outright, and Michael Gartner, president of NBC News, resigned over it. In the furor that erupted after the broadcast, the events themselves tended to get lost. Here is what happened, based on interviews with Gartner and the segment's producer Robert B. Read, and on a report from an internal investigation at NBC following the uproar over the broadcast.

In the late 1980s and early 1990s, more than a hundred people had sued General Motors, alleging that GM pickup trucks built between 1973 and 1987 had a serious design flaw that made them prone to burst into flames when they were hit from the side in an accident. The allegations centered on the truck's two gas tanks, which were mounted behind the cab outside the truck's frame like saddlebags, making them vulnerable to rupture.

The *Dateline* story was a fifteen-minute segment on the case against GM, based on interviews and industry documents that appeared to indicate that GM had continued to build the trucks with the safety flaw even though the company was aware of the dangers the sidesaddle fuel tanks posed.

The show interviewed a wide range of people in preparing the segment: families involved in lawsuits against the giant automaker, auto safety experts—some neutral and others who regularly side with plaintiffs in lawsuits against the industry—as well as current and former GM employees. A GM senior executive, Robert Sinke, the company's director of engineering analysis, was allowed to make the company's defense.

However, then came the last fifty-five seconds. In that final minute, NBC ran a tape of what it called two "unscientific crash demonstrations" of the trucks' susceptibility to fire in the event of a side impact. On the tape, which was made at NBC's request, an unoccupied car was sent hurtling into the side of an unoccupied GM pickup truck. In one collision, nothing happened. Then a second car was sent into the side of a second pickup. In that second crash, both car and truck erupted into a spectacular ball of fire. The explosion is repeated in slow motion and then again from a camera mounted inside the car, approximating the view from the driver's seat.

GM complained to NBC that the piece was not fair, and it asked for NBC's evidence, including access to the trucks. NBC refused, and GM called a news conference to announce that it was suing the network for the *Dateline* segment, charging, among other things, that *Dateline* had committed one of the most serious sins in journalism: it had made up part of its story. A senior GM executive decried NBC for "cheap, dishonest sensationalism."

There were several problems with the *Dateline* setup of the crash, but the most serious was that devices—variously called "igniters" or "sparking devices" or even (by GM) "rocket engines"—were hidden on the truck body.

Read, the producer of the segment, wanted footage to illustrate the fundamental contention of the show: the danger of fire from a side-impact collision. The *Dateline* segment featured family members of people who burned to death in two different side-impact collisions, and said there had been more than three hundred other fatal pickup-truck fires over the many years the popular truck was in production.

To ensure that a ruptured gas tank would have a spark to ignite the spilling fuel, the company that ran the crash demonstration for NBC secreted sparkers, or igniters, under the fuel tank on the side designated to be hit in the demonstration crash. On the first crash shown in the segment, the fuel tank did not rupture and there was no fire. But on the second, the tank did rupture and the gasoline burst into flames.

Read later explained to a skeptical audience at the Poynter Institute for Media Studies in St. Petersburg, Florida, that he had initially intended to include in the televised story information about the presence of the igniters as well as the fact that the spark, although a common occurrence in real accidents, had been set up for the taped demonstration. However, Read said, a close examination of the tape of the fire showed that the fire had been started, not by the igniters hidden in the truck, but by the headlight of the crash car as it plowed into the side of the truck. Thus, he explained, the fire started without the igniters at all. He said that he thought it would be confusing to the audience to include the information that there had been hidden spark generators but that those igniters had not started the fire after all. So the piece ran without any mention of the igniters. It is important to note that the NBC report on the whole incident, which is otherwise quite critical of Read, states clearly, "There is no evidence that anyone at 'Dateline,' including Read, conceived of the idea to use igniters as a means of rigging the test results. They did not, in our view, deliberately set out to falsify the 'test.'"

Nevertheless, what the report did accuse Read of was fuzzing up the distinction between a test and a demonstration. The difference is crucial. As the lawyers who prepared the internal report for NBC put it, the journalists doing the *Dateline* segment set up the fifty-five-second controversial scene because they wanted "to tape a crash fire—and that this was as important to the decision to do the test as was the desire to determine whether the trucks were unsafe."

Although the piece was titled, "Waiting to Explode?"—with the question mark—the thrust of the piece was not equivocal at all. The segment clearly depicted the trucks as unsafe, and it presented evidence that appeared to indicate that all three major manufacturers—GM, Ford, and Chrysler—knew that fuel tanks located outside the truck frame next to the sheet-metal skin were more vulnerable in a side-impact crash than were tanks located inside the heavy steel frame. The *Dateline* segment even included GM documents indicating that increased safety was one of the arguments made for moving the tanks inside the frame.

So the show was not really asking the question: Are these trucks dangerous? The show was saying, in effect, "Warning! These trucks are dangerous." So Read, the show's producer, set up the two crashes to illustrate that danger, not to test whether the danger was there. The point, he said, was to illustrate a danger that other evidence had proved to be there. Therefore, he argued, the igniters were not a serious intrusion.

What was gained by the use of that last fifty-five-second clip of the unscientific crash demonstration? Wonderful tape, a strong visual record of what the show was trying to show. And that, of course, goes to the heart of what television does better than any of its rival media: showing what things look like. By nearly all measures, the fundamental strength of print and online journalism is their ability to deal with complexity and with nuance, to provide intellectual and historical context and, especially with the better online news sites, references to various sources of additional information. And the fundamental strength of television (and, by extension, online video) is its ability to provide the visual dimension of a story.

In a later interview, Read stressed "something that print reporters sometimes do not understand, and that is the need for strong visuals, especially on a news magazine, but even on the nightly news as well."

Interestingly, Gartner, a former top editor at the *Louisville Courier-Journal* and the *Des Moines Register*, two of the nation's most highly respected papers, disagreed and argued that television was sometimes at its best when it ignored pictures altogether. "There are some things you can't tell with pictures, but that doesn't mean you can't do them on television," Gartner said in an interview. By way of example, he cited a conversation he had with John Chancellor, the longtime NBC correspondent and commentator, toward the end of Chancellor's career. Gartner recalled that he had expressed amazement to his old friend Chancellor about how much information Chancellor could pack into a ninety-second commentary. Chancellor reminded Gartner that the visual dimension of the spot was "just my face," no other pictures at all. Television is a visual medium, Gartner and Chancellor agreed, "but that doesn't mean you can't tell a story without pictures," Gartner said. "There is news that doesn't have pictures."

If it may fairly be said that *Dateline* reached too hard for a visual element for the GM truck story, what was lost by doing so? Several things. Several NBC employees were fired over the incident, and Gartner resigned in an effort to quell the firestorm of criticism. (Gartner said in an interview that he had long planned to leave NBC later in 1992 and had merely accelerated his departure by a number of months. He has since held a number of journalism and public-service posts, including several years in the 1990s as editor of *The Daily Tribune* in Ames, Iowa, and, in 2005, he was president of the Iowa Board of Regents, which provides oversight for public universities in that state.)

Far more important, NBC lost the story it was trying to present to the public. Once the bogus details of the unscientific demonstration—essentially an event staged for its visual appeal—became public, the attention shifted immediately to the serious challenge to the network's integrity and away from the contention of *Dateline* that GM had built dangerous trucks for more than a decade and did not do anything about it. Except for the last fifty-five seconds, the program was legitimate journalism, which took on a problem that needed addressing. In early April, the federal government asked GM to recall voluntarily the million-plus trucks at issue in the *Dateline* segment. The revelations about the *Dateline* show gave the whole journalism profession a major black eye. When all is said and done, the most important dimension to journalism is its integrity, and that integrity is based primarily on honesty. Anything that damages the trust between the journalists and their audiences lessens the chances that the citizens will be able to make the rational decisions necessary to manage their own affairs or the affairs of their communities.

Gartner saw another major problem with the segment; he said that the show's staff had become too enthusiastic about making their point because they had gotten too close to a major source for the piece—in this case, the Institute for Safety Analysis, which regularly helps plaintiffs in suits against the auto industry. Gartner was quick to add, however, that he was not trying to say that reporters should never take information and ideas from people or institutions with their own agendas to advance. On the contrary, journalists do that all the time, and legitimately so. Routinely, Gartner said, "They are using you and you are using them. That's OK." Nevertheless, journalists need to keep their sense of balance. The significance of using igniters in the crash sequence is open to debate, but the appearance of deception in journalism will always be a problem.

QUESTIONS TO CONSIDER

1. *Dateline* labeled the crash tests "unscientific crash demonstrations." Should that have let *Dateline* off the hook? (After all, newspapers and magazines run "photo-illustrations" with feature stories all the time.) Was there any way *Dateline* could have used the igniters in the crash demonstrations without being accused of deception?

2. If the igniters were clearly shown not to be the cause of the fire in the crash demonstrations, why was their presence relevant to the story?

3. Were there any other ways to illustrate the story that would have been just as good without getting into the crash-demonstration issue at all?

4. NBC, which is owned by General Electric, quickly backed away from the *Dateline* story when GM complained and had an apology to GM read on the program. Was NBC being responsible in doing this, or was it a case of one big corporation inappropriately caving in to the demands of another big corporation (and advertiser)?

5. When you are handling a consumer safety issue and you are trying to cover the issue fairly, what problems with sources do you need to anticipate and handle?

27

Avoid Deception
Is It Okay to Use Deception to Reveal Shady World Politics?

In Chapter 25, we considered a case in which journalists went undercover to catch a Bollywood actor asking a young reporter, posing as an aspiring actress, for sexual favors in exchange for helping her career. In this chapter, we consider another instance of a journalist going undercover to get the information he wanted, but the goal was to reveal a sinister aspect of world politics, not the seedy side of the Indian movie industry.

In its July 2007 issue, *Harper's Magazine* published an article by Ken Silverstein titled "Their Men in Washington," in which he wrote about high-priced lobbying firms in Washington, D.C., that try to curry favor among U.S. politicians for corrupt and violent regimes around the world. The piece was insightful and (typical of Silverstein's work) very well written, but it had one substantial black mark: To get the story, Silverstein pretended to be somebody he was not.

Ken Silverstein is a veteran journalist with a penchant for taking on some of the most powerful entities in U.S. and world politics, and has investigated topics such as alleged collaborations between the U.S. Central Intelligence Agency and the governments of dangerous despots in Libya and Sudan, corruption in the powerful American oil industry, and, for many years, corruption in and around Washington, D.C. Controversial and outspoken, Silverstein's work often is the target of considerable criticism, although some of his reports have led to investigations into corporate and congressional corruption. One topic he takes on with some regularity is the unseemly connections between the U.S. government and the dangerous rogue nations of the world.

For his exposé in the July 2007 issue of *Harper's*, Silverstein set out to demonstrate the process by which a notoriously brutal and repressive foreign government can hire a Washington lobbying firm to improve its image and curry favor among high-ranking U.S. lawmakers and officials. Posing as a consultant ("Kenneth Case") for a fictitious London-based investment firm ("The Maldon Group") with interests in working with a notoriously corrupt and repressive government (that of Turkmenistan under President Kurbanguly Berdymukhamedov), Silverstein began contacting Washington-based lobbying groups that would be willing to, he explained in the article, "convey to American policymakers and journalists just how heady were the reforms being plotted by the Berdy-mukhamedov government." To complete the ruse, Silverstein printed up business cards for the Maldon Group, purchased a cellular telephone account with a London phone number, and created a simple Web site listing contact information for the fictional firm along with a corresponding (and functioning) e-mail account.

Turkmenistan is one of the former states of the Soviet Union, a nation of about five million people located on the eastern banks of the Caspian Sea in Central Asia and on the northern border of Iran. The nation is almost four-fifths desert, but through irrigation has become one of the world's major producers of cotton. It has huge natural gas reserves as well, much of which it exports to Russia and other former Soviet states. Although a constitutional republic, Turkmenistan has been run as a dictatorship, and is considered among the worst nations in the world in terms of allowing free speech, personal freedoms, political dissent, and freedom of the press. Still, it does have official relations with the West, and the U.S. government provided Turkmenistan with $7.65 million in aid in fiscal year 2006, mostly to support programs that promote democracy and socioeconomic reforms, according to the U.S. Department of State. Silverstein's description of Turkmenistan was a damning account of political repression and economic corruption, and he argued that the only nation he could think of with a worse overall reputation in the free world was North Korea.

To begin his investigations, Silverstein, in the guise of Kenneth Case, made contact with APCO Associates, a Washington-based lobbying firm that Silverstein said had provided Capitol Hill advocacy for controversial governments in the past in such nations as Nigeria and Azerbaijan. His article recounts e-mail exchanges, boardroom presentations in APCO's downtown offices, discussions of what APCO's services would cost (Silverstein estimated the quote at $600,000 for one year), talks about which tactics would be used (and how), and discussions of how to deal with public-disclosure laws and information requests from the press. He established similar dialogues with another well-connected lobbying firm, Cassidy & Associates, which offered to help the Maldon Group at an annual price tag of between $1.2 million and $1.5 million, after associates of the firm bragged to Silverstein about their efforts at somewhat improving the reputation of Teodoro Obiang Nguema Mbasogo, the president of Equatorial Guinea and considered one of the world's most corrupt and oppressive dictators.

After his meetings with both APCO and Cassidy, Silverstein was contacted by both firms, and he told them that The Maldon Group regretted that it would not be able to use either's services. Silverstein then set to writing his piece, and a few months later, it was published. The end result provided great detail about both firms' sales pitches, their bragging about all of the heavy hitters in their employ (such as former members of the U.S. Congress and of foreign governments), the ease with which they could keep confidential any information about The Maldon Group (and its supposed goals in Turkmenistan), and their success in providing effective public relations for controversial governments and global corporations. Although the tone of Silverstein's report was less than flattering toward the firms, they were portrayed as operating legally and effectively for their clients, and although lobbying firms in general have poor reputations among the general public, within the lobbying industry both firms are highly respected.

In a response to Silverstein's article, a representative of APCO, B. Jay Cooper, did not refute the facts of the report, but did challenge Silverstein's own ethics, and the ethics of *Harper's Magazine* editors, for pulling such a stunt of journalistic deception. In a letter published in the September 2007 issue of the magazine, Cooper noted that although the article, "ostensibly written to expose the sleazy side of Washington lobbying, displays instead a stunning lack of ethics in the media. Silverstein lied to get an appointment with APCO Worldwide, printed fake business cards, created a phony website, and made up a story about whom he represented. . . . From APCO he received a polite reception and a straightforward presentation of what we could do for his 'client.'" Cooper also stated that his firm had checked with U.S. officials "for their reaction to our being approached by people from Turkmenistan. They were, in fact, pleasantly surprised that someone was making such overtures and saw it as a positive sign for the new leadership in the country." Cooper went on to say that his firm has been approached by other "questionable regimes" in the past, and had represented them "after doing some due diligence."

In his rejoinder to Cooper's critical letter, Silverstein was unapologetic, suggesting that what he had done was not nearly as unethical as public-relations firms that represent "rulers with horrible records on human rights and corruption." Wrote Silverstein: "I tricked APCO and Cassidy & Associates, which I openly disclosed to readers in the report, in order to demonstrate just how easy it is for lobbyists to manipulate political and public opinion. The lobbyists, on the other hand, offered to go to work on behalf of one of the world's most heinous regimes in exchange for the lavish fees they proposed to charge.... I'm absolutely certain who the ethically compromised party is in this affair—and based on the overwhelmingly positive response the story has received, the public is too."

This case study certainly raises shades of the adage two wrongs do not a right make, as the core questions seem to revolve around whether a journalist who lies is more ethical than a public-relations firm engaged in seemingly sleazy honesty. After all, Silverstein did not reveal any illegal activity in his report, nor any official dishonesty. He simply revealed that at least two of the largest lobbying firms in Washington are perfectly willing, perhaps even eager, to take on clients who are unpopular and probably (or even demonstrably) corrupt. Both Cooper of APCO and Kathy Cripps of the Council of Public Relations Firms (which lists APCO as one of its members) pointed out that Silverstein could have obtained information about how and why such firms take on questionable clients without resorting to deception.

The case also challenges the idea that journalism is ethically superior to public relations. Assuming that both APCO and Cassidy & Associates did "do due diligence," there is some truth to their claims that even "questionable regimes" deserve to have their opinions heard in the global arena of public discourse. In the courts, for example, notorious criminals still have legal counsel assigned to them to ensure a fair trial—should the situation be any different in the court of public opinion? If the free nations of the world truly do embrace free and open discourse as an inherent human right, then shouldn't they also consider the opinions of those who are seen as living on the fringes of the global society?

It's hard to say if Silverstein would have been able to get the information he was after if he had been honest and forthcoming about who he was and what he was looking for. He was, as he stated, honest and forthcoming about the ruse to the readers of *Harper's Magazine*. In the complicated profession of investigative journalism, many times the question of *should* boils down to who the journalists are most accountable to—the powerful people they write about, or the general public they write for.

QUESTIONS TO CONSIDER

1. When is lying about one's identity acceptable in either journalism or public relations? Are the truths discovered through such charades in any way tarnished by the fact that they were revealed only by using lies?

2. Silverstein's goal was to reveal how eager some public-relations firms would be to take on clients who are seen as some of the most corrupt and oppressive dictators in the world. What other, more ethically acceptable methods could he have used to achieve the same goal? How could he have approached the story differently and still gotten the information he obtained?

3. *Harper's* published two letters that were highly critical of Silverstein's article, and allowed Silverstein to comment on those letters using about the same amount of space. When, in your opinion, should publications allow authors to respond to letters that are critical of their work? Who should get the last word—the sources in news stories, or the reporters who wrote the stories? Why?

4. Critics of Silverstein's article said his actions had a negative impact on attitudes toward the press in general. Do you agree, and why or why not? To what extent do you think any one journalist's actions can cause harm to journalists in other locations?

28 ▪ ▪ ▪

Correction and Clarification
The Brilliant Student with the Dark Past: How Much Is Relevant in Follow-up Reports?

The first week of April 1995 was an emotional roller coaster for Gina Grant, then a nineteen-year-old honor student and star athlete at the prestigious Cambridge Rindge and Latin High School just outside Boston.

On Sunday, April 2, the *Boston Globe*'s Sunday magazine ran a story about children who overcome difficulty to lead successful childhoods. Part of that story focused on Grant, who was described as an orphan who had triumphed over adversity. She was co-captain of the tennis team. She tutored poor children in biology. She was an honor student with an IQ of 150. And she had won a most coveted high school academic prize—an offer of early admission to Harvard.

After the uplifting story was published, it all began to fall apart for Grant. A package of old newspaper clips, mailed anonymously, had arrived at Harvard, her high school, and at Boston's newspapers. The stories, by then nearly five years old, were news accounts from Lexington, South Carolina, of how Grant, then fourteen, had bludgeoned her mother to death with a candlestick and then, with the help of her boyfriend, had tried to make the death look like a suicide by slitting her mother's throat with a kitchen knife and then wrapping the dead woman's fingers around the handle. The defense called the killing self-defense against an alcoholic and abusive mother, a woman who had blamed the girl for her father's death from cancer three years before, who had fought with her daughter the night of her death, and who was drunk that night (her blood-alcohol level was 0.30 percent, three times the limit used to determine drunken driving in many U.S. states). The prosecution called it a vicious murder, spoke of the thirteen blows with the lead crystal candlestick, and the clumsy attempt at a cover-up. Grant pleaded no contest to manslaughter charges and spent six months in a juvenile detention center before being released into the custody of an aunt and uncle living in Cambridge, Massachusetts.

The original *Globe* profile included none of the information about the murder. All it mentioned regarding Grant's troubled past was that she had had a falling out with the aunt and uncle and had been on her own in Cambridge since the age of sixteen, living on a trust fund she had inherited at her mother's death. The story did not say how Grant's mother had died, instead quoting Grant as saying it was "too painful" to talk about. For her part, the writer—Maria Karagianis, a freelancer regarded highly by the *Globe*—did not press Grant on the issue of her mother's death because she was writing a child-overcomes-adversity story, not, as she told reporters, a story about "the Mafia or political corruption."

Walter V. Robinson, then the assistant managing editor of the *Globe*, said Karagianis, a former staff writer for the paper, "felt taken in" by Grant, but, given the nature of the story, she had seen "no need to do a clip check" on Grant's background.

When Harvard withdrew its offer of admission from Grant, it gave few details, saying only that it sometimes did so if it turned out that an application contained false information. However, Harvard's action, along with the old news clippings, transformed the story from one of a young woman making good to a rehashing of her troubled past. *The Globe* faced a situation in which it needed to follow up on a feel-good feature with a recounting of horrifying old news.

The newspaper's hand was certainly forced by other news media. Over the next two days, Grant's story had made the national wires, the front page of major newspapers, ABC's *Nightline* program, and more. As Harvard did not go into detail explaining its action, reporters were left to try to figure out what had happened. Speculation centered on Grant's having answered "no" to a question about whether she had been on probation.

As part of the terms of her release from the juvenile facility, Grant had been on probation until she reached the age of eighteen. Nevertheless, the question was worded ambiguously and could be read as asking only if the applicant had been in any academic difficulties, including academic probation. A Boston-area lawyer, Margaret Burnham, whom Grant's Massachusetts friends had found to represent the student, told reporters that Grant should not have had to disclose anything that had happened while she was a juvenile. Grant's trial lawyer from South Carolina, Jack Swerling, agreed, telling the *New York Times*, "This girl has paid her debt.

That chapter in her life should have been closed and she should have been able to start over." After many news outlets had republished details of her crime, Grant issued a statement though her Boston attorney saying that she was "deeply disappointed" that Harvard had withdrawn its offer of admission, saying she was worried that her collegiate career had been jeopardized, and noting that "the promise of a juvenile justice system" was a fresh start. "I deal with this tragedy every day on a personal level," she said in the statement. "It serves no good purpose for anyone else to dredge up the pain of my childhood."

That last issue, whether Grant should have had to disclose to Harvard (and, separately, to *The Globe*) anything that happened while she was a juvenile, is but one part of the ethical dilemma for journalists.

Similarly, Judge Marc Westbrook of Lexington County, South Carolina, who had ordered her to be released to relatives in Massachusetts, told reporters that it had been in Grant's best interests to release her. "There was nothing else in her record that indicated any other problem," Westbrook said. "She was on the right track, by what society deems to be the right track. What's happened since then bears that out. She was certainly not a menace to anybody."

The notion of allowing juveniles "a fresh start" lies at the heart of most of the many judicial restrictions on what can be reported out of the juvenile justice system. Most judicial records are sealed and most proceedings are closed to the public, which means that the names of many juvenile defendants are never made public. The reason to withhold the names of juveniles is to avoid tagging them with their offenses, labels that could follow them around for the rest of their lives.

However, John Allard, the reporter for the *State* in Columbia, South Carolina, who covered the Grant trial, cautioned against being overly concerned with protecting the identity of juveniles. In the great majority of cases, he said, "Who in ten years or twenty years is going to remember" the name of this or that defendant? His paper identified Grant at the time even though she was still a juvenile. And Allard said the Grant case was one of the few that would not be forgotten. "Her story will probably follow her all the rest of her life," he said. "And maybe that's as it should be." For Grant's name to get into Allard's newspaper, it had to pass two gatekeepers, the local sheriff's office and then Allard and his editors at the paper. The sheriff "was so outraged by the brutality of the crime that he said it was his duty to release her name," Allard said. The second hurdle was the paper's own staff. "We handle it on a case-by-case basis," Allard said. A juvenile is more likely to be identified in the paper "if it is a very serious crime, especially one involving violence, and it generates a lot of community interest and concern." The Grant case certainly qualified on those grounds.

However, it is not just reader interest that justifies putting a story or a name in the paper, especially if the story may cause some harm. And the widespread publicity surrounding the Gina Grant case, arguably even in this book, could well cause her harm. Her name still pops up in news stories, often stories regarding colleges that rescind admission offers after allegations of wrongdoing are leveled against the applicant—for example, *The Globe* mentioned Grant in a 2003 article about Harvard withdrawing an admission offer from a New Jersey high schooler accused of plagiarizing in articles she wrote for her local newspaper. Especially in the Internet age, it is difficult for anybody to escape their past, even if the legal system provides some protections for children who commit serious crimes but could still become law-abiding adults.

In the argument of the authorities in Lexington, South Carolina, the apparent viciousness and brutality of the slaying justified the release of Grant's name. That is, the crime was so unchildlike that the normal extra protection afforded children was forfeited in that case. However, that issue, however legitimate it is, is primarily a question for law enforcement, or perhaps for society at large. Publishing a defendant's name in the news media tends to add to the punishment; withholding it would tend to support rehabilitation. Such ambivalence is behind the mixed response to such arguments as Judge Westbrook's, who said it had been in Grant's best interests to release her to relatives in Massachusetts. Grant's supporters agreed and expressed dismay at all the coverage the case received. Her critics asked, in effect, what about the mother whom she beat to death and then stabbed? (It should also be noted that releasing Grant to Massachusetts was also, in part at least, in Judge Westbrook's best interests as well. Grant had strong support in the community, and South Carolina was under a federal court order to reduce the number of juveniles in detention in its state facilities, Allard said.)

The first question for journalists is: Could the story of Grant's crime have been told, or told as effectively, without using the defendant's name? The answer is, in truth, no. Names, faces, and the living details of a case are what make it real and significant and memorable to readers. "To get a full picture of the story," you have to have a name to go with the events, Allard said. "Without a name, there is a distance" between the subject and the reader. "If there is a name, and maybe a picture, then you, as a reader, have to confront the issues the story raises." Allard sees a particular significance in his paper's decision to identify Gina Grant at the time of the slaying. It was copies of his stories, after all, that were sent to the schools and the newspapers in Boston, bringing the whole story to light. Nevertheless, even if foresight were as good as hindsight, he would still identify her. "If I had to do it over again, I'd do exactly what we did," he said. "I have no qualms about what we did."

The second question for journalists is what to do with such information years later, when that person is in the news for something very different. Should a profile of a professional athlete mention his discipline in college for academic misconduct? Should a feature story on a college professor's research dredge up decades-old criminal charges of drunken driving? What should a newspaper do if, after publishing a photo of that year's valedictorian, it receives printouts of that girl's Facebook pages in which she has published pictures of her getting drunk with friends? Deciding which personal details are germane to a profile is more than just a matter of telling a good tale—the moral dimensions of such choices are serious, as the repercussions could be quite harmful.

The third question is perhaps the most difficult: What should journalists do if damaging details are revealed only after a profile is published? Journalists certainly have a moral obligation to correct errors to set the record straight, but what if the original story contained no errors, only omitted details that were not germane to the story? For *The Boston Globe*, the fallout from what it originally published as a story of an impressive young woman became a series of articles and opinion pieces about that woman's inability to escape her dark past. Over the following days, weeks, and months, *The Globe* published dozens of articles about Grant: articles about her teenage crime, about her apparent rehabilitation into a model citizen, about her reaction to the renewed publicity and the trouble it caused her, and about her (successful) efforts to get into nearby Tufts University (from where she later graduated). Chances are, had *The Globe* never published the original story of Gina Grant the impressive young orphan, it would not have had to deal with the difficulty of the following efforts in setting the record straight. This case stands as a reminder that sometimes the choices journalists make today will have unforeseen repercussions tomorrow, and that correcting the record may be much more complicated and time-consuming than running a small note on page two.

QUESTIONS TO CONSIDER

1. Did it serve a legitimate journalistic interest to identify Gina Grant in news articles at the time she killed her mother? Would it serve a legitimate interest to identify all juveniles accused of crimes? If a news media outlet adopts a case-by-case policy on identifying juvenile suspects, what problems could arise from that?

2. Did it serve a legitimate journalistic interest to identify Grant and publicize her crime nearly five years later? Was the reporter who wrote the glowing profile of children who had overcome adversity remiss in not investigating Grant's background more thoroughly?

3. Do you see any violations of Grant's privacy in any of the coverage? Did she weaken her right to privacy through her criminal actions in 1990, or in agreeing to be interviewed in 1995? If a reporter were to resurrect this whole case twenty-five years from now, publicly linking Grant to her crime again, would her right to privacy be violated then?

4. Assume you were the reporter who interviewed Grant to profile her, and you found out about Grant's criminal past—either because Grant told you about it or because you did a background check. Would you include her in your article about children who had overcome hardships? Would you write about her at all?

29 ■ ■ ■

Correction and Clarification
Fact-Checking Candidates' Claims on the Busy Campaign Trail

Although fact-checking is supposed to be a normal part of a journalists' job, the sad truth is that verification is not always possible when news is breaking and competition is keen. That can be especially true when covering political campaigns, in which journalists are bombarded many times daily with statements, comments, press releases, and behind-the-scenes sniping from a rival campaign. Sometimes, reporters cut corners and simply report what each candidate says, and worry about checking the veracity of those claims only after somebody else challenges those statements.

An example of that phenomenon occurred in the early spring of 2008, during New York Senator Hillary Clinton's campaign to be the Democratic nominee for U.S. president. Starting as early as December 2007, Clinton had told and retold a tale about a harrowing diplomatic trip she had made to Bosnia in 1996, and her recollection of ducking sniper fire was reported several times in news reports. However, in March 2008, Clinton's story of landing under sniper fire turned out to be untrue, but it wasn't the campaign journalists who uncovered the falsehood, nor was it the journalists who accompanied Clinton on the Bosnia trip more than a decade earlier. Rather, the disparity between what happened at the airport and Clinton's account of the incident was raised by a comedian who had been on the 1996 trip to entertain the troops, and it still took the major news media more than a week to eventually correct the record.

Hillary Rodham Clinton was, at the time, one of the most recognized figures in U.S. politics. Clinton entered the national and global political scene in the early 1990s when she was the politically active First Lady to former President Bill Clinton. After her husband left office, Clinton started her own career as an elected official, successfully running for a U.S. Senate seat in New York State in 2000 and easily winning reelection in 2006. In January 2007, she announced her intentions to run for president. In a large field of contenders for the Democratic nomination, she was the clear front-runner, largely running on her record of experience. By spring 2008, the Democratic field had been narrowed to Clinton and Senator Barack Obama of Illinois, a relative newcomer to Washington. Clinton stressed her foreign policy experience as the candidate who was "ready on Day One" to lead the country in dangerous times.

For months, Clinton relayed an anecdote about a trip she made in 1996 to Tuzla, Bosnia, which was still experiencing internal violence at the time. In a March 17, 2008, speech at George Washington University, Clinton repeated the tale she had been telling for months: "I remember landing under sniper fire," she said, according to a transcript by *Congressional Quarterly* and recorded on tape. "There was supposed to be some kind of a greeting ceremony at the airport, but instead we just ran with our heads down to get into the vehicles to get to our base."

That day in March was the first time Clinton was asked by journalists to validate her anecdote. That's because one week earlier, *Washington Post* political writer Mary Ann Akers wrote in her online political gossip column "The Sleuth" that one of Clinton's companions on the 1996 trip, the comedian Sinbad, disputed her account. "I never felt that I was in a dangerous position," Sinbad said in Akers' column. "I never felt being in a sense of peril, or 'Oh, God, I hope I'm going to be OK when I get out of this helicopter or when I get out of his tank.'"

For the first time in months of reporting on Clinton's "sniper fire" anecdote, journalists questioned the accuracy of Clinton's account. After her March 17 speech, a reporter finally asked her about the disparity between her account and that of the comedian. At first, she dismissed Sinbad's version of events, saying "He's a comedian. There was no greeting ceremony, and we basically were told to run to our cars. Now, that is what happened." That evening, CNN reported on the disagreement between Sinbad and Clinton and played a clip of Clinton's defense of her anecdote. A few days later, CBS posted on its Web site footage from the 1996 trip by Clinton that indicated there had been no sniper fire.

It took nearly a week for the rest of the news media to actively correct Clinton's erroneous claims. It began in the form of a short report on *CBS News* by reporter Sharyl Atkisson, which showed video footage of Clinton's 1996 trip to Tuzla in which she and her daughter Chelsea were seen smiling and shaking hands with troops as they got off the plane—a very different and much more peaceful scene from the one Clinton described in her speeches. In the 1996 footage, Atkisson herself was shown talking to Clinton, and the video showed a number of other journalists on the same plane with Clinton and her daughter (another prominent U.S. journalist, *NBC News'* Andrea Mitchell, also had accompanied Clinton to Tuzla. Mitchell issued her own recollection of the trip, with no sniper fire, about a week after the March 17 speech). Atkisson—one of the most respected and accomplished investigative reporters for *CBS News*—concluded the segment with this: "Hundreds of thousands have viewed the video online in just the past few days, a reminder that, in politics, memories should always match the videotape."

For days after that, Clinton's fictional tale of "sniper fire" dominated political news reports and talk-show banter, and Clinton's credibility suffered a serious blow in public-opinion polls. Nevertheless, the fact that it took a comedian's recollection to trigger the skepticism of professional journalists did little to improve the public's attitudes toward the competency of mainstream news media.

For months, one of the most high-profile politicians in the United States, running for the most powerful elected office in the nation, had told and retold a lie to countless thousands of people and to the reporters assigned to cover the campaign. What's more, it was a lie about a trip that had been covered by the national news media and by journalists who were still on the job in 2008. Yet it was a comic's comments to a political gossip column that first challenged the candidate's claim, and it still took more than a week for the major news networks to dig back into their archives to find out what really happened. And when they did uncover the archival video that proved Clinton had been lying, the news programs didn't acknowledge their own negligence in not verifying information before reporting it—but instead framed their "corrections" as stories of "gotcha" journalism.

In the blogosphere, meanwhile, a smoldering sentiment was waved back into flames—"the mainstream media" was again caught sleeping on the job. Consider this March 29, 2008, post to the Web site of the *St. Petersburg Times* newspaper in Florida: "The thing that I took from this was that Andrea Mitchell and the others knew [Clinton] was not telling the truth and refused to say anything. They were too afraid to become 'part of the story' and then be subject ... to the same scrutiny that others are. . . . When the media are dependent on the candidates for their livelihood, they are too hesitant [to] voice an opinion."

Actually, it is more reasonable to assume that Mitchell, Atkisson, and others didn't think at all about the veracity of Clinton's campaign claims until after somebody else (in this case, Sinbad) made the point. Journalists are human beings, not computers, and all of us have very limited capacities to remember details of every experience. However, beyond the limitations of being human, those journalists also face the limitations of working in the daily news business, which puts great professional pressures for journalists to focus not on what happened before, but rather on what is happening now. Only on truly big stories—major scandals, huge disasters, deep investigations—are a newsroom's time and treasure expended on verifying the claims of news sources against the historical record. For the routine, day-to-day stuff, a lot of reliance is placed on the marketplace of ideas to call attention to published errors.

Obviously, much of the blame for the "sniper fire" errors rests with Clinton herself and her campaign staff—in what can only be described as an abysmal failure of public relations, her staff allowed the candidate to publicly repeat an anecdote without making sure the claim was true, setting her up for embarrassment and a serious blow to her credibility that lay at the core of her campaign. Truthfulness is a virtue of any form of public communication, whether it is political campaigning or reporting the news. That is why journalists who cover politicians should be especially concerned about the truthfulness of claims made by public officials, and should expend much more time and energy verifying such claims. That is also why journalists who allow false claims to enter into news reports should also share the blame for allowing those falsehoods to be reported in the first place.

Clinton's story of landing under sniper fire could just be chalked up to nothing more than another politician exaggerating and journalists' willingness to let it pass. It may be understandable that the story raised no red flags among journalists who are very accustomed to the braggadocio and hypocrisy that plague politics. And considering all of the much more serious issues of the presidential campaign that year—the ongoing and unpopular war in Iraq, the collapse of the U.S. housing market, skyrocketing fuel and food prices, and serious economic problems—the questionable accuracy of a short anecdote told at a few stump speeches may not seem that big of a deal.

However, this seemingly minor incident illustrates a serious problem in the journalism profession in the early twenty-first century: a lack of routine fact-checking in daily news reports. Had the comedian Sinbad not spoken out to refute Clinton's claims, the candidate's tale of dodging sniper fire might never have been refuted, and perhaps may have been repeated time and time again in news reports as the campaign continued.

In the end, it took a comedian talking to a gossip columnist to debunk months of fibbing by a top candidate for president of the United States. That is no minor failing of the Fourth Estate, and it's no laughing matter for a profession whose credibility with the public continues to slip.

QUESTIONS TO CONSIDER

1. How much responsibility do you think the journalists covering the Clinton campaign had in fact-checking the candidate's claims? Does

simply attributing such statements to the candidate absolve journalists of responsibility for validating the truth of such statements? Why or why not?

2. What reasons, do you think, allowed the national news media in the United States—particularly the reporters covering Clinton's campaign—to not question the veracity of the candidate's "sniper fire" anecdote for so many months? To what extent should journalists fact-check anecdotes told by politicians on a campaign trail?

3. In this case, the news media had in their own archives evidence to refute Clinton's claims, yet that archival footage was reviewed only after a nonjournalist, the comedian Sinbad, suggested that Clinton was lying. To what extent should Sharyl Atkisson's suggestion that "memories should always match the videotape" apply to the news media as well?

4. The Clinton campaign complained for months, and with some reason, that reporters were much harder on her than on her chief rival, Barak Obama (who eventually won the nomination). Do you think the reporters didn't try to verify the sniper fire story for fear of being accused of anti-Clinton bias? What should a journalist's response be in such a situation?

Conclusion
What Is a Journalist?

We began this book with a quote from one of the most influential people in the development of professional journalism, Joseph Pulitzer:

> What is a journalist? Not any business manager or publisher, or even proprietor. A journalist is the lookout on the bridge of the ship of state. He notes the passing sail, the little things of interest that dot the horizon in fine weather. He reports the drifting castaway whom the ship can save. He peers through fog and storm to give warning of dangers ahead. He is not thinking of his wages or of the profits of his owners. He is there to watch over the safety and the welfare of the people who trust him.

In today's increasingly complex media landscape, Pulitzer's definition may seem a bit outdated (a journalist today could just as likely be a she as a he), but viewed through more than a century of careful thought regarding the moral principles upon which journalism stands, much of what Pulitzer said then could apply today.

Take, for example, the question raised earlier in this book, primarily in Chapter 10: Does the fact that the public generally considers TV personalities Bill O'Reilly and Jon Stewart to be "journalists" make them so? Does the fact that their wildly popular (and influential) television shows embrace many of the trappings of professional journalism make them part of the profession? What about so-called citizen journalists, people often with little or no professional training or experience who publish information they feel is important? Having a notebook and a Web site doesn't make you a journalist any more than having a knife and a table makes you a brain surgeon. However, the profession of journalism is not only composed of people who graduate from journalism schools and work for the mainstream press. Journalism in the early twenty-first century is indeed a big tent, but that tent still has walls and a roof, and it doesn't include anybody who communicates anything about anything to everybody.

This confusion over who qualifies as a journalist is nothing new. Indeed, in Pulitzer's day, when many of the modern trappings of professional journalism were just being tested, that legendary publisher saw a need to both ask and answer the question, "What is a journalist?"

The question, it turns out, is more difficult to answer than it might seem to be. O'Reilly says he is a journalist, but many critics say he is not (or at least hasn't been for a long time). Stewart says he is not, but many viewers seem to believe he is, as do many respected journalists and journalism scholars. What about Ariana Huffington? Larry King? Oprah Winfrey? Rush Limbaugh? A leading academic journal, the *Journal of Mass Media Ethics*, devoted an entire special issue in the fall of 2007 to the question, and wound up without a fully satisfactory answer.

We shall attempt one here, and explain our rationale:

A journalist is one who gathers useful information and presents it to the public in a manner that embraces honesty, transparency, accountability, balance, and all the basic moral principles of the journalism profession.

In practice, it would seem that an easier task would be to define who isn't a journalist. A large part of the problem lies in the matter of definition. Unlike medicine or law, the journalistic profession does not require either specialized training or a qualifying exam. In that regard, and in much of the world, if you say you are a journalist, then you are one. Reformers from time to time suggest there should be a vetting process. They argue that quality of the profession would improve, and, along with it, the democratic self-government it supports, if practitioners had to prove their competence to somebody. The resistance to such licensing has come largely from journalists themselves, who have argued successfully that any sort of licensing or vetting is an infringement on freedom of the press. Free-speech absolutists maintain that only if journalists are able to say and write anything they want, at any time, without any restrictions whatsoever, will journalism be able to do its job of monitoring government and keeping citizens sovereign, that is, in charge of their government, not the other way around. If our nation's founders were bold enough to write a First Amendment that guarantees "no law...abridging freedom of speech...or of the press," then journalism's critics should be bold as well. There is more than a century of argument from some of the finest minds ever to sit on the Supreme Court—Justices Oliver Wendell Holmes Jr., Louis D. Brandeis, William O. Douglas, Hugo Black, and others—that the answer to bad speech (or incompetent speech or inept speech or dishonest speech) is more speech. Licensing would merely curtail the robust exchange of ideas upon which democracy depends.

It should be noted that absolute free speech does not exist and never has. Perjury, which is lying under oath, is a crime and is surely speech. So is extortion ("Give me X dollars or I break your kneecap/front window."). So are libel and most forms of treason. Child pornography laws are restrictions on speech and so are laws against treason. Still, given that free expression is critical to democratic self-government, the legal limitations on speech are always narrowly drawn and exceptions very reluctantly granted.

When the U.S. nation was being invented, the framers took a big gamble in declaring a free press to be a bedrock of the new government. Newspapers of the Colonial era were as partisan and as scurrilous as anything on Fox today, and the freedom was granted, indeed, to "the press" in general—i.e., mass communication in all its forms—and not just professional journalists. Only by allowing all voices to be heard, they believed, would the truth emerge. Then and now, there is great reluctance to limiting the exchange of thought in the metaphorical public square we call the marketplace of ideas. If anyone will accept (or buy) your ideas, the argument goes, you should be free to make or sell them. Requiring a license to publish them will surely take some ideas off the market. And, as John Stuart Mill and many others have noted, you can't tell the good ideas from the bad ideas without a full debate.

So, unless you run afoul of some other law, you can say more or less what you please.

That establishes the legal right to speak, but is not helpful in answering the question of whether to count Stewart or O'Reilly or your favorite blogger or an apocalyptic pamphleteer as a journalist. For more than three centuries—roughly from the early days of moveable type to well into the nineteenth century—there was a rough limitation on the number and outlandishness of journalists and their ideas imposed by that other marketplace, the marketplace of money. It cost money to express ideas in print, which meant either readers had to buy what one wrote, or a publisher had to think a journalist's ideas were sufficiently in synch with his own to pay a writer to express them. As long as printing was expensive, economic forces provided a limitation on the number of newspapers and other publications, and on the types of journalism that were acceptable to the paying public.

However, across the nineteenth century that changed, as technology made it easier, cheaper, and quicker to publish. The result was a flurry of newspapers, magazines, pamphlets, broadsides, screeds, and the

marketplace came to be quite littered, indeed, with the output of anyone and everyone who had something to say and believed the world was
waiting to hear it. By the early twentieth century, the jumble of voices competing in the marketplace approached a cacophany. There were so many
ideas of such wide variety that it was hard to sort out one from another, to
pick out the ideas to hold onto and the ideas to discard.

In a period of about two decades, perhaps beginning in 1908 when the
University of Missouri launched the first journalism school in the country,
the profession of journalism was born. The Society of Professional Journalists, then known as Sigma Delta Chi, followed a year after in 1909.
The point was not to regulate the press—the First Amendment generally
forbade that and the proponents of a professionalized journalism did not
support regulation anyway—but to improve it voluntarily. The idea was
that while legally you still *could* mix up truths and falsehood, opinion and
fact, with proper training, you wouldn't *want* to.

It was out of this reform period that the modern notion of the journalist
was born. No longer was being a printer or a writer or a polemicist the
same as being a journalist. No longer was opinion considered inseparable
from fact. No longer was the reader left entirely on his own to sort out
honest efforts to inform from scurrilous and dishonest rumormongering,
or shrouded attempts at spreading ideological propaganda as fact. The notion emerged of the journalist as a professional practitioner—not licensed
to be sure, but still bound by accepted standards of behavior.

Determining those accepted standards evokes another important and
perennial question: What constitutes journalism? That question will
be asked every time we see somebody try a new approach to informing the public about the news of the day. At the close of the first decade
of the twenty-first century, the vogue is to mix irreverent humor, pure
reportage, and in-your-face argumentation together into something that
entertains as much as (or more than) it informs. In the 1970s and 1980s,
it was to write long, probing, hard-hitting investigative pieces about regional and national problems. In the 1950s and 1960s, it was judgmental
commentaries on wrongdoing from respected celebrity broadcasters. One
of the authors has an original *Harper's Weekly* cover from 1876 featuring a
Thomas Nast cartoon ridiculing Boss Tweed—was *that* journalism?

With each new approach to journalism, those of us who work in the
profession should not lose sight of the hard-won moral principles of the
profession, nor of the distinctions between those who *do* journalism and
those who borrow from it.

The code of behavior adoped by SPJ and other professional organizations has changed in terminology over the years, but the guiding principles remain remarkably constant. A journalist should try hard to separate
fact from both fiction and opinion and label things accordingly. A journalist should try to be fair to all parties to a story, despite the journalist's own

biases and beliefs. In the words of the current iteration of the SPJ Code of Ethics, journalists "believe that public enlightenment is the forerunner of justice and the foundation of democracy." As Pulitzer suggested, a journalist puts his or her duty to inform the public in a manner that promotes public safety and welfare above such things as money, fame, and power. The measure of a journalist is perhaps best based not upon job title or the manner in which he or she delivers information, but how closely one adheres to the moral principles of professional journalism. Bill O'Reilly may work in journalism as a big name on a major news network, but he so routinely rejects the basic principles of moral journalism that he often comes across as a charlatan.

With that, we can answer our question about Bill O'Reilly and Jon Stewart, and Oprah and "Wonkette" and any of a host of famous people who use journalistic techniques to promote their own agendas and personal wealth. Are they journalists? If we take seriously the goals that have guided the profession for a century, then no, they are not. They do not always try to be fair, they do not always try to be neutral, they do not always try to separate facts from opinions. O'Reilly is primarily a polemicist who willfully distorts the truth to suit either his political beliefs or to gin up his ratings and his income. Stewart is primarily a satirist whose major objects of ridicule are newsmakers and the broadcast journalists who report on them. Neither *The O'Reilly Factor* nor *The Daily Show*, nor Rush Limbaugh nor HuffPost.com, nor any other hybrid of news and entertainment, would be possible if not for the work of countless real journalists who covered the events of the day, gathered facts and footage from all sides of the issue, and documented all of those memorable moments in a fair and balanced manner, and made them available to the public.

Regardless of what the media landscape looks like today or tomorrow, one thing remains constant: The need for morally grounded journalists— people who gather and present important information to the world for the welfare of all—should not be overlooked for the popularity of those on the fringe of the profession, like O'Reilly and Stewart.

Notes

CHAPTER 4

1. The term began when major New York publishers began experimenting with spot color in their pages, starting with a cartoon character called "The Yellow Kid." Both Hearst's *Journal* and Pulitzer's *World* had such comic strips, and as these two papers were the biggest and boldest of the sensationalist papers, the term *yellow journalism* was applied first to Hearst and Pulitzer and then to their many imitators.

CHAPTER 5

1. Richard Streckfuss, "Objectivity in Journalism: A Search and Reassessment," *Journalism Quarterly* 67:973–83 (1990).

2. "Picturing the Amish," by Sarah Childress, *Newsweek* online edition, October 19, 2006.

3. H. Eugene Goodwin, *Groping for Ethics in Journalism* (2nd ed.). Iowa State Press, 1987: p.50.

4. Canadian Newspaper Association, "2006 National Freedom of Information Audit," p. 1.

5. Jock Lauterer, "Who's on First: A community journalism perspective on the civic journalism debate," in Steven R. Knowlton, *Moral Reasoning for Journalists* (1st ed.), Praeger, 1997: pp. 43–49.

6. Ron Fournier, "Accountability Journalism: Liberating reporters and the truth," in *The Essentials* (the internal newsletter of the Associated Press), June 1, 2007. Accessed June 11, 2007, at http://poynter.org/forum/?id=32365.

7. Detailed facts about this case are laid out in the findings of an independent review of the incident by former U.S. Attorney General Dick Thornburg and Louis Boccardi, former CEO of the Associated Press. The report was downloaded June 12, 2007, at http://www.cbsnews.com/htdocs/pdf/complete_report/CBS_Report.pdf.

8. "Barroom Sting," *Time Magazine*, January 23, 1978. Accessed online June 12, 2007, athttp://www.time.com/time/magazine/article/0,9171,919328,00.html.

9. John Nolan, "Chiquita accepts apology, $10M from Enquirer." *Cincinnati Enquirer*, June 29, 1998: p. 1A.

10. "Chiquita Brands International, Inc., Pleads Guilty to Making Payments to a Designated Terrorist Organization," press release from the U.S. Department of Justice. Accessed online on June 11, 2007, at http://www.usdoj.gov/usao/dc/Press_Releases/2007%20Archives/Mar_2007/07088.html.

11. "Regret The Interview: A conversation with Seth Mnookin," *Regret the Error* Web site, September 7, 2005. Accessed online on June 15, 2007, at http://www.regrettheerror.com/2005/09/today_regret_ki.html.

12. "From the Editors: The *Times* and Iraq." *The New York Times*, May 26, 2004, Section A; Column 1; pg. 10.

13. "For the Record," *The Star*, June 13, 2007. Accessed online June 15, 2007, at http://www.thestar.co.za/index.php?fArticleId=3880631.

CHAPTER 6

1. H. Allen White, "The Salience and Pertinence of Ethics: When Journalists Do and Don't Think for Themselves," *Journalism and Mass Media Studies Quarterly* 73:1 (Spring 1996), 26.

CHAPTER 7

1. Written for this volume by Michael Dillon.

CHAPTER 9

1. Mitchell, B. (Sept. 4, 2005). "First person and then some," Poynter Online. http://www.poynter.org/column.asp?id=68&aid=88340. Accessed August 21, 2008.

CHAPTER 11

1. As many lawyers have tried to point out, a presumption of innocence holds true only within a courtroom and only after a trial starts. It is a legal fiction designed to protect those defendants who happen, in fact, to be innocent. However, in the broad sense in which the phrase is commonly used, it makes no sense at all. If suspects were really thought to be innocent, there would be no arrests and nobody would ever be held on bail.

CHAPTER 14

1. "Newspaper objects to police seizure of newsroom computer," *New Castle* (Pa.) *News*, August 3, 2007.

2. "Distinctions that Matter: Ethical Differences at Large and Small Newspapers," by Bill Reader, *Journalism & Mass Communication Quarterly*, Winter 2006, Vol. 83, Issue 4, p. 851–864.

CHAPTER 15

1. Literally, the term "beltway" refers to the District of Columbia and its immediate surroundings that lie within the 66-mile ring road of I-495 that circles the national capital. In common usage, it refers to the whole national political establishment, including politicians, lobbyists, hangers-on of all descriptions—and journalists. The term is sometimes used derisively to suggest that those inside the beltway become so absorbed with political minutia that they lose touch with what the rest of the country is thinking.

2. Disclosure: From 1998 to 2000, coauthor Bill Reader was opinion page editor of the *Centre Daily Times* in State College, Pennsylvania, for which Klein's mother, Miriam, was an occasional columnist on local issues. Mrs. Klein had gifted Reader with signed copies of some of her son's books, including *Primary Colors* (which is signed "Anonymous"); Reader uses the signed copy as a discussion piece in his media ethics classes, and plans in the future to donate the book to a journalism library.

3. Larry J. Sabato, *Feeding Frenzy: How Attack Journalism Has Transformed American Politics*. (New York: Free Press, 1991).

4. Janet Cooke was a reporter for *The Washington Post* who, in 1981, fictionalized an account of an eight-year-old heroine addict that won a Pulitzer Prize (the award was rescinded after the discovery of Cooke's deception). Stephen Glass was a young star writer for *The New Republic* in the late 1990s who was later discovered to have fabricated, in whole or in part, more than two dozen articles for the magazine (the story of Stephen Glass is fictionalized itself in the 2003 film, *Shattered Glass*). Both Cooke and Glass were fired and publicly humiliated, and their publications issued profuse apologies for the conduct of their "former employees."

CHAPTER 18

1. By Loren Ghiglione. Reprinted, with permission, from the (Southbridge, Mass.) *News*, Wednesday, December 23, 1992.

CHAPTER 21

1. It is worth pointing out that the book was written before television became so ubiquitous in American culture; the problems it describes are even more serious today.

CHAPTER 22

1. (Both CBS and USA TODAY have posted PDF files of the memos on their respective Web sites).

2. According to the document dated May 19, 1972.

3. According to the memo dated August 1, 1972.

CHAPTER 23

1. See William B. Blankenburg, "The Utility of Anonymous Attribution," *Newspaper Research Journal* Winter/Spring 1992, pp. 10–23.

2. See Douglas A. Anderson, "How Newspaper Editors Reacted to Post's Pulitzer Prize Hoax," *Journalism Quarterly*, 59:363–66 (Autumn 1982).

3. Steven A. Esposito, "Anonymous White House Sources: How They Helped Shape Television News Coverage of the Bill Clinton-Monica Lewinski Investigation," in *Communication and the Law*, 1999.

4. "The President, the Intern, and the Media: Journalism Ethics Under Siege," by Deborah Potter, The Poynter Institute, Feb. 16, 1988. Accessed March 17, 2008, at http://www.poynter.org/content/content_view.asp?id=5633.

5. "Survey Shows Many Newspapers Never Permit Use of Anonymous Sources," by David Crary, Associated Press Managing Editors, June 8, 2005. Accessed March 17, 2008, at http://www.apme.com/news/2005/060805anonymous.shtml.

6. "When The Post Banned Anonymous Sources," by Ben H. Bagdikian, *American Journalism Review*, August/September 2005, p. 33.

CHAPTER 24

1. "Age, Wealth, Education Predict Letters to Editor," by Bill Reader, Guido H. Stempel III, and Douglass K.Daniel. *Newspaper Research Journal*, Fall 2004, Vol. 25 Issue 4, pp. 55–66.

2. Telephone interview with Alan English, March 18, 2008.

3. "TTT Offered a Laugh to Start Off the Day," by G.B. McKinnon [letter to the editor], The Times, Shreveport, La., September 8, 2004, p. 11A.

4. "'Tell The Times' Was Like a Pit Bull with Distemper," by Keith Hightower. *The Times*, Shreveport, La., September 11, 2004, p. 11A.

5. Kaminski and Saladino, 1981: 320–321.

6. *Talking Back to The New York Times*, by Kalman Seigel. Chicago: Quadrangle Books. 1972. p. 8.

7. *Your Obedient Servant: A Selection of the Most Witty, Amusing and Memorable Letters to The Times of London, 1900-1975*, by Kenneth Gregory. Toronto: Methuen. 1976: p. 25.

8. Craig, 1968: 27.

9. Kapoor, 1995.

CHAPTER 25

1. This case study includes research conducted with the assistance of Ohio University graduate students Jaya Shroff and Mansi Tiwari for a graduate course in media ethics. Shroff and Tiwari presented their research at the 2006 convention of the Association for Educators in Journalism and Mass Communication in San Francisco, California

2. The original paper on this topic by Shroff and Tiwari was written for a media ethics class at Ohio University, taught by co-author Bill Reader.

3. Upala, KBR, and Zahra Khan. "Shakti's journey from fame to shame." *Midday*, March 14, 2005.

Bibliography

American Society of Newspaper Editors. *Thinking Big about Small Newspapers*. Reston, Va.: Small Newspaper Committee of the American Society of Newspaper Editors, 1993.

Bacon, Francis. *Novum Organum* [microform], edited by Joseph Devey. New York: P. F. Collier, 1901.

Bagdikian, Ben H. "Lords of the Global Village." *Nation*, June 12, 1989.

Beittel, K. *Zen and the Art of Pottery*. New York: Weatherhill, 1992.

Bennett, James Gordon. "To the Public—Enlargement of the *Herald*." *New York Herald*, January 1, 1836.

Bok, Sissela. *Lying: Moral Choice in Public and Private Life*. New York: Pantheon, 1978.

Boorstin, Daniel J. *The Image: A Guide to Pseudo-Events in America*. New York: Atheneum, 1961.

Breed, Warren. "Social Control in the Newsroom." *Social Forces* 33, no. 4 (1955).

Charity, Arthur. *Doing Public Journalism*. New York: Guilford, 1995.

Commission on Freedom of the Press. *A Free and Responsible Press*. Chicago: University of Chicago Press, 1947.

Facts about Newspapers. Reston, Va.: Newspaper Association of America, 1994.

Foucault, Michel. *Ethics: Subjectivity and Truth*. Edited by Paul Rabinow. New York: The New Press, 1997.

Frankena, William K. *Ethics*. 2d ed. Englewood Cliffs, N.J.: Prentice Hall, 1972.

Frankfurt, Harry G. *On Bullshit.* Princeton, N.J.: Princeton University Press, 2005.

Greeley, Horace. "A Great Journalist Dead." *New York Tribune,* June 3, 1872.

Hobbes, Thomas. *The Leviathan.* London: G. Routledge, 1907.

Klaidman, Stephen, and Tom L. Beauchamp. *The Virtuous Journalist.* New York: Oxford University Press, 1987.

Lauterer, Jock. *Community Journalism: The Personal Approach.* Ames, Iowa: Iowa State University Press, 1995.

Lewis, Anthony. *Make No Law: The Sullivan Case and the First Amendment.* New York: Random House, 1991.

Liebling, A. J. *The Press.* New York: Ballantine, 1961.

Lippmann, Walter. *Public Opinion.* New York: Macmillan, 1922.

Locke, John. *Two Treatises of Government* (orig. 1691). Hafner, 1947.

Marx, Karl. *Capital: A Critique of Political Economy.* Vol. 1. Translated by Ben Fowkes. New York: Vintage Books, 1981.

Merrill, John C. *The Imperative of Freedom.* New York: Hastings House, 1974.

Mill, John Stuart. *Utilitarianism.* New ed. with selections from Auguste Comte and positivism. Edited by H. B. Acton. London: Dent, 1972.

Milton, John. *Aeropagitica: A Speech of Mr. John Milton for the Liberty of Unlicensed Printing to the Parliament of England.* Edited by Isabel Rivers. Cambridge, Eng.: Deighton, Bell, 1973.

Niebuhr, H. Richard. *The Responsible Self.* New York: HarperCollins, 1963.

Pingree, Suzanne, and Robert Hawkins. "News Definitions and Their Effects on Women." In *Women and the News,* edited by Laurily Keir Epstein. New York: Hastings House, 1978.

Plato. *The Republic.* Translated by Robin Waterfield. Oxford: Oxford University Press, 1993.

Pulitzer, Joseph. "The Great Issue." *St. Louis Post and Dispatch,* January 10, 1879.

Rosen, Jay. *Getting the Connections Right: Public Journalism and What It Means to the Press.* New York: Twentieth Century Fund, 1995.

Sinclair, Upton. *The Brass Check.* Ayer, 1920.

Smith, Adam. *An Inquiry into the Nature and Causes of the Wealth of Nations.* 6th ed. Edited by Edwin Cannan. London: Methuen, 1961.

Stepp, Carl Sessions. "Public Journalism: Balancing the Scales," *American Journalism Review,* May 1996.

Stiff, C. *Untitled.* Abstract accepted for presentation to the Huck Boyd National Center for Community Media and National Newspaper Association Symposium on Community Journalism, Nashville, Tenn., March 20, 1996.

Thames, R. "Public Journalism: Some Questions and Answers." Handout accompanying session on public journalism at the ASNE annual convention, Washington, D.C., April 16, 1996.

Thomson, John. *An Enquiry, Concerning the Liberty, and Licentiousness of the Press and the Uncontroulable Nature of the Human Mind.* New York: Johnson and Stryker, 1801.

Trenchard, John, and Thomas Gordon. *The Third Collection of Political Letters in the London Journal.* London: n.p., 1720.

Warren, Samuel, and Louis Brandeis. "The Right to Privacy." *Harvard Law Review* 4, no. 5 (1890).

Wilson, James Q. *The Moral Sense*. New York: Free Press, 1993.

Winship, Thomas. "Jim Batten and Civic Journalism." *Editor & Publisher*, April 1995.

Wortman, Tunis. *A Treatise Concerning Political Enquiry and the Liberty of the Press*. New York: n.p., 1801.

Index

Berlusconi, Silvio, politician, 50
Bernstein, Carl, reporter, 128, 179, 183
Berst, Ron R., suicide, 147
bias and ethics 3–5, 43–51, 69–72,
    77–100, 102–3, 112, 126, 136, 176,
    225
Blair, Jayson, reporter, 63, 71, 173
Blankenburg, William, professor, 181
blogosphere, 57, 85, 92, 114, 177, 218
Bloomberg, Michael, mayor, 50
Bloomberg, news service, 50
Bloomsburg (Pennsylvania)
    Press-Enterprise, 78–79, 186
Boccardia, Louis, Associated Press
    president, 176
Bode, Nicole, reporter, 92–93
Bok, Sissela, author, 61, 72
Bollywood, 192–94, 205
Bolton, John, U.N. ambassador, 102–3
Boorstin, Daniel, author, 32–33, 109, 169
Bosnia, 47, 165, 216–17
Boston Globe, 106–10, 210–14
Boyd, Gerald, 63
Bradlee, Benjamin, editor 179, 183–84
Burkett, Bill, Lt. Col., 174, 176
Brandeis, Justice Louis, 25–26
"Brangelina," 40
Brass Check, The, 39
Bremner, John, professor, 57
British Broadcasting Corporation, xvi,
    35, 127, 180–181
Brody, Jane E., reporter, 149
Buddhism, 7
Bullard, Robert W., funeral director,
    144
bullshit, philosophical concept, 4
Burnham, Margaret, attorney, 211
Bush, Pres. George W., 27, 38, 50, 58,
    101–2, 130, 174–78

Calhoun, John C., politician, 24
Callinan, Tom, editor, 135–36
Campbell, Cole C., editor, 165–71
Canada, 26, 42, 159–60
Canadian Newspaper Association, 54
Cape Verde, 16
capitalism, 5, 30, 35–38
Capote, Truman, author, 92

Cassidy & Associates, lobbying firm,
    207–8
casting couch, 192–97
Cato, 21–26, 39, 53
CBS News, 46, 58, 66, 93, 128–29, 149,
    173–78, 200, 217–18
celebrity and journalism, 4, 57, 93, 104,
    127, 162, 192–97, 199, 224
Chancellor, John, television
    commentator, 202
Charter of Fundamental Rights, 16
Chicago Tribune, 188
Chile, 42
China, 35, 38, 50, 109
China Daily, newspaper, 50
Chiquita Brands International,
    61–62
Christiansen, Sabine, journalist, 111
Church of England, 20
citizen journalism, 86, 222
Cincinnati Enquirer, 61–62, 136
Clark, Sally, wrongly convicted, 133
Cleveland, Mary and Somalia
    photograph, 170
Cleveland, Sgt. William and Somalia
    photograph, 170
Clinton, Hillary Rodham, 84–85, 88–91,
    216–20
Clinton, Pres. Bill, 128–31, 148, 179–83
codes of ethics, 15–16, 45, 81, 165,
    224–25
CNN, 31, 50, 217
Cohen, William, U.S. senator, 105
Cold War, 17, 26
Cole, Adam, alleged graffiti "artist,"
    117
Collins, Susan, U.S. senator, 106
Columbia Journalism Review, 113–14,
    155
Columbia, S.C. State, 212
Columbia, space shuttle, 81
Commitee to Protect Journalists,
    158–59
composite cases as journalistic fiction,
    xv
confidentiality of sources, 59, 109–10
conflict of interest, 49–50, 64, 79–80,
    118, 123, 125, 132, 161

About the Authors

STEVEN R. KNOWLTON is Professor of Journalism at Dublin City University in Ireland. He has eighteen years of professional newspaper experience, and continues to freelance for *The New York Times* and other major newspapers in the United States and in Ireland. He is the author/editor of six books, including the first edition of *Moral Reasoning for Journalists: The Journalist's Moral Compass* (with Patrick R. Parsons) and, most recently, *Fair and Balanced: A History of Journalistic Objectivity* (with Karen L. Freeman).

BILL READER is Assistant Professor in the E. W. Scripps School of Journalism at Ohio University, where he teaches journalism reporting, writing, editing, and ethics. He has a decade of professional newspaper experience, most recently as opinion page editor of the *Centre Daily Times* in State College, Pennsylvania. His research of journalism ethics issues has been published in *Journalism & Mass Communication Quarterly, Journalism, Journal of Broadcasting & Electronic Media, Newspaper Research Journal,* and *Journal of Mass Media Ethics,* and he contributes to trade publications including *Quill, The Masthead,* and *Grassroots Editor.*